Following the Ark of the Covenant

THE TREASURE OF GOD

Solving the Mystery of Sanpete Valley, Utah

Following the Ark of the Covenant

THE TREASURE OF GOD

Solving the Mystery of Sanpete Valley, Utah

by

Kerry Ross Boren
&
Lisa Lee Boren

ISBN: 1-55517-459-0

v.2

Published by Bonneville Books

Distributed by:
925 North Main, Springville, UT 84663 • 801/489-4084

CFI Publishing and Distribution Since 1986
Cedar Fort, Incorporated
CFI Distribution • CFI Books • Council Press • Bonneville Books

Typeset by Virginia Reeder
Cover design by Adam Ford
Cover design © 2000 by Lyle Mortimer

Printed in the United States of America

Table of Contents

Acknowledgments

Special acknowledgment is extended to the following individuals, whose contributions to this work helped make it possible: Randy Lewis, Layton, Utah; A.C. & Bertha Wilkerson, Tridell, Utah; author Lee Nelson, Mapleton, Utah; Jeff Hanks, Orem, Utah; David McMurtry, Lexington, Kentucky; Terry L. Carter, Orem, Utah; Stuart Beattie, Rosslyn, Scotland; Randall Johnson, Orem, Utah; Alan Morehead, Rockville, Maryland; and a special thanks to the late Wade Warner, who believed and cared to the end.

Introduction

Sanpete Valley, in central Utah, has long been regarded by locals as a sacred place; but if one were to ask why it was considered sacred, chances are no one could tell you. There is usually a vague, non-specific explanation that it has something to do with religion and with ancient inhabitants of the valley, most often associated with Jaredites, or Nephites, or Lamanites, races of people mentioned in the Book of Mormon.

Isaac Morley, the Mormon patriarch who established the first pioneer settlement of the valley in 1849, proclaimed that an ancient Nephite temple once stood on Temple Hill, at Manti, and that it was mentioned in the Book of Mormon. Brigham Young confirmed Morley's proclamation and mentioned further in a sermon that it had been made known to him that this valley was a sacred place, and that he had offered up a prayer to the Lord that no man should ever profane it. This became the basis for a religious belief in the sanctity of Sanpete Valley among Mormons, but it did not explain why the valley was sacred to the Ute Indians long before the arrival of the first white settlers.

As early as 1849, when settlers first arrived in the Sanpete Valley, mention was made in pioneer journals of strange inscriptions on ledges throughout the region. Though faded with time, those same inscriptions can still be seen today. The symbols are strange and unusual, apparently very ancient, and in no way resemble the numerous Native American petroglyphs that are found throughout the region.

Then, in the 1960s, a nondescript resident named John Brewer claimed to have discovered a cave in the hill east of the Manti Temple containing the mummies of a man and a woman and metal plates engraved with strange characters. Brewer not only made the claim, but he even produced some of the plates which he submitted to the academic community for analysis. Results were mixed, but in spite of reviews, interest in the Sanpete site as a sacred place was revived.

Since then the mystery of Sanpete Valley has remained ethereal and the question of what comprised the secret of Sanpete Valley was left unanswered. Who were the mummies? What connection did they have with the stone boxes and engraved plates? What part did the strange rock inscriptions play in the historical scene? There had obviously been an ancient culture existing in this region, but who were they? Was there an ancient temple built on Temple Hill in Manti? If so, who built it? Jaredites? Nephites? Or was there some other answer heretofore overlooked?

These questions and more confronted us when we first set out to write this book. We first became drawn to the topic when it became apparent that there was some connection between the sacred gold mines of the Ute Indians, situated in the Uintah Mountains, and the mystery of Sanpete Valley. We had written two books on the sacred mines: *Footprints in the Wilderness: A History of the Lost Rhoades Mines* [Kerry Ross Boren & Gale R. Rhoades, Publishers Press, Salt Lake City, 1971] and *The Gold of Carre-Shinob* [Kerry Ross Boren & Lisa Lee Boren, Bonneville Books, Springville, Utah, 1998]. Our research into these works consistently indicated some connection between the gold source of the

Utes and their reverence for Sanpete Valley, especially the prominence regarded as Temple Hill. The common link with both places was Isaac Morley, pioneer colonizer of the Sanpete Valley, and his unusual friendship with Chief Walker of the Utes, "Keeper of the Yellow Metal."

Isaac Morley, third great-grandfather of Kerry Ross Boren, a most remarkable man in his own right, was a pioneer, a colonizer, a theologian, a legislator, a soldier, and an authority on the Book of Mormon; but we were to discover that Isaac Morley was much more than this—he was the key to the mystery of Sanpete Valley.

This is not a book of expected outcomes. If the reader is expecting a story about Jaredites or Nephites, this book will be a disappointment. However, if you enjoy mysteries and surprises, there is ample material to incite the most curious mind.

We have ventured to present in *The Treasure of God,* a hypothesis supported by substantial evidence, both circumstantial and real, that reveals the solution to the mystery of Sanpete Valley, and it transcends anything that has heretofore been postulated. It takes the reader on a journey through history from 2000 B.C. to 2000 A.D., and explores the earliest voyages to America and their connection to the mystery of Sanpete Valley.

Wherever possible we have drawn upon established sources in an effort to demonstrate the basis for our claims. It goes without saying that not all of the claims made in this hypothesis can be proved by documentation, especially when it is shown that very careful effort has been made through the centuries to protect the secret of Sanpete.

If *The Treasure of God* does anything, it unsettles history and views it in a new perspective. It takes a remote and obscure valley in the State of Utah and places it in the mainstream of world history. If *The Treasure of God* does nothing more than open up the reader's mind to new possibili-

ties, then it shall have been worth the effort to write.

Kerry Ross Boren

Lisa Lee Boren

Salt Lake City

The temple furniture showing the Mercy Seat being the lid of the Ark.

Chapter One

THE ARK OF THE COVENANT

The Ark of the Covenant is the greatest treasure the world has ever known, and the oldest sacred relic in the religious iconography of the Hebrews. It is also the most revered religious relic in the Egyptian pantheon of gods, and in the religious tradition of Christians. It is, in addition, the least understood object of worship in history, and...it is missing.

During the wandering desert life of the Twelve Tribes of Israel, they were shaped into a cohesive and well-defined community under the leadership of Moses. They had established a union with the Lord, a system of laws and a priesthood headed by Moses' brother Aaron and Aaron's two sons, Nadab and Abihu. The Shekinah, or Divine Presence, traveled with them, in the Ark of the Covenant.

The earliest mention of the Ark occurs in the Bible, in the book of Exodus. Moses had received the two Tables of Stone, containing the Ten Commandments written by the Finger of God while on Mount Sinai. God himself gave instructions to Moses for the construction of the Ark, wherein the Tables of Stone would be kept. An artificer named Bezaleel was chosen to build the sacred container. He is described as a man "filled with the spirit of God, in wisdom, and in understanding, and knowledge, and in all manner of workmanship, to devise cunning works" [Exodus 31: 2-4]. He was "the son of Uri, the son of Hur, of the tribe of Judah."

The Ark was a rectangular box made of acacia wood, measuring three feet nine inches by two feet three inches by two feet three inches (extrapolated from the ancient cubit which measured approximately eigh-

teen inches). It was plated, inside and out, with pure gold, and decorated around the top with a gold moulding. Four gold rings were fixed to the top corners, two on each side, and through these were inserted shafts of acacia wood plated with gold, by which the Ark could be carried.

The cover or lid of the Ark was fashioned of gold nine inches thick, and was called the Mercy Seat. Two golden cherubim were positioned on either side of the Mercy Seat, facing each other, without blemish and of beaten gold, with outstretched wings forming a protective shroud over the Mercy Seat. The Lord had instructed Moses:

> There I will meet with you, and from above the Mercy Seat, from between the two cherubim that are upon the ark of the testimony, I will speak with you of all that I will give you in commandment for the people of Israel. [Exodus 25: 22]

When the Ark was finished, Moses placed inside it the two Tables of Stone, inscribed with the Ten Commandments. The Ark, now pregnant with its precious contents, was installed behind the veil or curtain in the Holy of Holies of the Tabernacle — a portable tent-like structure which served as a place of worship by the Israelites during their wanderings in the wilderness.

No sooner had the Ark of the Covenant been installed in the Holy of Holies than terrible things began to happen, demonstrating the object's supernatural powers and force. The first concerned Nadab and Abihu, two of the four sons of Aaron the High Priest. Aaron's sons, as members of the priestly family, had access to the Holy of Holies, where they assisted in performing sacred rituals. One day they entered carrying metal incense burners in their hands. According to the book of Leviticus they "offered strange fire before the Lord, which He commanded them not," and as a consequence fire leapt out from the Ark "and devoured them and they died." [Leviticus 10: 1-2]

And the Lord spake unto Moses after the death of the two sons of Aaron, when they offered before the Lord and died; And the Lord said unto Moses, speak unto Aaron thy brother, that he come not at all times into the holy place within the veil before the throne of mercy, which is upon the Ark; That he die not: for I will appear in the cloud upon the Throne of Mercy. [Leviticus 16: 1-2, amalgam of King James Version and Jerusalem Bible.]

"The cloud upon the Throne of Mercy" which threatened death to Aaron manifested itself between the cherubim. It was not always present, but when it did appear the Israelites believed "that the demons held sway," and when it did materialize even Moses dare not approach.

Other supernatural phenomena manifested "between the Cherubim" that faced each other across the Mercy Seat. Just a few days after the consuming by fire of Aaron's two sons, Moses entered into the Holy of Holies of the Tabernacle, which was then still pitched in the shadow of Mount Sinai. As soon as he entered, Moses "heard the voice of one speaking unto him from off the mercy seat that was upon the Ark...from between the two cherubim." [Numbers 7: 89]

Ancient Jewish legends maintain that this voice came from heaven "in the form of a tube of fire," and fire seems often to have been associated with the cherubim. One account states, for example, that "two sparks" or "fiery jets" issued from the cherubim which shaded the Ark—sparks which occasionally burned and destroyed nearby objects. [see *The Legends of the Jews*, Rabbi Louis Ginzberg, The Jewish Publication Society of America, Phila., 1911, vol. 111, p. 210.] The earliest mention of cherubim (which are otherwise never described) is found in the book of Genesis where, after Adam and Eve were cast out of the Garden of Eden, two cherubim were placed to guard the way with "Flaming Swords" to prevent them from returning.

Among its many other powers and attributes, the Ark of the Covenant had the ability to counteract gravity and levitate itself (and frequently its bearers) off the ground. In other words, the Ark could fly! The first example of this is found when the Israelites departed from Mount Sinai and the Ark "went before them in the three days' journey, to search out a resting place for them. And the cloud of the Lord was upon them by day, when they went out of the camp. And it came to pass, when the Ark set forward, that Moses said, "Rise up, Lord, and let thine enemies be scattered; and let them that hate thee flee before thee." And when it rested, he said, "Return, O Lord, unto the many thousands of Israel." [Numbers 10: 33-36]

The Ark of the Covenant was normally borne upon the shoulders of "the Kohathites," i.e. "the sons of Kohath" [Numbers 7: 9], a sub-clan of the tribe of Levi to which both Moses and Aaron also belonged. According to rabbinical commentaries on The Old Testament, these bearers were occasionally killed by the "sparks" which the Ark emitted. [Ginzberg, op. cit. vol. III, p. 228.] These "sparks" or "fire" are mentioned frequently in connection with the Ark. For example, in Leviticus 9:24 we read of a fire which came out of the Ark and consumed a burnt offering on the altar.

When the size and dimensions of the Ark are studied, and consideration of the weight of the tremendous amount of gold utilized in its construction is taken, it seems impossible that the bearers could have lifted it at all. The lid or Mercy Seat alone was solid gold, measuring three feet nine inches by two feet three inches and was nine inches thick. It would have been impossible for four or even eight men to lift this weight alone, without the remainder of the Ark, also heavily plated with gold.

The answer seems to be the Ark's ability to levitate. Several learned Midrashic exegists testify that the Ark sometimes lifted its bearers off the ground (thus relieving them of a considerable burden) [*The Jewish Encyclopedia*, Funk and Wagnalls, New York, 1925, vol. II, p. 105]. Another Jewish legend reports an incident during which the bearers of the Ark were "tossed by an invisible agency into the air and flung to the ground again and again." [Ginzberg, op. cit., vol. III, p. 194.] Another tradition describes an occasion when "the Ark leaped of itself into the air." [Ibid. vol. III, p. 395.] Midrashic commentaries also say that during the wilderness wanderings: "The Ark gave the signal for breaking camp by soaring high and then swiftly moving before the camp at a distance of three days' march." [Ibid., vol. III, p. 243.]

Imbued as it was with such strange powers it was only natural that the Israelites would recognize the Ark as a terrible weapon. One Jewish chronicle has written:

The oldest Biblical references to the Ark agree absolutely in representing it as discharging two specific functions, that of choosing the way it wished to go, and that of going into battle with the army of Israel and giving it victory over its enemies.... These two important functions the Ark was able to discharge, all the evidence indicates, because of a positive divine power resident in it. And all these earliest sources agree in identifying this divine power with Yahweh. [*The Book of the Covenant*, Hebrew Union College annual, KTAV Publishing House, New York, 1928, vol. V, pp. 27-28.]

One battle account describes the Ark as first uttering "a moaning sound," then rising up off the ground and rushing towards the enemy, who were plunged into disarray and slaughtered to a man. [*The Jewish Encyclopedia*, op. cit., vol. II, p. 106.] Conversely, when the Ark was not carried into battle, the Israelites lost. For example, on one occasion the Israelite army, flushed with victory, mounted an attack upon the war-like Amalekites. Moses withheld the Ark from them because they ignored his advice against mounting the assault. Moses had warned them, "Go not up, for the Lord is not among you; That ye be not smitten before your enemies." [Numbers 14:42] But the army went up, without the Ark: "Then the Amalekites came down...which dwelt in that hill country, and smote them and discomfited them." [Numbers 14: 44-5]

Thereafter, during the forty years spent wandering in the wilderness, the Israelites learned that it was wisdom to follow Moses's advice. Under his leadership and with the help of the Ark, they successfully subdued the fierce tribes of the Sinai peninsula, conquered Transjordania, spoiled the Midianites, and laid waste to all those who opposed them. After four decades of wandering, they "pitched their camp in the plains of Moab...opposite Jericho." [Numbers 22:1] They were just across the Jordan River from the Promised Land.

"Joshua spake unto the priests, saying, Take up the Ark of the Covenant, and pass over the people...And it came to pass...as they that bare the Ark were come unto Jordan...[that] the waters which came from above stood and rose up upon an heap...and those that came down were cut off...and the priests that bare the Ark of the Covenant of the Lord stood firm on dry ground in the midst of Jordan and the soles of the priests' feet were lifted up onto the dry land...The waters of Jordan returned unto their place...And [Joshua] spake...saying...the Lord your God dried up the waters of Jordan from before you, until ye were passed over." [Joshua 3: 6, 14-17; 4:18, 21,

23.]

The assault on Jericho followed the triumphal crossing of the Jordan. While the main body of Israelites stood back a distance of two thousand cubits (more than half a mile), priests blowing trumpets marched around the walls of the city bearing the Ark. They repeated this procedure every day for six days. Then, on the seventh day, beginning with the dawn, they marched around the city seven times. On the seventh time, when the priests blew the trumpets, Joshua bade the people to shout: "...and when the people shouted with a great shout...the wall fell down flat, so that the people went up into the city...and they took the city...and they utterly destroyed all that was in the city." [Joshua 6:20-21]

The Ark continued to be utilized to achieve victory in battle throughout the term of Joshua's leadership. However, within about a hundred and fifty years of Joshua's death, the relic was no longer routinely being carried into battle; instead it had been installed in the tabernacle at a place known as Shiloh.

Then, at the battle of Ebenezer, at which the Israelites were defeated by the Philistines and four thousand of their men were killed, they consulted the elders of Israel, who said, "Let us fetch the Ark of our God from Shiloh so that it may come among us and rescue us from the power of our enemies." [I Samuel 4:3]

The battle was joined again and to the utter astonishment of all concerned: "Israel was smitten, and they fled every man into his tent: and there was a very great slaughter; for there fell of Israel thirty thousand footmen. And the Ark of God was taken." [I Samuel 4: 10-11]

This catastrophe had been unthinkable, unimaginable; never before had they been defeated when they had carried the Ark into battle and never before had the Ark itself been captured. When this news was brought to Eli, the High Priest at Shiloh (who was ninety-eight years old and blind),

he "fell backward off his seat...His neck was broken and he died, for he was old and heavy." His daughter-in-law, who was pregnant, when she heard the news that the Ark had been taken, "crouched down and gave birth, for her labor pains came on." [I Samuel 4: 13-19] She named her child Ichabod meaning "where is the glory?"

The Victory of the Philistines was short-lived, however. They jubilantly brought the Ark of the Covenant from Ebenezer to Ashdod and placed it in the temple of their deity Dagon, setting it down beside the statue of that god. Next morning they found the statue of Dagon lying face down on the ground before the Ark. They put it back in its place, but early next morning they found the statue of Dagon on the ground again, with its head and hands severed and lying before the Ark.

Then the people of Ashdod were afflicted with tumors called "emerods." Some scholars equate these "emerods" with "hemorrhoids," but this seems to have been an unfortunate phonetic assumption, because afterwards the priests of Dagon fashioned solid gold models of the emerods as an offering to the Hebrew God. This could not have been done with hemorrhoids. Jewish tradition maintains that the tumors caused a swelling of the testicles, accompanied by great pain and suffering; these were likely the forms taken by the gold replicas of the emerods.

The Philistines took the Ark to Gath, which town also became plagued with the tumors, so they removed it to Ekron which also suffered the plague. "The people who did not die were struck with tumors and the wailing from the town went up to heaven." [I Samuel 5]

After seven months the Philistines decided to return the Ark to the Israelites. They loaded it onto a "new cart" hauled by "two milch kine" and sent it on its way to Bethshemesh, the nearest point inside Israelite territory.

The cart came to rest in the field of a

Bethshemite named Joshua, and the Israelites came to offer sacrifices and praise God for the return of the Ark. But they made a drastic mistake when some of the men took it upon themselves to look into the Ark, to see if the contents were still in tact. Because they looked into the Ark, seventy men were struck dead (more recent translations agree that the scriptural number of "fifty thousand and threescore and ten" is incorrect). Nowhere is it stated exactly how the men were killed, but it is clear that they were killed by the Ark, in a manner sufficiently terrible to lead the survivors to conclude: "No one is safe in the presence of the Lord, this holy God. To whom can we send it to be rid of him?" [I Samuel 6:20, New English Bible translation] Suddenly and mysteriously a group of Levitical priests appeared and carried away the Ark to a place called Kiriath-Jearim where it was installed in the house of Abinadab on a high hill, where it remained, isolated and guarded, for the next half century.

Sometime between 1000 and 990 B.C., David became King of Israel. Having recently captured the city of Jerusalem, he intended to consolidate his authority by bringing up to his new capital the most sacred relic of his people.

They placed the Ark on a new cart and brought it from Abinadab's house on the hill above Kiriath-Jearim. Uzzah and Ahio were in charge of the transfer. Uzzah walked alongside the cart and Ahio went in front. When they came to the threshing floor of Nacon, the cart started to tip when a wheel dropped into a depression, and Uzzah instinctively put out his hands against the Ark to steady it. "Then the anger of Yahweh blazed out against Uzzah, and for this crime God struck him down on the spot, and he died there beside the Ark of God." [I Samuel 6: 3-4; 6-7]

David was afraid to bring the Ark into Jerusalem, saying, "How can I harbour the Ark of the Lord after this?" Instead he "turned aside and carried it to the house of Obed-edom the Gittite." Here the Ark remained for three months while King David waited to see if it would kill anyone else. There were no more disasters and in fact "Yahweh blessed Obed-edom and his whole family." The Bible is not explicit about the nature of this benediction, but an ancient tradition states that "it consisted in Obed-edom being blessed with many children...The women in his house have birth after a pregnancy of two months only and bore six children at one time." [Ginzberg, op. cit., vol. VI, p. 275.]

When at last David brought the Ark into the city, he placed it in a simple tent, because the Lord forbade him to build a temple because he was a man of war. It was left to David's son Solomon to erect a house for the Ark of the Covenant.

At Solomon's command, work was started on the Temple around the year 966 B.C. [*Jerusalem Bible*, op. cit., Chronological Table, p. 344.] and was completed probably in 955 B.C. [I Kings 6:38 states that the Temple took eleven years to build.] When the great structure was finished, Solomon ordered the Ark to be brought forth:

> Solomon assembled the elders of Israel, and all the heads of the tribes...that they might bring up the Ark of the Covenant of the Lord...And all the elders of Israel came, and the priests took up the Ark. And they brought up the Ark of the Lord...And King Solomon, and all the congregation of Israel that were assembled unto him, were with him before the Ark, sacrificing sheep and oxen that could not be told nor numbered for multitude. And the priests brought in the Ark of the Covenant of the Lord to its place in the Temple...in the Holy of Holies. [I Kings 8: 1-6, amalgam of King James Version and Jerusalem Bible translations.]

The Biblical account states that the glory of the Lord filled the Temple in the form of a cloud, as the King knelt before the altar and blessed the Temple, and offered up sacrifices. The dedication feast lasted for seven days.

The Holy of Holies, or "Dvir," wherein the Ark was kept within the Temple, was 33 feet square and windowless. "The Lord has set the sun in the heavens but has said that he would dwell in thick darkness." [I Kings 8: 12] The Holy of Holies was completely covered with gold—walls, ceiling, and floor. The Ark of the Covenant was between two cherubim (in Hebrew, heruvim) sixteen feet high, made of olive wood and covered with gold. Their outstretched wings spanned the chamber from wall to wall, larger images of the two small cherubim which had flanked the Ark of the Tabernacle in the time of Moses.

The Tractate Erubin of the Jerusalem Talmud [v. 22c.] records that the Temple was so constructed that on the two equinautical days the first rays of the rising sun shone directly through the eastern gate. This gate was kept closed during the year, but was opened on equinautical days for this purpose: The first ray of the equinautical sun shone through the eastern gate and into the very heart of the temple, coming to rest upon the Holy of Holies and the Ark of the Covenant. [*The Gates of Righteousness*, Julian Morgenstern, Hebrew Union College Annual VII, 1929.]

Moreover, the Holy of Holies was built directly over the Eben Shetiya, or "fire stone," better known as the Foundation Stone. One scholar writes:

The stone on which the Temple of Solomon was built—Eben Shetiya, or Fire Stone—is a bolide that fell in the beginning of the tenth century, in the time of David, when a comet, which bore the appearance of a man with a sword, was seen in the sky. [*Worlds in Collision*, Immanuel Velikovsky, Doubleday Co., New York, 1950; Tractate Sota 48b; Ginzberg, op. cit.]

Eben-Shetiya, or Foundation Stone, was so-called because it was said to be the central core from which the whole world was formed. A fourth century rabbi recorded:

The Land of Israel is the middle of the earth. Jerusalem is the middle of Israel. The Temple is the middle of Jerusalem. The Holy of Holies is the middle of the Temple. The Holy Ark is the middle of the Holy of Holies. And the stone of Foundation is in front of the Holy of Holies. [*The Temple of Jerusalem*, Joan Comay, Rinehart & Winston, New York, 1975, p. 45.]

It became necessary, for a more complete understanding of the Ark, to quote the biblical passage regarding the placing of the Ark of the Covenant within the temple:

And the priests brought in the Ark of the Covenant of the Lord unto his place, unto the oracle of the house, to the most holy place, even under the wings of the cherubims. For the cherubims spread forth their two wings over the place of the Ark, and the cherubims covered the Ark and the staves thereof above. And they drew out the staves, that the ends of the staves were seen out in the holy place before the oracle, and they were not seen without: and there they are unto this day. There was nothing in the Ark save the two tables of stone, which Moses put there at Horob, when the Lord made a covenant with the children of Israel, when they came out of the land of Egypt. And it came to pass, when the priests were come out of the holy place, that the cloud filled the house of the Lord. Then spake Solomon, The Lord said that he would dwell in the thick darkness. [I Kings 8: 6-12]

Two points stand out in the foregoing passage: "...They drew out the staves," and "...There was nothing in the Ark save the two tables of stone..." When God commanded Moses to build the Ark, He specified that "The shafts must remain in the rings of the Ark and not be withdrawn..." [Exodus 25: 10-22] The shafts or staves remained in the rings throughout the wandering of the Israelites, but when the Ark found a permanent place in the Holy Temple, the staves were permanently removed. The significance of this ritual is never explained.

The second declaration, that the Ark contained only the two "Tables of Stone," is more highly significant, and puzzling inasmuch as the book of Hebrews in the New Testament mentions the "jar of manna" and other sources list even more relics kept within the Ark. The manna was the "bread that the Lord has given you to eat" [Exodus 16:15] during the forty years the children of Israel wandered in the wilderness. The implication is that it was somehow produced by the Ark to fall from heaven. It is described as "a fine flake-like thing, fine as hoarfrost on the ground...like coriander seed, white, and the taste of it was like wafers made with honey." [Exodus 16:14,31] The jar of manna (made of gold) was preserved in the Ark.

Tradition also tells us that the Ark contained the following holy relics: a jar of manna; a bolide that fell from heaven; the rod of Moses (in Hebrew, *Shamir*); the rod of Aaron which magically flowered; the genealogy of the Jews; the mystical Sword of Methusaleh; the vestment or "luminous" suit of Adam; the Urim and Thummim; and other relics and symbols. Because of their significance to the Ark which housed them, a brief review of these items is helpful in understanding the sacred nature of the relic.

The jar of manna we have already explained above.

The bolide that fell from heaven has never been fully explained. Some scholars believe it might have been a part of the Eben-Shetiyah that ostensibly fell from heaven at the time of David; however, if the stone dates from the time of Moses, this would abolish that theory. More recent investigations support the theory that the

stone was the "Pillar of Jacob," the stone upon which he rested his head while dreaming the vision of the staircase to heaven. Afterwards, Jacob (Israel) erected the stone at Beth-el ("House of God"), ostensibly on the site where Solomon built the Temple. According to tradition, this was the stone "rejected by the masons" who constructed the foundation of the Temple, and it was the stone upon which every king of Israel was crowned from David to Zedekiah. This stone was ostensibly brought by the Prophet Jeremiah from Jerusalem to Ireland circa 585 B.C. where it became known in Irish tradition as the Lia Fail (Stone of Destiny). This relic is discussed elsewhere in this text in greater detail.

The rod of Moses, called the Shamir, is inextricably connected to the powers of the Ark of the Covenant. Yet virtually nothing of it is mentioned in scripture. The word "Shamir" appeared only four times in the Old and New Testaments (Joshua 15:48; Judges 10:1; Judges 10:2; Chronicles 24:24)—thrice as a place name and once as the name of a man. None of these could have been the "magical" Shamir, the secrets of which the Masons claimed had been concealed in the Bronze pillars that held up the portico of Solomon's Temple.

According to the Bible, the Temple's builder and master mason, Hiram (Hiram Abif of the Freemason tradition), fashioned

...two bronze pillars; the height of one pillar was eighteen cubits, and a cord twelve cubits long gave the measurement of its girth; so also was the second pillar.... He set up the pillars in front of the vestibule of the sanctuary; he set up the right-hand pillar and named it Jachin; he set up the left-hand pillar and named it Boaz, so the work on the pillars was completed. [I Kings 7:15, 21-22]

According to the "old ritual" of Masonic tradition these two great pillars had been hollow [*The Royal Masonic Cyclopedia*,

Kenneth Mackenzie, Aquarian Press, Wellingborough—first published 1877–1987, pp. 349-50]. Inside them had been stored the "ancient records" and the "valuable writings" pertaining to the history of the Jewish people [*King Solomon's Temple in the Masonic Tradition*, Aquarian Press, Wellingborough, Alexander Horne, 1988, p. 219], and amongst these records had been "the secret of the magical *Shamir* and the history of its properties." [Ibid.]

Simply because the Shamir is not mentioned in the Bible does not discount its authenticity. Both the Talmud and the Midrash refer to the Shamir in some detail. These sources state that because Moses had commanded the Israelites not to use "any tool of iron" in the construction of holy places [e.g. Deuteronomy 27: 5 "And there shalt thou build an altar unto the Lord thy God, an altar of stones: Thou shalt not lift up any iron tool upon them." [See also Joshua 8:31], Solomon had ordered that no hammers, axes or chisels should be used to cut and dress the massive stone blocks from which the outer walls and courtyard of the Temple had been built. Instead he had provided the masons with an ancient device dating back to Moses. Moses was said to have used the Shamir in the desert to engrave writing on the precious stones worn in the breastplate of the High Priest. [Ginzberg, op. cit., vol. I, p. 34 & vol. IV. p. 166] The Shamir was capable of cutting the toughest of materials without friction or heat [Ibid. vol. I, p. 34], and was also known as "the stone that splits rocks" [Ibid. vol. IV, p. 166], and

The Shamir may not be put in an iron vessel for safekeeping, not in any metal vessel: it would burst such a receptacle asunder. It is kept wrapped up in a woolen cloth, and this in turn is placed in a lead basket filled with barley bran.... With the destruction of the Temple the Shamir vanished. [Ibid. vol. I, p. 34]

Ancient tradition claimed that the Shamir had possessed "the remarkable property of cutting the hardest of diamonds." [Ibid. vol. I, p. 34] A collateral version of the same story adds that it had been quite noiseless while in operation. [Islamic traditions, reported by Alexander Horne, op. cit., p. 165.] In some accounts the Shamir is said to have cut stone with "a worm of light," after which it was utilized to levitate the great stones in place.

The Shamir figured prominently in the wonder-making of Moses. It was used, for instance, in the parting of the Red Sea, to create the miracles of the plagues in Egypt, and when held above Moses' head secured success in battle against the Amalakite armies and to strike fresh water from the rocks of the desert.

The legends of the Jews and esoteric tradition maintains that it was the Shamir with which Enoch anciently constructed the Great Pyramid of Giza in Egypt and hid up within it arcane sciences and knowledge to preserve it from the impending deluge (see Ginzberg, op. cit.).

An independent Arab source states that the stones which were used to construct the pyramid were wrapped in papyrus and then "struck with a rod by a priest." They thus became weightless and were transported through the air for about 50 meters and the procedure was repeated until the stones were in place. [*We Are Not The First*, Andrew Thomas, Bantam Edition, New York, 1973, p. 99] It is interesting that the author of the Book of Mormon was apparently well acquainted with the concept of the Shamir when it is stated: " And the Lord hath said: I will raise up a Moses; and I will give power unto him in a rod..." [2 Nephi 3:17].

The Shamir has been described as a metal rod about one cubit (18 inches) in length, and is the prototype of the later "magic wand." It may have been the source of much of the power of the Ark of the Covenant.

The Rod of Moses (Shamir) is not to be confused with the Rod of Aaron. The latter was a shepherd's staff, six to eight feet long, or the shorter version which was actually a club about three feet long with a knob on the end to beat off wolves from the sheep. The latter version appears the most probably in order to fit within the Ark. Aaron's rod or staff (in Hebrew, *Khoter*, a twig or branch) was also imbued with power, bringing about some of the plagues of Egypt. For example: "...for Aaron stretched out his hand with his rod, and smote the dust of the earth, and it became lice in man, and in beast; all the dust of the land became lice throughout all the land of Egypt." [Exodus 8:17]

It should be pointed out, however, that the Rod of Aaron seems to have derived its power from the Shamir or from the Ark itself, for we read in scripture:

And Moses spake unto the children of Israel, and every one of their princes gave him a rod apiece, for each prince one, according to their fathers' houses even twelve rods; and the rod of Aaron was among their rods. And Moses laid up the rods before the Lord [i.e., before the Ark] in the tabernacle of witness. And it came to pass, that on the morrow Moses went into the tabernacle of witness; and, behold, the rod of Aaron for the house of Levi was budded, and brought forth buds, and blossomed blossoms, and yielded almonds.... And the Lord said unto Moses, bring Aaron's rod again before the testimony, to be kept for a token against the rebels; and thou shalt quite take away their murmurings from me, that they die not. [Numbers 16:6-10]

Tradition maintains that among the many relics preserved in the Ark of the Covenant were scrolls containing the genealogical record of the twelve tribes of Israel, as well as other important histories and records concerning the origins of the Jews.

The Sword of Methuselah, traditionally one of the holy relics kept within the Ark, is perhaps the most historically significant; yet few people are aware of its amazing history. This sword is said to have been brought to this planet from another world by Adam, together with the Luminous Suit of Invulnerability. [Ginzberg, op. cit.] The sword was handed down to Enoch who used it to slay the giants who were in the earth in those days, and to Methusaleh, from whom it has often been called the "Sword of Methusaleh." In addition, it belonged to Jacob and various other Patriarchs in succession, as also Hercules, Atlas, and numerous others of the Greek and Roman Pantheon.

According to the legends of the Jews, the Sword of Methusaleh had mystical powers. It could only be wielded by a "rightful heir," and the sword recognized this person by his handprint upon the sword's hilt; it could not be wielded by an impostor. In the hands of a rightful heir, the sword made him an invincible champion of just causes.

The miraculous sword, mentioned only vicariously in the scriptures as "the sword of the Lord," or "the mighty sword of God," played an important part in the Arthurian legends of the Knights Templars, and has come down to us as "Excaliber." To the Welsh it was "Caliburnus," and it has had a myriad of other names and incarnations throughout history. It was said to have been the sword of Hector the Trojan, captured by his assassin Achilles, who passed it down through the generations to his descendent, Alexander the Great (other accounts state that Alexander removed the sword from Achilles' tomb). Alexander, by its power, conquered most of the known world. It was "Durandal" of Roland the Paladin, nephew of Charlemagne, who with it defeated the Moors; and according to legend, Roland obtained the sword in Ireland from Morgana le Fay, the sister of King Arthur, who was a Druidic priestess who had achieved immortality via the famous Philosopher's Stone.

Excaliber was called the "sword of Kings

since the foundation of the world." It allegedly had the power of light and levitation, much like the Shamir, and was activated only by the hand of the rightful king of the royal blood by virtue of his handprint on the hilt. Thus, only Arthur could activate the sword and remove it from the stone—the stone being either Jacob's Pillar or the Ark of the Covenant, which contained a bolide.

All of history is replete with mentions of the sword of God: Muhammad's cousin and son-in-law Ali the Shiah hero, had a miraculous sword called Dhual-fiqar [*Encyclopedia Brittanica*, 9:950; Quran (Koran), Surah 11:9], and Joan of Arc is said to have defeated her foes with a magical sword, found in the ruins of a castle or cathedral in France, directed by the voice of God. Beowulf, Scandinavian ancestor of the English race, defeated mystical monsters with a magical sword he discovered in an underwater cave, while his ancestor Thor, a nephew of Hector the Trojan, came down in history as a god, bearer of a mighty hammer, which interpreted from the early Norse actually meant "sword." This sword was supposedly carried from Troy to Persia and from thence into the North countries by Woden, who became Odin, god of the Norsemen.

In the Holy Kabballah a magical sword was hidden in a cave beneath Solomon's Temple, and in Masonic tradition with it the Master Masons slew the evil men who killed Hiram Abif, builder of the Temple. Also in this cave were gold and brass plates, the Urim and Thummim, and a mystical ball similar to the Liahona of the Book of Mormon.

To Joseph Smith the sword of God was an important element in the Book of Mormon, having been the sword of Nephi with which he slew Laban to obtain the brass plates upon which were engraved the genealogy of his family.

Joseph Smith and Oliver Cowdery allegedly entered a cave in the Hill Cumorah where, in addition to the gold plates of the Book of Mormon, they found the sword of Laban hung upon the wall, and later unsheathed, lying upon a table. The sword, according to Brigham Young, had the following inscription: "This sword will never be sheathed again until the kingdoms of this world become the Kingdom of our God and his Christ.... [*Journal of Discourses*, 19:36-39, from a sermon given at Farmington, Utah, 17 June 1877.]

The Luminous Suit of Adam was supposedly a vestment (garment) given to Adam by God to cause him to be invulnerable against the attacks of Satan [Ginzberg, op. cit.], and was handed down through his descendants until it came into the hands of Nimrod. Nimrod used the garment to become the mightiest of kings and, according to esoteric tradition, he also possessed the Shamir, and with it constructed the Tower of Babel. Abraham was able to defeat Nimrod when God caused a beetle to crawl into Nimrod's ear while he slept and "vexed" him to insanity. Abraham thus secured the return of the holy relics.

The suit was also alleged to have been the garment which was stolen by Ham while his drunken father Noah slept after leaving the Ark (ship), and with which Ham and his descendants (through Nimrod) claimed the priesthood.

The vestments of Aaron the High Priest used in the Tabernacle and later in the Temple were copied upon this garment. The Lord warned Aaron that he must put on these protective clothes to approach the Mercy Seat or die. [Leviticus 16.]

There are other relics associated with the Ark of the Covenant which space does not permit details: the harp of David (which played music by itself), David's pipe or flute. Most revered of all, however, was the remarkable Urim and Thummim.

The High Priest alone (with the exception of Moses, David, and Solomon) could invoke the powers of this miraculous device. The High Priest wore an ephod, an apron-like garment with a pouch, over which he wore a breastplate set with twelve precious stones engraved (by virtue of the Shamir) with the names of the Twelve Tribes. The Urim and Thummim were contained in a pouch within the ephod and beneath the breastplate over the heart of the High Priest. When so worn, the High Priest became an oracle, receiving direct communication from the Lord.

> And thou shalt put in the breastplate of judgment of Urim and Thummim: and they shall be upon Aaron's heart, when he goeth in before the Lord: and Aaron shall bear the judgment of the children of Israel upon his heart before the Lord continually. [Exodus 28: 30. See also: Lev. 8:8; Num. 27: 21; Deut. 33:8; I Sam. 28:6; Ezra 2:63; and Neh. 7:65.]

The foregoing passage indicates that the Urim and Thummim worked in conjunction with, or by virtue of, the Ark of the Covenant. Some scholars equate the Urim and Thummim with the Holy Grail because both are said to have had the ability to project words and images much like a modern television screen. However, most scholars now agree that if any such comparison could be made, it is more likely that the Grail was synonymous with the Ark itself.

The Ark of the Covenant was unique to scripture. No other holy relic is so revered as to be equated with God Himself, and it was matchless in its awesome deeds. It was the *only* artifact explicitly and unambiguously portrayed as being imbued with supernatural powers. Thus it continued to lift itself, its bearers, and nearby objects off the ground; it continued to emit unearthly light; it continued to fly and find its own way; it continued to be associated with a strange "cloud" that materialized "between the cherubim"; it continued to kill those who accidently touched or opened it, sometimes by deadly fire, sometimes by something akin to electrocution; it

continued to afflict people with ailments like "leprosy" and "tumors"; and it continued to communicate by image and voice.

Before passing from the subject of the Ark, some additional explanation must be made of the Tables of Stone. The traditional image of the two stone tablets that supposedly contained the Ten Commandments as being large blocks of granite or other such stone, as portrayed for example in Cecil B. Demille's motion picture *The Ten Commandments*, must be discarded. The most detailed descriptions of the tablets are contained in the Talmudic-Midrashic sources and reveal the following information: 1- They were "made of a sapphire-like stone"; 2- They were "not more than six hands in length and as much in width" but were nevertheless enormously heavy; 3- Though hard they were also flexible; 4- They were transparent. [Ginzberg, op. cit., vol. III, pp. 118-19.]

It was upon these objects that the Ten Commandments were supposedly written by Yahweh himself, as the Bible is at pains to point out:

> When He had finished speaking with Moses on the mountain of Sinai, He gave him the two tablets of the Testimony, tablets of stone, inscribed by the finger of God.... And Moses turned and went down from the mount with the two tablets of the Testimony in his hands, tablets inscribed on both sides, inscribed on the front and on the back. These tablets were the work of God, and the writing on them was God's writing. [Exodus 31:18; 32: 15-16]

But these were the tablets that Moses threw down and broke in a fit of pique because the perfidious Israelites had fashioned a golden calf to worship. Accordingly God instructed Moses to return to the mountain top to receive two new tablets. However, this time there was a distinct difference: on his second descent from the mountain " the skin of his face shown."

[Exodus 34:29] What caused this divine radiance, which had not occurred previously? The Talmudic-Midrashic sources again provide an answer: When God handed the tablets to Moses, "He seized them by the top third, whereas Moses took hold of the bottom third, but one third remained open, and it was in this way that the Divine radiance was shed upon Moses's face." [Ginzberg,op. cit., vol, III, p. 119.]

This effect upon the face of Moses was so pronounced, perhaps even gruesome, that when he arrived in the camp all the Israelites were "afraid to come nigh him." [Exodus 34:30] To spare their feelings "he put a veil over his face" [Exodus 34:33] and ever afterwards, except when he was alone in his tent, he wore this veil. [Exodus 34: 34-5]

It would be possible to speculate endlessly about the true nature of the Ark of the Covenant—and of its contents. But we cannot ignore one important tradition, based upon a myriad of substantial evidence, strongly held by Cabalistic and Knights Templar orders: That the Ark contained the fabulous and mysterious relic known as the Emerald Tablet.

The Emerald Tablet was a miraculous device, composed of translucent emerald crystal, that contained all of the secrets of the universe and included the secret word or name of God by which all things were created, and by which utterance could unravel that same creation. For that cause, it was placed in the Ark of the Covenant for absolute protection.

One of the properties of the Emerald Tablet was the ability for its inscription to change as required for instruction (not unlike the description given of the Tablets of Stone containing, supposedly, the Ten Commandments), and it sometimes vibrated or "groaned" by virtue of its power. It also on occasion emitted a powerful light and was "influenced" by the rising of the constellation Pleiades (perhaps the "sweet influences of the Pleiades" mentioned by Job in the Old Testament).

According to tradition, the Emerald Tablet was obtained by the patriarch Enoch, either as a relic descended from Adam, or obtained by Enoch during his visit to seven celestial worlds (the basis of *The Book of Enoch*: R.H. Charles, trans., Society for the Propagation of Christian Knowledge, London, 1987). Enoch, according to the same tradition, became deified in Egypt as "Thoth," who taught language, writing, and the sciences to the Egyptians, and built the Great Pyramid at Giza (by use of the Shamir) wherein he placed the Emerald Tablet and other holy relics to preserve them from the impending great flood. These relics were eventually retrieved by Moses and became a part of the contents of the Ark of the Covenant. [For additional information on the Emerald Tablet, see: *The Secret Teachings of All Ages, An Encyclopedic Outline of Masonic, Hermetic, Qabbalistic, and Rosicrucian Symbolical Philosophy*, Manly P. Hall, Philosophical Research Soc., Los Angeles, 1928.]

The Ark of the Covenant was not only the most revered relic in history, but the most feared. Its power could hardly be contained and during its sojourn in the wilderness it had literally destroyed thousands of people, both friend and foe alike. The writer Graham Hancock summarized his conclusions in these words:

There was, I felt, a real sense in which the Temple appeared to have been built less as an earthly palace for a dearly beloved but incorporeal deity than as a kind of *prison* for the Ark of the Covenant. Within the Holy of Holies, above the two cherubim that face each other across the relic's golden lid, Solomon had installed two additional cherubim of giant size—grim guardians indeed, with wingspans of fifteen feet or more, all covered in gold. Meanwhile the Holy of Holies itself— the purpose of which, the Bible stated explicitly, had been "to contain the Ark of the Covenant of Yahweh" [I Kings 6:19]—had been a perfect cube, foursquare and immensely strong. Measuring thirty feet long, by thirty feet wide, by thirty feet high, its floor, its four walls and its ceiling had been lined with pure gold, weighing an estimated 45,000 pounds [2 Chronicles 3:8 states that 600 talents of fine gold were utilized; a talent weighed 75.6 pounds, therefor the total weighed more than 45,000 pounds—more than twenty tons], and riveted with golden nails. [2 Chronicles 3:9] [*The Sign and The Seal*, Graham Hancock, Crown pub. Inc. New York, 1992, p. 366]

It does appear from the evidence that the only way the Ark of the Covenant could be contained safely from its power was within a chest and walls of solid gold, and in thick darkness. Where did Solomon obtain so much gold? The Bible provides the answer as follows: "And Hiram sent in the navy his servants, shipmen that had knowledge of the sea, with the servants of Solomon. And they came to Ophir, and fetched from thence gold, four hundred and twenty talents, and brought it to King Solomon." [I Kings 9: 27-28]

This voyage across the sea, to the mysterious land of "Ophir," which has never been identified, brought back more than 32,000 pounds of gold—sixteen tons—and was but one of many voyages to take place.

Sometime prior to 587 B.C., when the Babylonian destruction of the Temple occurred, the Ark of the Covenant came up missing, removed and hidden to preserve it from capture. The Apocalypse of Baruch states that the relic had been swallowed by the earth below the great "Foundation Stone" known as the *Shetiyyah*. Reinforcing the belief that a cavern might have been located directly beneath the

Holy of Holies, the Talmud states that "the Ark was buried in its own place." [*Tractate Yoma*, 53b, Hebrew-English Edition of the Babylonian Talmud, Soncino Press, London, Jerusalem, New York, 1974.] This entombment, it appears, had been the work of King Josiah, who had ruled in Jerusalem from 640 to 609 B.C. [*Jerusalem Bible*, op. cit., Chronological Table, p. 345], just a decade before the first Babylonian seizure of the city. Near the end of his reign, the tradition maintained, foreseeing "the imminent destruction of the Temple, Josiah hid the Holy Ark and all its appurtenances, in order to guard them against desecration at the hands of the enemy." [*Tractate Yoma*, 52b, op. cit.; Ginzberg, op. cit., vol. IV, p. 282; *New Standard Encyclopedia of Judaism*, W. H. Allen, London, 1970, p. 158.]

In the final version of the tradition, either the Prophet Jeremiah removed the Ark from its hiding place and took it to Ireland circa 587 B.C., or the Ark was discovered by the Knights Templar circa 1118 A.D., or it was brought to Glastonbury in England shortly after the crucifixion of Christ by Joseph of Arimathea; the important issue is that it disappeared from the pages of history, never to be heard of again in scripture. The Old Testament reveals more than two hundred separate references to the Ark of the Covenant up until the time of Solomon, but after the reign of that great King (970-931 B.C.) it is almost never mentioned again. [*The Interpreter's Dictionary of The Bible, An Illustrated Encyclopedia*, Abingdon Press, Nashville, 1962, p. 222.]

Where is the Ark of the Covenant today? It is unlikely, considering its power to defend itself, that it should have been destroyed. Wherever it is, it must be contained within a place of thick darkness, probably a cavern, within a cubical lined with pure gold.

The premise of this book is to trace its possible return to the source of the sacred gold, the mysterious land of Ophir which, by this and other names, may well have been within the confines of present-day Utah.

Chapter Two

Brewer's Cave

We have never met John Brewer, but we have certainly heard a great deal about him. So has anyone else with an interest in ancient Utah artifacts, or who has read the defamatory article about him which appeared in the Wednesday, 26 November, 1975, edition of the *Deseret News*.

The newspaper displayed a large banner headline which read: "John Brewer has a cave, but he's not giving tours!" The description given of Brewer is not very flattering: "quiet, in his mid-forties, frail, amateur collector (of arrowheads)...has worked at (a) sewage plant...held odd jobs to support his wife and five children...has been on public welfare at times."

This was followed by a tirade from local university archaeologists who claimed to have "wasted their time exposing the man's works." Those works, in Brewer's case, happened to be "finding inscribed tablets and plates" of very ancient origin. It was noted that between 1963 and 1975, Brewer claimed to have found tablets and plates made of limestone, lead, copper, brass and gold. Dr. Ray Matheny, BYU archaeologist, concluded that they are "the meaningless work of a forger."

From the scholars' point of view, their professional opinions seem sound, exposing the limestone and lead plates as forgeries. Dr. William S. Adams, a cryptologist, examined the inscriptions and concluded that he "found so very few clusterings that from a language point of view I am forced to conclude that instead of a meaningful script, the work was the haphazard scratchings of a forger." What Dr. Adams appears to be saying is that merely because he cannot read the inscriptions, they are meaningless.

To make matters even worse, Adams ostensibly later visited the home of a cattle rancher's widow in Manti and during lunch opened a napkin which depicted some local cattle brands. He was dumbfounded, he said, to see some of the signs he had copied from the Brewer plates. Dr. Adams claimed that further investigation revealed that nearly one-fifth of the signs on the tablets were apparently inspired by registered Utah cattle brands. Dr. Adams, at the very least, was being very subjective; perhaps it did not occur to him that the brands could have been inspired by the signs, for the same signs are inscribed into ledges throughout the region.

It is not our purpose to defend John Brewer but to present information withheld by the so-called authorities and the biased press. If, by presenting the other side of the coin, the truth vindicates John Brewer, then justice will have been served.

Dr. Jesse Jennings, University of Utah archaeologist, stated that the tablet which the U. of U. obtained from Brewer was a "ridiculous" hoax. "Utah is peculiarly 'blessed' with antiquities frauds," Jennings postulated. "Many old gentlemen and eager youths have brought me things, and were upset when I told them they weren't real. Yet I had the general feeling they didn't believe me and went away pitying ME. I don't pay any attention to them anymore."

Dr. Jennings, often called the "Father of Utah Archaeology," was not being completely honest himself. In 1960, Brewer took eight small copper plates to Dr. Jennings at the University of Utah. After sharing them with some of his colleagues,

Dr. Jennings pronounced them fakes, but then curiously kept four of the smaller plates for further analysis, promising their return. Brewer never saw the plates again.

My late cousin, Gale Rhoades, discovered information to the effect that two of the copper plates in possession of Dr. Jennings had been spray painted with gold and sent to an eastern museum for evaluation. The museum returned the plates together with a report declaring them as fakes. Gale located Dr. Jennings, who by then had retired to another state, and queried him by telephone about the plates. Jennings adamantly denied that any such plates had ever been brought to the university. He very pointedly stated that anyone who thinks the Native Americans had metal records is in great error and that anyone professing to have found metal plates in Utah should be considered a fraud.

I had contacts at the University of Utah who permitted me to examine the acquisition accounts for the year 1960. There, plainly written, under date of 12 October 1960, was the acquisition receipt of "four small plates of pounded copper bearing inscriptions of unknown origin." It was signed by none other than Dr. Jesse Jennings. More significantly, another reference indicated that two of these plates had been subsequently (1962) donated to the Church of Jesus Christ of Latter-day Saints!

I placed my own telephone call to Dr. Jennings and confronted him with my discoveries, and asked him for an explanation. My question was met with silence. I then asked if he could at least explain why two of the plates subsequently ended up in possession of the Mormon Church. His tentative reply was that "the Mormon Church exerts a tremendous amount of influence in Utah."

The *Deseret News* interview of John Brewer revealed more details in regard to his unusual cave discoveries (he had not yet discovered the second cave):

"I found the cave about 20 years ago, when I was 22. George Kelley [sic: Keller], a Negro that lived in Manti, showed it to me after I gave him a couple bottles of wine. Inside the cave are big boxes with plates in them, two mummies (male and female), and a lot of gold stuff and figurines and stick-like things."

After the natural entrance to the cave fell in a few years later, Brewer said he dug his own thirty-foot tunnel, which is now beset with natural booby-traps for anyone who might discover it. He feels it's a private place, his own little work area, and says he spends hours tinkering around in the cave, widening it, bringing plates out into the open.

For years there was a snag—the cave was on private property. But the "old man" who refused to sell died, and his son now has sold Brewer ten acres, including the cave site, Brewer claims. Dr. Paul Cheesman of Brigham Young University's Religion Dept. has been trying to get Brewer to show him the cave, but Brewer has balked.

"Whenever I don't understand anything, I stall," Brewer said, and his actions verify that. He has put Cheesman off for four years and, in fact, hasn't shown a single person the cave—including his wife and children.

"Most people don't understand why I keep it a secret," he noted. The three reasons he gave this reporter were: "I value my privacy highly. Who gets the credit for finds like this? Always some professor working on his master's thesis, never the guide that showed him the place. I have three boys, and I don't have much money. I want to leave something for them."

Brewer maintains that at least three private collectors have "offered me six and seven place figures" for the cave....and its contents. I'm deep in debt, but so is everybody else. I just won't sell."

"I don't expect anybody to believe me," Brewer says. "And I'm not worried, either, because I know what I've got," he said, with an emphasis on the "I".

Meanwhile, while Jennings, Adams, Matheny and their colleagues were insisting that the plates were fraudulent, Dr. Paul Cheesman expressed mixed feelings. "They could be real," he stated. According to Brewer, the discoveries came about in the following manner.

On 30 March 1955, Brewer met George Keller and discussed the former's desire to enter his arrowhead collection in the county fair. Keller casually mentioned knowing about a cave behind temple hill (whereupon is situated the Manti Temple). He said there were a lot of arrowheads to be found there. On May 10th Brewer went alone to look for the cave but couldn't find it. On May 19th Brewer went out to the Keller place and offered him some wine to show him the place, which he did. Brewer entered the cave and found thirty arrowheads.

In the course of time, Brewer discovered numerous artifacts of apparent ancient origin, many of which he brought out in the hope of making an identification through the universities. But the greatest discovery was two well-preserved mummies entombed within a large stone sarcophaguses—a man and a woman.

Brewer made pen-and-ink sketches of the two mummies looking downward into each of the stone coffins. Each of the stone coffins was inscribed, according to Brewer, with a "Dragon motif." Brewer ascribed the mummies, in his journal, to be of Book of Mormon origin. He believed they might be Jaredites. According to "The Book of Ether" in the Book of Mormon, the Jaredites came from the vicinity of the Tower of Babel (in what is now central Iraq) and established themselves on the American continent, until their civilization was destroyed between 600 and 300 B.C.

Brewer also removed a number of stone boxes from both caves, some of which contained inscribed plates. Many of the stone boxes themselves, weighing about ninety pounds each, were inscribed with strange hieroglyphics and symbols. Those in the second cave appeared to be several centuries "newer" by virtue of their "fresher" appearance. Many of the inscriptions closely resemble Mayan glyphs, though the symbols do not appear to be related.

I recall my first reaction upon viewing photographs of the stone boxes removed from Brewer's caves. I had seen nearly identical stone boxes and symbols in the caves of Carre-Shinob in the high Uintah Mountains of northeastern Utah [see *The Gold of Carre-Shinob* by Kerry Ross Boren & Lisa Lee Boren, Bonneville Books, Springville, Utah 1998].

John Brewer's life became something of a nightmare after his discoveries were made public. George Keller, who had been a party to the initial discovery, was killed in an unexplained accident, and shortly thereafter threats were made against Brewer's own life if he continued to publicize his find. When he ignored the threats, his eldest son was killed under mysterious circumstances. He has been ridiculed, spurned, disparaged and shunned. Since that time, John Brewer has understandably avoided further publicity. It was with some trepidation that we decided to recount Brewer's story in these pages, not wishing to bring him more unwanted publicity. It is our hope that after our evidence has been presented, Brewer's reputation will be seen in a better light, and he may yet be credited with bringing forth discoveries that may lead to one of the most important treasures in the history of mankind.

Templar Knight—Brewer's Cave

—Male Mummie

—Believed to be of the Gunn/Sinclair clan

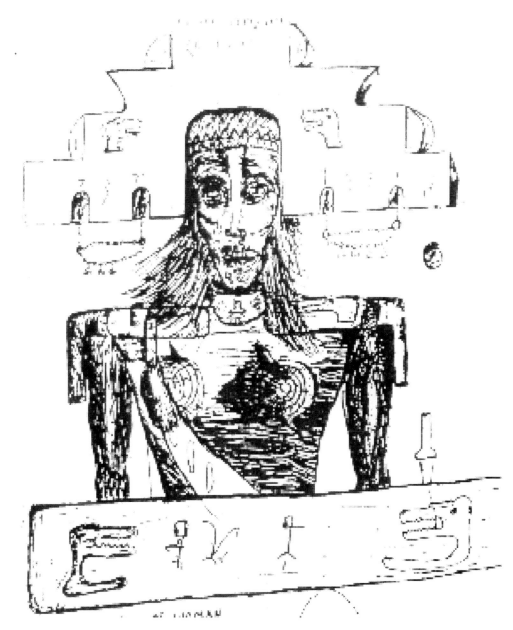

Female Mummie—resides with the Knight Templar Mummie
—Brewer's Cave

Chapter Three

The Secret of the Golden Fleece

The Hellenes (Greeks) are among the most ancient maritime nations in history. Proof of this was discovered by anthropologists at Franchthi Cave in Argolis (Pelloponnese) according to which Hellas seems to have had navigation since 7000 B.C.! The appearance of large quantities of obsidian from Melos and quantities of large fish bones (probably tuna) shows that the inhabitants of Franchthi Cave not only traded afar at this early date but also fished in oceanic waters.

The first recorded maritime expedition, a glorious and audacious common enterprise by Hellenes, was the Argonautic Expedition which took place around 1400 B.C. and by some accounts much earlier, around 2000 B.C. This was the expedition of Jason and the Argonauts in quest of the Golden Fleece.

Jason was the son of Aeson. King Cretheus of Iolcus, son of Aeolo, had two sons, Aeson and Pelias. As the eldest son, Aeson stood to inherit the throne by birthright upon the death of Cretheus, but when the old king died, Pelias usurped the throne. Pelias immediately consulted the oracle concerning the future of the kingdom and was warned to beware Aeolo's descendants because one of them would kill him. To protect himself, Pelias ordered the death of the Aeolides.

Jason's parents, concerned about their son's life, sent him away to be raised by the famous pedagogue Cheiron on Mount Pelion. Cheiron is often depicted in classical mythology as a centaur, a creature possessing the head, trunk, and arms of a man, and the body and legs of a horse. In reality he was a great teacher, bringing up Jason in all the arts, including medicine in which he excelled.

When Jason came of age he returned to Iolcus to reclaim the throne from his uncle Pelias. Pelias agreed to yield the throne to Jason if he brought him the Golden Fleece from the fabled land of Colchis. Pelias knew that what he asked from Jason was a hazardous and foolhardy venture from which he would likely never return. Jason, however, craving for heroic glory (cleos), accepted the challenge and went to Cheiron for advice. Cheiron exhorted all the Greek heroes—most of whom had spent a good portion of their lives being taught by him—to take part in the heroic expedition to the glory of Hellas and its people.

The ship was named *Argo* after her shipbuilder Argos, the first known ship in history to be given a name. The *Argo* was built near Mount Pelion, probably at Pagassus. The ship was shaped oblong, so it is often referred to as the "long vessel," the first of its kind at that time, as they used only small, round-shaped ships. By some accounts the *Argo* was a fifty-oared ship while by other accounts there were thirty oars on each side. This means that the ship's length was between 22 and 25 meters—over eighty feet. The wood used was probably oak and pine and the ship was equipped with all implements and tackling necessary for the operation of the *Argo*. Its solid construction enabled it to sail in open seas and to stand up well to the pounding of huge waves.

Because of her low draught she could easily and safely approach a sandy coast. Moreover, after the removal of the mast, the rudder, the ropes, the anchors, the oars and all else that could be carried away, the ship could be hauled by the Argonauts on the beach by means of "Falangia"—cylindrical pieces of wood which they always carried with them (*Argonautica* by Orpheus, 272- 273, 1104). Because the ship had to be hauled up the beach to avoid possible destruction by storms, it had no deck to avoid extra weight.

At the prow of the *Argo* was a "koraki" or "speaking" timber which would serve as a compass to advise the Argonauts on the right course. It was said that the goddess Athena had provided the "koraki" from the sacred oak of Dodona. It corresponded to the North while the steering oar "diaki" corresponded to the South. The imaginary line between the steering oar and the "speaking" timber extended towards a certain point on the horizon which was determined by the positions of stars and the sun, for tracing an approximate course by day or night.

The voyage of Jason and the Argonauts can be recounted from various sources, including the writings of Orpheus. The places mentioned must be surmised in consideration of the ancient names applied.

Now we come to the crux of the matter. Recent revolutionary hypotheses maintain that the primary voyage of Jason and the Argonauts brought them to the Americas! Having said that, we present the following account of one authority's search for the route of the Argo.

The *Argo*, having crossed the Mediterranean and passed through the Pillars of Hercules, was carried to the American Continent by the Gulf Stream. They sailed to the south of the Sargasso Sea ("the floating islands," Apollonius Rhodius, Book II, 285, 295, 298) and landed at Puerto Rico. The Sargasso Sea was named after the sea-weed known as Sargassum, which floats in island-like patches over hundreds of square miles of the Caribbean.

At Puerto Rico the Argonauts met the king and seer Phineus and freed him from the "Arpyias" (Harpies) which are not a poetic exaggeration but according to Apollonius' description these birds must have been the "Hoatzin" as they are now called in South America. From that place the Argo passed through the Windward Passage between the two islands of Haiti and Cuba—the Cyanean Rocks or Clashing Rocks.

According to Henriette Mertz the detailed and accurate description of this natural phenomenon would be possible only by eyewitness and this phenomenon exists precisely as described and exists in no other place. On the other hand, such tides do not take place in inland seas like the Black Sea or the Mediterranean; hardly of sufficient force to match Apollonius' description: "The current whirled the ship around."

After passing through the Clashing Rocks the *Argo* was said to have sailed into another broad sea, "where the two seas met," according to Apollonius. The two seas here would be the Caribbean and the Atlantic. Upon entering the warm Caribbean Sea after leaving the cold Atlantic, we read about a windless calm and airless silence where the Argonauts were compelled to bend over the oars with sweating and panting.

Following down the eastern coast of South America, the Argonauts came to the Rio De La Plata River (Phasis), according to Mertz's calculations. Sailing up the river they came to the south of Titikaka Lake where the tribe of Colchicourous lived. Mertz claims that the word "Colchicourous" is the Spanish equivalent for the Hellenic "Colchis."

To us, however, it appeared that the name "Colchicourous," applied to a tribe in South America, was less a Spanish term than a combination of the words "Colchis" and "Dioskouri." We are willing to agree with Henriette Mertz that the *Argo* sailed up the Rio De La Plata, for her extensive research seems sound. Additionally, ancient Hellenic inscriptions have been found there. There are also ancient Hellenic words in the languages of the Incas and the Mayans, as well as among the people of Hawaii. The Aegean origin of the architectural style of several buildings of the Mayans, the Aztecs and the Incas has been noted, and there have been ancient Hellenic finds in the Bahamas, as well as in Inca country. All of this constitutes further evidence that ancient Hellenes were capable of navigating tremendous distances, and that they crossed the Atlantic and visited the Americas in the remote past.

In summary, we had learned that Jason and the Argonauts were real historical figures, and that the voyage of the *Argo* in quest of the legendary Golden Fleece was a matter of record. But it appeared to us that some important points were missing or overlooked.

For example, we were unwilling to accept Mertz's theory that the Cyanean or Clashing Rocks were the Windward Passage straits between the islands of Haiti and Cuba. They simply did not fit the description of Apollonius Rhodius that they were fraught with sea-storms and waves crashing like mountains. Only one place on earth matched this description: the Straits of Magellan at the tip of South America. This also fits the description of "where the two seas met"—in this case the Atlantic and Pacific. If so, this would be a remarkable achievement and would mean that the Argonauts sailed up the west coast of South America and possibly even to the west coast of North America. This seems to be confirmed by the statement that because Aeetes had blocked their way back at Bosporus, the Argonauts sought a new way back to Iolcus. It is in fact tempting to believe that, having chosen this northern route through the Pacific, they may have circumnavigated the globe!

From other sources we learn that they sailed north, having learned of much gold to the north of Colchis (*Odyssey*, Z.P.

Petrides). Herodotus, in his book *Melpomeni* (27, 104), speaks of the existence of gold to the north of the Euxinus Pontus, though he equates it with the Scythian steppes. Herodotus says that "According to Issidones (Scythian nation) there are 'one-eyed people' and 'grypes' (winged monsters) guarding the gold..." And he adds, "Agathyrisi (another Scythian nation) live a life of luxury and wear a lot of golden jewellery...." The Scythians were a nomadic people, horseback warriors dwelling in skin houses. Though gold jewelry has been found in the tombs of their kings, they were never so wealthy as the people mentioned by Herodotus. What if they were not Scythians? What if they were another race that lived in the north of another continent—America? There were great civilizations in America at this time, with temples and gold and much luxury. And the "grypes" mentioned by Herodotus were references to Griffins—fabled creatures with the head and wings of an eagle and the body of a lion. No such creature exists in the mythology of the Scythians, but did exist among the inhabitants of America—the Mayans, the Incas and later the Aztecs. The "one-eyed people" who guard the gold may be a reference to the long-held belief of Greeks that there were cyclops in faraway places (e.g., *The Odyssey* by Homer) who guarded caves filled with great treasures.

But the best evidence that the Argonauts were in northern climes other than those of Scandinavian Europe is the mention that among other nations the Argonauts passed by were a people called "Hyperboreans." These strange people have never been identified. It is clear from the name that these people were not just to the north of the Euxinus Pontus but to the upper north (Hyper boreans). Ancient sources place them near the North Pole, but it is equally clear they were not Eskimo or Siberians.

There was in fact an intimate relationship between Hyperboreans and Hellenes, especially those from Delos Island because Apollo used to be the greatest god for Hyperboreans, and Delos was Apollo's birthplace. The Hellenes had apparently been visiting the Hyperboreans for ages. Diodorus Sykeliotis (B47) gives us a most intriguing statement: "Hyperboreans have their own language and they are favorably disposed towards Hellenes particularly Athenians and Delians—a friendship which they inherited from their ancestors. Tradition says that Hellenes had visited Hyperboreans leaving behind them some valuable votive offerings with Hellenic inscriptions."

Apollo was god of the sun; Native Americans worshiped the sun god. And ancient Hellenic inscriptions have been found in the Americas. What could be more clear? The Hyperboreans were the native race of North America, a distinction made to separate them from the race of Colchis farther south. But if the Hyperboreans lived far to the north in polar regions, then the land of Colchis, the land of the Golden Fleece, was somewhere in the continental United States!

———

Having placed Jason and the Argonauts in the Americas, and circumstantially in the western region of the United States, we developed our own hypothesis: in our opinion, the land of Colchis was located in the Great Basin, and more particularly in the Utah-Colorado-New Mexico-Arizona region. Subsequent research would narrow our focus to the Uintah Mountain-Sanpete Valley area. In subsequent chapters we hope to convince the reader not only of this fact, but also of the identification of the Golden Fleece. Moreover, we maintain that the Colchis were the ancestors of the Aztecs, who in turn were the ancestors of the Utes who revered both the Uintah Mountains and Sanpete Valley as sacred.

The capital city of Colchis was called Aeas, and Aeetes was king of that land. He was the appointed guardian of the Golden Fleece. Love blossomed between Jason and Aeetes' daughter Medea, who helped him to seize the Golden Fleece. Taking Medea with him, Jason fled to the *Argo* and put out to sea, pursued by the Colchians. Aeetes blocked their way back at Bosporus (Straits of Magellan) and the Argonauts had to find a new way back to Iolcus; the only way this could have occurred logically was for the Argo to sail westward, circumnavigating the globe. Perhaps it was on this return voyage, later to be confused as a second voyage, that they sailed through the lands of the Kimmereans and Scythians.

We can no longer ignore the presence of Hercules on the expedition. According to myth, Hercules (whose true name was Heracles) was son of the beauteous Alcmene; his father was the god Zeus who had seduced Alcmene by disguising himself as her husband Amphitryon. Zeus' wife, the goddess Hera, jealous over her husband's interest in Alcmene, delayed Hercules' birth, then sent two giant snakes to kill the infant in his cradle. Accounts differ as to whether it was Zeus or the remarkably strong baby Hercules who strangled and killed the serpents.

It is not necessary to recount here all of the amazing feats of Hercules. Suffice it that he was renowned for this tremendous strength and became legendary when he performed twelve superhuman labors. One of those labors is of particular interest to our hypothesis: Hercules was to retrieve the "golden apples" from the Garden of the Hesperides.

The Hesperides were the daughters of Atlas, whose kingdom lay somewhere west of the Pillars of Hercules on an island (or continent) in the Atlantic Ocean (which takes its name from Atlas). Some scholars believe that Atlas was king of the lost continent of Atlantis which also bears his name. Of interest to us was the fact that in order to obtain the "Golden Apples" in the Garden of the Hesperides, Hercules had to sail west into the Atlantic Ocean, virtually the same route taken by the *Argo*; and inasmuch as

Hercules was an Argonaut, it seems logical to conclude that this labor of Hercules was identical in legend to Jason's quest for the Golden Fleece.

It is further noteworthy that the name "Aztec" derives from the same root word as "Atlas," and according to Aztecan tradition the ancient king of their nation was a man equated with Atlas. When the Aztecs left the northern land to migrate south to Mexico, the city they established was called "Aztlan" which means "city of Atlas" and bears a remarkable similarity to the name of "Atlantis." Moreover, the symbol of the Aztecs was a griffin-like creature not unlike the "grypes" mentioned by Herodotus, winged monsters which guarded a fabulous treasure of gold.

———

We have established our hypothesis: Jason and the Argonauts sailed to the Americas; they sailed through the Straits of Magellan (the Clashing Rocks) and up the Pacific Coast to the western coast of the present-day United States; they penetrated inland to the Great Basin, specifically to the land of Colchis, which we believe to be the present-day Sanpete region of Utah; with the aid of Medea, Jason seized the Golden Fleece, loaded it aboard the *Argo*, and returned to Iolcus by a western global route.

What was the Golden Fleece? What relic could induce such a hazardous epic journey? Researchers have put forward a plethora of theories. One of them says that there was gold in the rivers of Colchis and the natives collected it by using fleeces. There may have been an actual relic known as the Golden Fleece, but like the Golden Apples in the Gardens of the Hesperides it appears to be more a symbol of a vast source of gold which was considered sacred by several nations, though guarded by the Colchians.

It should also be mentioned that Jason and the Argonauts, under the religious direction of Orpheus, erected a temple in the land of Colchis to mark the completion of their epic voyage; this will become an important factor in subsequent chapters.

The most significant member of the Argonautic Expedition, other than Jason himself, was Orpheus, the mystical religious leader who went on to be revered as a god. Orpheus was a Thracian, on which isle he constructed a temple, also connected to the Dioskouri. He was a musician who, when he played on his lyre, charmed rivers, stones, and even wild beasts. He was the son of Calliope, the muse of epic poetry. He was also said to be a Thracian river god and, interestingly, some have equated him with Apollo, the sun god. The Aztecs worshiped a sun god equivalent to Apollo.

Orpheus married the nymph Eurydice, who soon died by being bitten on the heel by a snake. Orpheus, in mythology, followed her to the underworld where he played his lyre to charm the deities to release her. He had to escort her to the upper world without looking at her, but he succumbed to the temptation, looked, and she disappeared before his eyes.

From that day forward Orpheus rejected women. Part of the Orphic Mysteries concerned the abstinence of sex and wine. Because he rejected the advances of powerful Thracian women, they tore him to pieces. In mythology, Orpheus was dismembered by Maenads at the urging of the god Dionysus who resented his worship of Apollo. The singing head and lyre of Orpheus is said to have floated to Lesbos where his oracle was established.

Orpheus is a significant figure in our hypothesis because he came to be revered among later hermetic societies such as the Knights Templar (who also worshiped a dismembered head) and the Freemasons. And those societies were to play a major part in the greatest golden treasure in recorded history, which would ultimately lead us directly to the Sanpete Valley region.

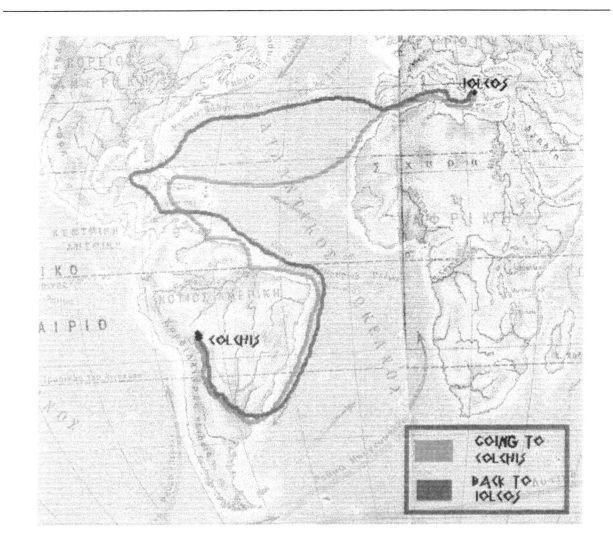

As per Henriette Mertz's Theory

As per Orpheas' Argonautica

As per Apollonius' Argonautica

Chapter Four

The Secret of Solomon's Temple

Three Temples have been associated with Mount Moriah in the city of Jerusalem. The first was the Temple built by King Solomon three thousand years ago. The second was that built by King Zerubabel in the early part of the sixth century B.C. after the Jews returned from their Babylonian captivity. The third and final Temple was being erected by Herod at the time of Jesus Christ and was destroyed by the Romans in 70 A.D., just four years after its completion.

But it is the Temple of Solomon that has obtained legendary status. It has remained associated with mysticism, ritual, power, and one of the greatest treasures the world has ever known.

It had been King David whose collaboration with the Philistines enabled him to take the throne of a divided Israel and make Jerusalem the center of his kingdom. The city was already established on a wealthy crossroads on the trade routes by the Jebusites, who called it Yerushalayim, meaning the "Foundation of the god Salem." Salem was their god of prosperity. And it was already sacred.

Here in the time of Abraham there ruled the mysterious and mystical King of Salem named Melchizedek—from "Melchior" and "Zadok," both of which mean "King"; thus Melchizedek means "King of Kings."

A table-like rock behind the city, named Moriah, was considered sacred long before the arrival of the Israelites. It was called Eben Shetiyah—the Foundation Stone— and was said to be a giant bolide which fell from Heaven. A Jebusite farmer named Araunah owned the rock, which he used as a threshing floor for grain, and sold it to King David who renamed it Sion (Zion). A Jebusite priest, Zadok, anointed Solomon king on the rock. And on the rock Solomon built his great Temple.

The workforce needed to construct the Temple was numbered at one hundred and eighty thousand, which included thirty thousand workers imported from Phoenicia. The Jews themselves had no architectural heritage, being primarily pastoral nomads, while the Phoenician architects and masons had more experience in building cities.

Beneath the city was the tunnel of Gihon, a large shaft that went down into a tunnel that led from the spring of Gihon, which served as a source of water to Jerusalem when the city was besieged by an enemy. It was this tunnel that allowed the Hebrews to capture Jerusalem. The mount beneath the Temple was honeycombed with natural caverns and manmade excavations.

The Temple was built about 950 B.C. Yahweh's Temple was almost a carbon copy of a Sumerian Temple erected for the god Ninurta a thousand years earlier. It is erroneous to assume that Solomon's Temple was a place where the Jews worshiped their God; it was not constructed to be visited by men—it was, quite literally, the House of God, a home for Yahweh himself.

The Temple was less than half as large as the palace Solomon had built for himself. It was not intended as a slight, however, but was constructed to the specifications of Yahweh himself. Mystics such as Sir Isaac Newton believed the architecture to contain mystical numerology which were codes to explain the mysteries of the universe.

The walls are said to have been nine cubits (about 13 feet 6 inches) thick at their base and supported a flat timber roof of cedar topped with fir. The interior was 90 feet long and 30 feet wide and the whole building was aligned from west to east with a single entrance at the eastern end. A partition divided the interior by a two thirds to one third measure, creating a cube 30 feet in height, width and length. A pair of folding doors was built into the partition to permit access.

This cubicle was the Oracle of the Old Testament, better known as the Holy of Holies, also known in Masonic rituals as the Sanctum Sanctorum. It was completely empty except for a rectangular box of shittim wood (acacia) 4 feet long by 2 feet wide and 2 feet high, placed in the exact center of the floor. On top of this box, which was covered with a thick sheet of solid gold, were two wooden cherubim, heavily covered with gold, with outstretched wings guarding the precious contents.

This was the legendary Ark of the Covenant which contained the two tablets of stone bearing the Ten Commandments of Yahweh and other holy relics: the mysterious Shamir, a small metal rod with supernatural powers, including what Solomon called a "worm of light" which cut the stones for the Temple (it was forbidden for metal to touch the stones) and levitated them into place; a small bolide that fell from the sky; a golden laver containing samples of the manna which had miraculously fallen from the heavens to feed the Jews at the time of the Exodus; the Rod of Aaron, a staff of wood which miraculously flowered on specific occasions; scrolls containing the genealogy of the Jews; the miraculous Sword of Methuselah, and more.

But the Ark of the Covenant was much more than a holy reliquary, for the Mercy Seat, between the wings of the cherubim, was the place where Yahweh himself appeared from time to time to speak to the Holy Priest, as He had spoken in more ancient times to Moses.

Legends from medieval times told a story of the Ark being hidden in a cavern within the foundation of the Temple before the Babylonian captivity. The laity also had to be protected from the power of the Ark, which could exert supernatural force against the uninitiated. The High Priest was compelled to wear protective vestments upon entering the Holy of Holies; two of the sons of Aaron were killed by a "holy fire" emanating from the Ark for failing to take precautions. Uzziah, who innocently put his hands upon it to keep it from being tipped over while being transported in a cart, was instantly struck dead. In I Chronicles 15:2 it is said that "none ought to carry the Ark of God but the Levites" and in Deuteronomy 10:8, "At that time he separated the tribe of Levi, to carry the Ark of the Covenant." The warnings are clear. The Ark was used to win battles, kill people, and even to cause sickness. Its power was so great it became the object of capture, but when the Philistines captured it and placed it in their own temple of Dagon, it caused their statue of that god to fall and shatter. They begged the Hebrews to take it back.

The Holy of Holies was kept in permanent darkness except for once each year on the Day of Atonement when the High Priest, dressed in his protective vestments, entered with the blood of a scapegoat, the national sin-offering. On that occasion the sunlight was permitted to enter the chamber through an oval aperture in the exterior Sun Gate and to fall in a shaft of light on the Ark. After the High Priest left, a large chain of gold was placed across the doors sealing off the smaller chamber from the larger. The outer chamber, used exclusively by Priests and Levites, contained a gold-covered cedar altar placed squarely in front of the eastern doors. Just outside the doors stood two mysterious pillars called Boaz and Jachin. Jachin, the right-hand pillar, represented Judah in the north, and the other, Boaz, the left-hand pillar, represented Israel in the south—yet they had other arcane and mystical significance known only to the initiated.

The interior of the Temple was decorated in both Hebrew and Egyptian motif. The walls were lined with cedar brought from Tyre—the famous "Cedars of Lebanon." The most distinguishing characteristic, however, was the tremendous amount of gold which covered the floor, walls and ceiling—tons of it—set amongst carvings of Egyptian cherubim and open flowers, with both Hebrew and Egyptian characters inscribed throughout.

The massive Temple complex that King Solomon ordered to be built included an annex that would serve as the treasury, but this was not the only place where treasures would be hidden. Throughout the turbulent history of Jerusalem, the Temple was looted several times, yet mysteriously the treasure was replaced.

After Solomon's reign, the wealth of Jerusalem also attracted enemies. Sheshonk, a Libyan pharaoh, forced Jerusalem to ransom itself when the Hebrews were ruled by Reheboam. Asa, the grandson of Reheboam, used the treasury to fight off a contender to the throne. Joas found the treasury entirely depleted when he took over. But the treasure was always somehow mysteriously replenished. In 716 B.C. Hezekiah added to the tunnel system beneath the city and was enabled to resist siege by the Assyrians. The Babylonian captivity began in 586 B.C., putting an end to the rule of the Davidic kings, and the history of Israel thereafter became a list of outside conquerors.

The mystery of Solomon's Temple deepens when examined at length. Solomon barely had enough money to complete the construction of the Temple, since virtually all of the expertise and raw materials were foreign and imported at great expense. King Hiram of Tyre provided the skilled workforce and most of the materials. Solomon sold many cities to pay off the mounting debts. The Jews had to endure forced labor, with ten thousand workers monthly, on a rotation basis, being sent to Lebanon to work for Hiram. The kingdom was split into twelve regions, with each region responsible for providing taxes to the palace for one month of each year. Tax levels became oppressive and Solomon's popularity suffered accordingly among his subjects.

The Kingdom was nearly bankrupt supporting Solomon's desire for grandeur, and towards the end of his reign Solomon gave himself over to the sole worship of gods other than Yahweh, which caused great consternation with the priests of the Temple. This "wickedness" of Solomon's was not punished by Yahweh; in fact, Yahweh praised Solomon as a favorite and bestowed upon him "wisdom."

Nevertheless, when Solomon died, the country was not only virtually bankrupt, but Godless. Under the kingship of Solomon's son Rehoboam, the unity of the two lands quickly fell apart and the northern kingdom of Judah had no more to do with Israel. But Solomon died leaving the secrets of the Temple to be handed down amongst a royal group—the precursors of later secret societies.

The question then remains unanswered: if Solomon mortgaged his kingdom to build a Temple, where did the immense amounts of gold with which it was adorned come from? Tons upon tons of gold were utilized in interior decoration, and uncountable tons more of it were stored in the underground chambers beneath the Temple mount. While Solomon's kingdom was bankrupt and impoverished, his Temple was the wealthiest treasure trove in the world.

The one thing that is certain is that the gold came from outside of the Holy Land, for no such gold source exists there. The gold, like the other raw materials for the Temple, came by ship from foreign ports. Ships from faraway places like Sheba (in Arabia) brought goods that originated in the Orient. Ships of the Dan, a sea people of the Mediterranean who traded with the Phoenicians, sailed far west to Spain and the isles of Britain and a mysterious kingdom near Spain, called Tortessus. Solomon even had his own fleet. Rumors still persist that Solomon acquired his gold from famous lost mines in Africa, and people still search for "King Solomon's Mines."

The transportation of the gold from its source was most probably accomplished by the Phoenicians under the direction of King Hiram of Tyre. The Phoenicians were the greatest sailors in the world. Long before Solomon's time they had plied most of the seas of the world, and there is strong evidence that they visited the Americas. Certainly by 600 B.C., prior to the destruction of Solomon's Temple, Pharaoh Necho II of Egypt commissioned a fleet of Phoenician ships, together with some of his own Egyptian sailors, to sail around the Cape of Good Hope and return to Egypt by way of the Arabian Sea. Their voyage took four years, during which time they were blown off course and landed in South America, where the Phoenician inscription of their journey has been found carved in stone [*Explorers of the New World*, Katherine & John Bakeless, G.Bell & Sons, London].

It is an interesting side note that the Phoenicians, who were great stonemasons, left evidence of their travels in various parts of the world by carving their symbols on rock walls, on ledges, and in caverns wherever they went. The same is true of the Egyptians and the Greeks, who frequently combined their voyages with the Phoenicians. Collectively they were known as the Peleset, or Sea Peoples.

———

Near the time of the building of Solomon's Temple, 250 years after the voyage of Jason and the Argonauts, the Milesians invaded Ireland. We know this from a very good source. The best preserved and most complete chronicles of

Ireland known as the "Plantation of Ulster" date from about 700 B.C. One section thereof are the "Milesian Records." The name "Milesian" in the Greek means "warrior" or "mercenary." The Milesian Records give the account and genealogy of Gallam [William the Conqueror of Ireland, the last person mentioned in the genealogy, who is also called Miletus and Miletius (or Milesius)].

Milesius was a Greek mercenary, a soldier of fortune, who spent time in Egypt connected to the army of Pharaoh Sheshonk (a.k.a. Shishak). He rose in power and esteem and married Scota, the pharaoh's daughter. It should be explained that "Scota" is not a personal name, but a title, much like "princess." So it comes as no surprise to learn that two other daughters of Pharaoh Sheshonk were also called Scota; one of them married a man named Nile; the other became one of the many wives of King Solomon (apparently an important wife, because for her he built a separate palace).

Nile was the grandson of a man named Gadhael Glas, a Scythian Celt who founded the Gaelic race of Ireland. Gadhael Glas had led a migration of his people from the steppes near the Black Sea to the northern Mediterranean coast of Africa (present day Libya), a land they called Gaetulia. Nile left Gaetulia with a contingent of followers and settled in Egypt. Having married a daughter of Pharaoh Sheshonk, he became brother-in-law of Milesius and also of Solomon.

Milesius was a renowned sailor and explorer who had sailed "all the known seas" of the world. He was admiral of the Phoenician fleet and thus in charge of gathering and transporting the raw materials for the construction of Solomon's Temple. In this venture he was accompanied by his brother-in-law, Nile.

Upon completion of the Temple, Milesius and Nile sought new lands to settle. According to legend, because Nile's race had saved Moses from snakebite, Moses prophesied that the Gaels would find a home on an island where there were no snakes. That island was, of course, Ireland. It is likely that Milesius, at least, was already aware of the existence of Ireland. Some review of the early history of Ireland is important to our text.

Judah, son of Jacob (Israel), was the father of twin sons, Pharez and Zarah, by his union with Tamar. Pharez, the first born, was a breach birth. Zarah had first extended his hand from the womb and a scarlet thread had been tied around the tiny wrist, the hand withdrew, and Pharez came forth, and therefore received the birthright. From Pharez descended David, the first king from the tribe of Judah, and father of Solomon. The royal line of Pharez, established in David, was unbroken until the command of the Lord was given concerning Zedekiah, "...take off the crown; exalt him that is low, and abase him that is high."

When Zedekiah was dethroned there was a breach in the line of Pharez, for not another king had reigned over the tribe of Judah. The scriptures relate: "And the sons of Zarah: Zimri, and Ethan, and Herman, and Calcol, and Dara; five of them in all." Two of Zarah's descendants are given as authors of certain of the Psalms. And Solomon is described as having wisdom greater "than Ethan, the Ezrahite, and Herman, and Calcol, and Darda."

Historical records show that Darda, "the Egyptian", son of Zarah, was "Dardanus" the Egyptian founder of Troy, and his brother Calcol was "Cecrops" of Greece. One early account states:

Hecataeus, therefore, tells us that the Egyptians, formerly, being troubled by calamities, in order that the divine wrath might be averted, expelled all the aliens gathered together in Egypt. Of these, some, under their leaders Danaus and Cadmus, migrated to Greece.

The "calamities" referred to were obviously the plagues which God brought down on the Egyptians, and the "aliens" were the Israelites, some of whom migrated to Greece with Danus and Cadmus, while others, under the leadership of Moses, made their Exodus. Diodorus gives another version:

Now the Egyptians say that...a great number of colonies were spread from Egypt all over the inhabited world. ...They say also that those who set forth with Danaus, likewise from Egypt, settled what is practically the oldest city of Greece, Argos, and that the nations of *Colchi in Pontus* [italics added; "Colchi in Pontus" means literally "Colchi in the Ocean"] and that of the Jews [remnant of Judah] which lies between Arabia and Syria, were founded as colonies by certain emigrants from their country, and this is the reason why it is a long-established practice instituted among these peoples to circumcise their male children, the custom having been brought over from Egypt. Even the Athenians, they say, are colonists from Sais in Egypt. [*Diodorus of Sicily*, G.H. Oldfather, London, 1933, Vol. 1, Books I-II, 1-34, p.91]

Turning once again to Calcol or Cecrops (Calcor of 1 Chron. 2:6 and Chalcol of 1 Kings 4:31), *The Harmsworth Enclopedia* claims him as the mythical founder of Athens and its first king. He was believed to have been originally a leader of a band of colonizers from Egypt.

The descendants of Calcol migrated along the shores of the Mediterranean Sea, establishing Iberian (Hebrew) trading settlements. One settlement was called "Saragossa," in the Ebro Valley in Spain, and was originally known as "Zarah-gassa," meaning "The Stronghold of Zarah." From Spain they continued westward as far as Ireland. The Iberians gave their name to Ireland, calling the island "Iberne" which was later abbreviated to "Erne" (Erin) and subsequently Latinized to "Hibernia." Thus the "Hibernians" or "Iberians" (after Eber or Heber, ancestor of the Hebrews) who came to Ireland about 1700 B.C. were undoubtedly Hebrews, descended from

Abraham through Judah's son Zarah and grandson Calcol. Gladstone's *Juventus Mundi* and the old *Psalter of Cashel* both state that some of the Grecian Danai left Greece and invaded Ireland. Petanius and Hecataeus of Abdera (6th Century) speak of Danai as being Hebrew people, originally from Egypt, who colonized Ireland. Moore's *History of Ireland* states that the ancient Irish, called the "Danai" or "Danes," separated from Israel around the time of the Exodus from Egypt, crossed to Greece and then invaded Ireland.

Of pertinent note is that Milesius sailed to Saragossa, Spain, following the completion of his voyages for Solomon, accompanied by Nile and his family. Milesius died in Spain, and his wife Scota and his grown sons continued on to Ireland's west coast and engaged in battle with the native races of Firbolgs and Tuatha de Danaan, where Scota, wife of Milesius, was killed. Subsequently, Ireland was divided between the two sons of Milesius, and has remained divided—north and south—ever since.

The "other" Scota, wife of Nile, settled in Alba, lending her name to that place which came to be known as "Scotia" or "Scotaland"—modern day Scotland.

Modern theorists have deduced from the description of the voyage of Jason and the Argonauts that the land they visited—Colchis—was the American Continent. If the Golden Fleece was in fact a great golden treasure, it might well explain the source of Solomon's gold. But we would first have to establish a connection.

Milesius was a renowned sailor who had visited foreign lands, and was one of those Greeks who lived in Egypt and who, according to Diodorus, established "a great number of colonies...from Egypt all over the inhabited world." He was also admiral of the Phoenician fleet belonging to King Hiram of Tyre, the same fleet which transported the wealth of raw materials—including the gold—for the construction of Solomon's Temple. And Milesius was Solomon's brother-in-law.

But there is yet another connection of considerable importance: Milesius was a direct descendant of Jason! It seemed to us more than coincidence that Jason had sailed in quest of a fabulous source of gold, ostensibly somewhere in the New World, and 250 years later his descendant Milesius, also alleged to have sailed to the New World, supplied Solomon with the greatest treasure of gold in recorded history.

In summary, it appears that a fabulous gold source was known of in the New World from very ancient times, visited by Jason and his Argonauts circa 1194 B.C., and which became the basis of the legend of the Golden Fleece. Milesius, a descendant of Jason, apparently knew of both the New World and the gold source, and sailed there in behalf of his brother-in-law Solomon, for the benefit of the construction of Solomon's Temple. This seems to be the basis of the legend of "King Solomon's Mines."

However it came about, Solomon's Temple was adorned with gold beyond measure, and the cavernous vaults below the Temple in the bowels of Mount Moriah were stuffed with even more. It was the greatest treasure in the history of the world, and in subsequent chapters we will present evidence that it came from the Sanpete region of present-day Utah.

Chapter Five

The Knights Templar

For almost two hundred years the Templars were more powerful than kings, with a reputation for wealth and fighting ability that has made them legendary. The modern image of the crusading knight is that of a bearded warrior in armor, wearing a white mantle decorated with a red cross, slaying the wicked and protecting the good, while in fact it pertains only to that mysterious group of mystic warriors known as the Knights Templar.

The Muslims had ruled Jerusalem since the seventh century. During their reign they had allowed Jews and Christians access to the city for their own religious purposes. Near the end of the eleventh century Seljuk Turks took control of Jerusalem and banned Christians from making pilgrimages. Christians united to form "holy armies" to battle for control of the Holy Land, which came to be known as the "Crusades."

The conflicts were far from holy and the Crusaders proved to be little more than merciless self-seeking Christian invaders. For example, they believed that the Muslims were in the habit of swallowing their gold and jewelry to hide them from invaders and consequently many Muslims died in agony with their bellies torn open. The Jews of Jerusalem, who had lived side by side with the Muslims for centuries, fared no better. On 14 June 1099 they were slain beside their Muslim neighbors. Thousands of women, children and the elderly fled to the Temple mount and climbed upon the domed roof of the mosque which had replaced the Temple, and herded inside in droves. But the Crusaders, led by Tancred, Norman King of Sicily, rode into the mosque on the Dome of the Rock and mercilessly slew every living person there assembled, trampling them beneath their horses' hooves until "there was blood to the horses' wethers [sic: withers]." Refugees on the Dome itself became bloody target practice for Tancred's archers.

During the years that followed the capture of Jerusalem, Christians from all over Europe began to make the pilgrimage to the Holy City. It was a journey replete with danger from pickpockets, con artists, pirates and highwaymen. Often, dishonest shipowners sold their entire cargoes of Christian pilgrims into slavery in northern Africa.

In 1118 AD a French nobleman from Champagne by the name of Hugues de Payen, together with eight other knights, established the unofficial Order of the Poor Soldiers of Christ and the Temple of Solomon. King Baldwin II, the patriarch of Jerusalem, gave his support to the new Order and provided quarters for them in the eastern part of his palace which joined the former Al-Aqsa Mosque and stood on the site of King Solomon's Temple. The Knights Templar, as they came to be called, ostensibly came into existence for the purpose of providing protection for the increasing number of pilgrims as they made their hazardous journeys between the coastal port of Jaffa and Jerusalem. This was a strange claim. How could nine knights, who were so poor in the beginning that they had to ride two to a horse, protect a throng of pilgrims from overwhelming numbers of Saracens?

These original knights took an oath of poverty, chastity and obedience as though they were monks. Initially they wore no special clothing and behaved as though they were members of a religious order, praying fervently. It was not until they had lived on the site of Herod's Temple for nine years that Hugues de Payen left for Europe in search of worthy recruits who would swell the Order to a much greater size.

Why would King Baldwin give nine poor knights unrestricted use of the portion of his palace directly over the ruins of the Temple? The French historian Gaetan Delaforge provides us with an answer:

The real task of the nine knights was to carry out research in the area in order to obtain certain relics and manuscripts which contain the essence of the secret traditions of Judaism and ancient Egypt, some of which probably went back to the days of Moses. [*The Templar Tradition in the Age of Aquarius*, Gaetan Delaforge, Threshold Books, Putney, VT, 1987]

There is ample evidence that the Templars did excavate beneath the Temple ruins. In his landmark book *The Sign and the Seal*, Graham Hancock quotes from an Israeli archaeologists' official report concerning the Templar's excavations:

The tunnel leads inward for a distance of about 30 meters from the southern wall before being blocked by pieces of stone debris. We knew that it continues further, but we had made it a hard-and-fast rule not to excavate within the bounds of the Temple Mount, which is currently under Moslem jurisdiction, without first acquiring the permission of the appropriate Moslem authorities. In this case they permitted us only to measure and photograph the exposed section of the tunnel, not to conduct excavation of any kind. Upon concluding this work...we sealed up the tunnel's exit with stones. [*The Sign and the Seal*, Graham Hancock, Crown Pub. Inc., New York, 1992]

Writers have speculated that the Templars may have been looking for the lost treasures of Solomon's Temple, searching for the Holy Grail, or even trying to find the Ark of the Covenant. They obviously found something—but what? Whatever it was, it shook them up considerably and even challenged their Christian beliefs.

A few months after the death of their benefactor, Baldwin II, in October 1126, Hugues de Payen made a journey west to seek recruits for the Order for the first time. A letter he wrote while traveling through Europe clearly illustrated his concern that his fellow knights in Jerusalem needed a bolstering of their convictions. The letter referred to the knights' original mission being weakened by the devil and quoted biblical passages to reassure his seven remaining knights.

Payen was accompanied on his journey by Andre de Montbard, one of his knights, who was the uncle of the very young but highly influential Abbot of Clairvaux (destined to become St. Bernard). Bernard became the instant champion and benefactor of the Templars, praising them thus:

They go not headlong into battle, but with care and foresight, peacefully, as true children of Israel. But as soon as the fight has begun, they rush without delay upon the foe...and know no fear...one has often put to flight a thousand; two, ten thousand....gentler than lambs and grimmer than lions, theirs is the mildness and the valour of the knight. [*Holy Blood, Holy Grail*, Michael Baigent, Richard Leigh, Henry Lincoln, Dell Publishing, London, 1982, 1983; New York, 1983]

Bernard brought the fledgling Order to the attention of Pope Honarius II, who granted them a "Rule", i.e. a constitution that laid out requirements for conduct and practice which would give them legitimacy within the jurisdiction of the Catholic Church. The Rule was granted on 31 January 1128 when Hugues de Payen appeared before the specially convened Council of Troyes, presided over by the Cardinal of Albano, and comprised the Archbishops of Rheims and Sens, no less than ten bishops and a number of abbots, including Bernard.

The new Rule required joining members to probations for the first year, to take a vow of poverty, handing over their personal wealth, not to the Church but to the Order. Candidates were required to have been born in wedlock, be of noble birth, sound body, and free from any vow or other tie. His only possession would be his sword, which was dedicated to the service of the Order, and when he died his grave carried no inscription except the shape of his sword carved on a rectangular stone. Entrants were obliged to cut their hair but forbidden to cut their beards. On the battlefield Templars were not allowed to retreat unless the odds against them exceeded three to one. The Order became highly respected and feared for its fighting skills.

We noted with interest that the Rule of the Temple Knights, with the exception of some Catholic requirements, was nearly identical to the Orphic vows taken by Jason and the Argonauts on the island of Samothrace prior to their expedition. It was no coincidence, as we later discovered.

The Templars became more arrogant with their increased wealth and power. They rewrote the Latin Rule into a French Rule, adding the amendment: "...we command you to go where excommunicated knights are gathered." This boldly implied that they were outside Vatican law.

While inductees took the vow of chastity, Hugues de Payen, the Grand Master of the Order, remained married to Catherine de St. Clair, a Scottish woman of Norman descent, and set up the first Templar Preceptory outside the Holy Land on her family's land in Scotland.

The Saracens retook Jerusalem in 1188, and the Templars returned to Europe. They had suddenly amassed a vast treasure and their power rivaled that of kings and governments. Bernard of Clairvaux was apparently the recipient of much of the Templar wealth for he built dozens of chapels and cathedrals throughout France. The Templars established one of the largest private fleets in the world, sailing to virtually every port in the known world and beyond. They created and established practices that would lead to modern banking. They made loans to kings and nobles which gave them immense control in politics, but also gained them the enmity of those jealous of their wealth and power.

One of their worst enemies was Philip IV, King of France, who owed the Templars vast amounts of money which he was unable to repay, and had been insulted by being denied entrance into the Order. Moreover, because he levied such high taxes on his subjects to pay his debts, the people rebelled and he was further shamed by having to seek refuge for a time in the Paris temple under the protection of the Knights Templar. Their power was so great they could protect the king when he could not protect himself. Jacques de Molay, who was then Grand Master of the Order, had been godfather to one of Philip's sons and pallbearer for the king's brother-in-law, Charles of Valois.

In spite of the Templars' benevolence, King Philip resented their wealth and power and coveted it for himself. He had not even the ability to tax the Templars, who were exempt by decree, nor could he simply confiscate their vast properties without repercussions. In order to rid himself of the Templars and secure their wealth he accused them of heresy and devil worship, adding sexual perversion for good measure. In order to effect this scheme he needed an ally in Pope Clement V, the only man on Earth to whom the Templars answered. The Pope had reason to fear Philip who had supported one military action against Clement's predecessor, Boniface VIII, who had excommunicated him. The next Pope had been poisoned.

On Friday the thirteenth, 1307, with the Pope's sanction, Philip ordered all the Templars to be arrested. The Templars were then subjected to the worst tortures imaginable by the Inquisition. Many died and some even committed suicide as a result of the torture. Only four of one hundred and thirty-eight captured French Templars failed to confess to the crimes their torturers invented, which included devil worship; abortion; infanticide; spitting on, repudiating and trampling on the Christian cross; homosexuality; and the worship of a skull or bearded head named Baphomet.

Philip pressed the Pope to carry the ban on Templars to other lands. England procrastinated after the papal decree, and Edward II waited until the second order came on 15 December 1307. The Pope then ordered Edward to allow his own torturers access to the imprisoned Templars, and Edward at last capitulated. The Pope signed the order to torture in the name of God on Christmas Eve.

The scourge reached Naples and Sicily, but most of the Templars escaped. In Germany (a confederation of principalities) they found a haven with the Teutonic Knights. Only in Portugal and Scotland was the Order safe from the Pope's edict. Scotland, then at odds with England, became the safest sanctuary of the Templars, and many fled there to be welcomed heartily by Robert the Bruce and the Sinclair family, the latter of whom had been instrumental in organizing the Templars nearly two centuries earlier.

King Philip managed to seize the Templar lands in France, and some monies, but the bulk of the Templar precept in Paris, where the Order kept its massive hoards of gold and sacred treasure, they found empty. The Templars had removed their treasure by wagon train under cover of night to the port of La Rochelle where they loaded it aboard their ships. The principal ports of La Rochelle and nearby Le Havre were where the Templar fleet harbored; the fleet was so substantial that some ports banned it because they were afraid it would rival the trading ability of private fleets.

By some accounts it took seven ships to carry the load; by other accounts there were nine or twelve. Various legends say the treasure was taken to the Mediterranean, Portugal, Ireland, and even Scandinavia. But all reliable evidence indicates that Scotland was the destination of the Templar treasure. And the choice was no coincidence.

———

Scota was one of the earliest names in Ireland, so-called from the title Scota, the "daughter of Pharaoh." We noted three Scota's previously, circa 950 B.C., three daughters of Pharaoh Sheshonk, who had married respectively King Solomon, Nile the Gael, and Milesius the Greek.

Solomon's Temple lasted a little over 360 years when, in 587 B.C., the Babylonian army of King Nebuchadnezzar razed it to the ground and carried the Jews away into captivity. The sons of Zedekiah were killed before his eyes and then his eyes were burned out; Zedekiah was the last King of Judah.

The Prophet Jeremiah, who had consistently warned the Jews of the impending destruction, managed to rescue the Ark of the Covenant and hide it up in Egypt, together with other holy relics, in the tomb of Pharaoh Necho II, who had been succeeded by Pharaoh Hophra (Apries) in 589 B.C.

Jeremiah fled to Egypt with the Ark and the Temple relics, but also with a treasure of another kind, his two great-granddaughters, Tamar and Mirabel, daughters of Zedekiah. They found sanctuary with the Milesian garrison, which according to secular records was stationed at Tahpanhes, Egypt. Tahpanhes has been identified with the Greek fortress "Daphnae" (modern Tel Defneh) which is on the caravan route from Egypt to Palestine. Tel Defneh is also known to this day as "Qast Bint el Yehudi"—"The Palace of the Jew's Daughter."

One noted biblical scholar, Rev. Glover,

English Chaplain to the Consulate at Cologne, came to the conclusion that Jeremiah had escaped with a remnant of the royal blood, and reported his findings more than one hundred years ago in these flamboyant words:

If the Legend be sound, which may be assumed, as having been spoken by one who had authority, and who could be no other but Jeremiah;...who will venture to say that it be not?...In order to have made the prediction of possible realization, the Prophet must have been accompanied by some member of the Family of David. For to a "Sceptre" of what Stock could a Hebrew prophet promise continuance, but to the "Sceptre of Judah?"—And how could a "Throne of David" be re-established, but in the presence of those by whom a perpetuation of the Royal Line of David, would be possible? Therefore, a man of the Seed Royal [Sang Real—Royal Blood], or woman, must have been present, to make the promise possible and reasonable.

But the kings and princes of the royal house [sons of Zedekiah] had been cut off; consequently none of them were there. "The King's daughter," had not been cut off. They were manifestly in the Prophet's company on his two forced journeys from Jerusalem; first, [Jer. 41:10] with Ishmael the son of Nethaniah, towards Ammon; and last, [Jer. 43:6] with Johanan the son of Kareah, to Tahpanhes in Egypt. When there against his will, the Prophet was commanded to escape from it, and promised safety in flight, [Jer. 44:12-14] to return to Judea; and consequently, safety to those with him, who should, in so escaping, obey the Voice of the Lord. [*England, The Remnant of Judah & The Israel of Ephraim; The Two Families Under One Head; A Hebrew Episode of British History*, The Rev. F.R.A. Glover, M.A., Rivingtons, Waterloo Place, London, 2nd Ed. 1881]

At Tahpanhes, the Milesian garrison, Jeremiah and his companions, with their precious cargo, met the leader of the Greek colony, a sailor-mercenary named "Gallo" (Gathelus) a "Miletus" (Milesian) chieftain. Gathelus, as fate or fortune would have it, was a descendant of Milesius, and like his illustrious ancestor, married a "Scota," who was a daughter of Pharaoh Necho II. The alliance of Gathelus with Jeremiah at Tahpanhes was no coincidence, for the mother of Tamar and Mirabel had also been "Scota," a sister of the wife of Gathelus.

The marriage of Scota to Gathelus is said to have occurred during the reign of a Pharaoh who was "drowned" in the Red Sea. This would have been the Pharaoh Hophra of the XXVI Dynasty, successor of Pharaoh Necho II. Hophra had provided refuge to Jeremiah and the daughters of Zedekiah, and was later murdered in his boat in 566 B.C.

The *Chronicles of Scotland* tells us the ancestor of the Scots was "one Greyk callit Gathelus, son [sometimes used to denote a descendant] of Cecrops [Calcol] of Athens, untherwayis [founder] of Argus, King of Argives," who came to Egypt when "in this tyme rang [reigned] in Egypt Pharo ye scurge of ye pepill of Israel." [*Chronicles of Scotland*, Hector Boece, Trans. into Scottish by John Bellenden, 1531, Vol 1, pp. 21-27]

Gathelus gained a great victory for Pharaoh against "the Moris and pepil of Yned" and "King Pharo gaif him his dochter, callit Scota, in marriage." Gathelus left Egypt with his wife Scota, his friends, and a company of Greeks and Egyptians rather than "to abyde ye manifest wengenance of goddis" (reference to God's judgment on the remnant that had fled to Egypt to escape Nebuchadnezzar's armies). Traveling by sea (Mediterranean) after "lang tyme he landit in ane part of Spayne callit Lusitan" (later called Portigall). After this he built the city of Brigance and "callit his subdittus [subjects] Scottis in honour and affection of his wyiff." And, peace having been secured, "Gathelus sittand in his chayr of merbel within his citie."

This chair of "marble" had such fortune and omen that wherever it was found in any land the same land "shall became the native land of the Scots."

The Scottis sall ioyis and brouke the landis haill

Quhair ya: fynd it, bot gif weirdis faill.

(The Scots shall brook that realm as native ground

If words fail not, where'er this chair is found.)

Keeping in mind that the account is a confusion of the several Scota's, it is reasonable to assume the "marble chair" referred to was the Coronation Stone (which may have once been the foot-stool of Solomon's fabulous marble and gold throne) or the Bethel Stone, which the Irish called Lia Fail—the Stone of Destiny.

Jeremiah and his sacred cargo traveled on the ship with Gathelus. What an epic voyage was this! The Ark of the Covenant was in the ship's hold, and on deck the royal blood of Judah coursing through the veins of Zedekiah's daughters, and a Prophet of God on the prow, praying to God for their preservation, while the Greek Gathelus steered their course; and here too was Scota, a daughter of the Pharaoh of Egypt. It is the stuff legends are made of.

We are told that the "ship wrecked on the coast of Ireland, they yet came safe with Lia Fail...Eochaidh [King of Ireland] sent a car for Lia Fail, and he himself was placed thereon." The Coronation Stone, upon which every King of Israel and Judah was crowned from David to Zedekiah, became the Coronation Stone for every Ard-Righ (High King) of "Eireann" for a period of about 1040 years, from King Eochaidh to the 131st Ard-Righ named Murcheartach. A myriad of scholars have written of the Stone since that time. We quote here the scholar Weaver:

It appears that the Irish kings, from very ancient times until A.D. 513, were crowned upon a particular sacred stone, called "Liath Fail," "the Stone of Destiny;" that so, also, were the Scottish Kings until the year 1296; when Edward I of England brought it here: and it is a curious fact, that this Stone has not only remained in England until now, and is existing still under the Coronation Chair of our British Sovereigns in Westminister Abbey, but that all our Kings, from James I, have been crowned in that Chair. [*Essay of Certain Monuments of Antiquity*, by R.A. Weaver, London, 1871, p.118]

In 513 AD Fergus, brother of the Irish King Murcheartach, "borrowed" the Stone to have himself crowned King of Scotland (Alba) and it was never returned.

Another biblical scholar, Rev. W.M.H. Milner, capsulizes subsequent tradition as follows:

That the Royal party escaped Egypt seems certain; also that they returned to Jerusalem as foretold, and rescued from the ruined temple the Stone of Israel...then...Jeremiah transported his precious cargo (by ship of Tarshish) to an Israel Settlement overseas. Shortly after this, Spanish Tradition describes the arrival on their shores of two eastern princesses, accompanied by an ancient prophet and Brug (Baruch) his scribe, bearing with them a sacred Stone. ...Here the younger princess [Mirabel] appears to have married the ruler of the Sara-Gaza (Saragosse) colony...the older princess [Tamar], with Jeremiah and Baruch set sail for Baal-boa (Bilbao) intending to land in Denmark (or Danmark). They were, however, ship wrecked off the north coast of Ulster (Ireland)...at this time Eochaidh, a Prince of Judah, newly elected Heremon of all Ireland, was awaiting his coronation when tidings of the shipwreck were brought to him. Meeting the Princess Tamar Tephi, Eochaidh...married her...(both) standing on the sacred Stone of Destiny. She did not long survive her marriage. A mound known as The Hill of Tara was erected over her remains. [*Chronicles of Eri*, Rev. W.M.H. Milner, London, 1931, Vol. 2; *The Heritage of Anglo-Saxton Race*, Rev. W.M.H. Milner, Covenant Pub. Co., London, p.5]

The great "Mergech," the name given to her tomb, is Hebrew for "Repository" and denotes a place of deposit for treasures, secrets, mysteries, etc. Considering the Ark of the Covenant, Title Deeds to Palestine, and the "Evidences" (believed to be deeds to the Temple mount, for the eventual rebuilding and restoration of the Temple) in Jeremiah's possession, the term is pertinent.

But the Coronation Stone went to Scotland, where it was known as the "Stone of Scone," and it established Scotland as the "land of promise." It was the logical destination—other than Ireland itself—for the Templar treasure.

———

Scholars have searched diligently for a place in Scotland where such a fleet of treasure laden ships could have landed. The most likely place was the Orkney Islands. Scapa Flow in the Orkneys was the place where the Germans scuttled seventy of their own ships at the end of World War I, rather than surrender them to the British. In World War II the British fleet itself hid there.

Across from Scapa Flow is a landmark called Saint John's Head, where the cliffs rise 1,141 feet from the sea, among the highest in the British Isles. Saint John, the beheaded Baptist, played an important role in Templar iconography. The Feast of Saint John, June 24, is the most sacred day in the Templar year. Templars were charged with worshiping an idol of a skull named Baphomet.

There was another reason why the Orkney Islands were the probable site of the Templar destination: the Sinclairs were the Earls of Orkney.

Chapter Six

The Rosslyn Sinclairs

During the ninth and tenth centuries the Scandinavian Norse grew restless. The Vikings streamed out of Norway, Sweden and Denmark in droves, raiding and colonizing wherever they went. In the north of France, Rollo led Norse invaders in search of new lands to colonize. His son Rognwald not only demanded land from the French king, Charles the Simple, but also the king's daughter in marriage. At the place where they met to forge an alliance, the Norsemen built a castle. The Norse who settled in France became known as the Normans (i.e. Northmen).

Among the early Normans was the clan Möre. In fact, the Mörenowned the castle that was built at the treaty site in 912 A.D. Shortly thereafter they changed their name to St. Clair, after that of a saintly martyr who lived as a hermit near a holy well on the bank of the River Epte, north of Paris. This holy man had been murdered by the order of a "cruel woman" whom he had rebuked. His statue depicts him holding his severed head in his outstretched hands, reminiscent of the "severed head" symbol of the Templars.

William the Conqueror, himself a descendant of Rollo, invaded and conquered England with the aid of his fellow Normans. Nine members of the St. Clair family accompanied the Conqueror and were present at the Battle of Hastings, for which service they were rewarded with extensive grants of land in England. They anglicized the spelling of their name from St. Clair to Sinclair. It was the Normans who, for purposes of taxation and administration, introduced surnames into Europe.

The nine Sinclairs, who were related to the Conqueror by marriage, became very prominent in England. Walderne Sinclair married Margaret, daughter of Richard, Duke of Normandy. His son William founded what became the Rosslyn (Roslin) branch of the family. Another Sinclair, Agnes, married the head of the Bruce clan, who had anglicized their name from the French "De Brus," and would soon come to challenge England.

William Sinclair and the Bruce clan had a serious falling out with the English King and removed to Scotland where they allied themselves with Malcolm III. Malcolm, a Celtic ruler, had first married the widow of a Norse ruler in northern Scotland. After Malcolm's death his sons, Alexander and David, ruled by their widespread loyalties to the north, and welcomed imported Normans to reinforce their power. The distinction between Norman and Scot became somewhat blurred after two centuries.

In March of 1286, Alexander III, the reigning King of Scotland, attended a wild drinking bout with some of his knights, after which he rode home alone in the dark inebriated. Somewhere along the way he fell from his horse and died of a broken neck, leaving no heir.

There was an immediate battle for succession. Norman families were split in their alliances and the King of England took advantage to send military excursions to impose his will on the north. The French and the Pope backed John Balliol, and the Scots found themselves being manipulated by foreign interests. Robert the Bruce of Carrick rose to the forefront of this newly inspired nationalism.

Robert the Bruce was of Norman extraction, but he opposed the choice of Balliol and won the enmity of many other Norman families, including that of John of the Red Comyn. An effort was made to get Robert the Bruce and John Red Comyn together to settle their differences. In February 1306 the two met at the church of the Minorite friars in Dumfries, known as the Grey Friars church. It was believed that violence could be avoided in such austere surroundings.

Bruce and Comyn entered the church alone. Bruce stabbed Comyn at the altar with a dirk (a short Scottish dagger). Robert the Bruce seized the opportunity. He instructed his men to seize Dumfries Castle while he rode to Bishop Wishat for absolution. Five weeks later the bishop crowned Robert the Bruce king on the ancient Stone of Scone. The bishop's approval was a calculated move on Bruce's part to divide the Scottish Church and the Church in Rome, as well as to separate the English in the south and the Scots in the north. As a result, Edward of England led his army into Scotland, beginning an era of bloodshed unparalleled in Scottish history.

In 1314 the English returned to reclaim Scotland, after having been driven out by Bruce. This time they came in force, one hundred thousand strong, stretching in a column over two miles long. They outnumbered the Scots three to one and had superior arms.

They met at Bannockburn and the battle seemed over before it began. But Bruce rode onto the field and met the English champion, Henri de Bohun, in single combat, and unnerved the English force by killing their best knight against all odds. In the confusion the Scots attacked. The English were routed and Scotland achieved its independence.

The Battle of Bannockburn united numerous Scottish families under the banner of nationalism, including the Sinclairs. Allied by marriage to the Bruce family, William Sinclair was rewarded for his stand with additional lands in Pentland and near Edinburgh. His son William married Isabel, the daughter of Malise, the Earl of Orkney, bringing even more land into his wealthy and powerful family. William's second son Henry became the first Sinclair to bear the title Earl of Orkney. It is with William Sinclair, champion of the Bruce cause, that the story of the mysterious Rosslyn Chapel begins.

———

William Sinclair owned a large fleet of ships with which he visited his many holdings in the islands and foreign trade. His ships plied the Mediterranean to Italy, Spain, North Africa and Asia; how much more beyond these places they sailed is unknown. When he was not at sea, Sinclair lived at his castle at Rosslyn.

William Sinclair began the construction of the Rosslyn Chapel and personally supervised every phase of its building from its inception to his death in 1484, just two years before its completion. Every carving, however small and seemingly insignificant, was first created in wood and submitted for approval, and once approved it was then carved in stone. William Sinclair had brought some of Europe's finest masons to Scotland for this great project, building the village of Rosslyn to house them. He paid them £40 per annum and the lesser masons £10 per annum, a huge amount in those days. Even £10 would be today's equivalent of $140,000.

A careful investigation, however, indicates that Sinclair's "masons" were in reality Freemasons, former Templars who built forts around the world. Their guild was formed near Edinburgh in 1475, and this "trade" organization's members included knights who fought in the Crusades and knights who fought for Bruce: Sinclairs, Setons, Stewarts, Hamiltons and Montgomerys, not an ordinary "stonemason" among them. Under the guise of a trade guild and under the protection of the Sinclairs the Templars survived intact. In turn, they became the hereditary protectors of the Templar treasure housed beneath Rosslyn Chapel.

In fact, however, Rosslyn Chapel is not a chapel at all; it is not even Christian. It is a temple of the Knights Templar, a replica of the underground vault on Mount Moriah from whence came the treasure. There is no altar, for one thing. A later William Sinclair, who became the first elected Grand Master of the Grand Lodge of Scotland, had been in trouble with King James VI for having Sinclair's children baptized at Rosslyn which was not a Christian place of worship. The chapel had to be reconsecrated by the Church in 1862.

A careful examination of the chapel shows that the symbolism is Egyptian, Celtic, Jewish, Templar and Masonic, but nowhere Christian. It has a star-studded ceiling, vegetation coming forth from the mouths of the Celtic Green Men, entangled pyramids, images of Moses, towers of Heavenly Jerusalem, engrailed crosses, squares and compasses. The only Christian imagery—stained glass windows, a baptistery and a statue of the Madonna and child —were later Victorian alterations.

Some of the decoration has been described as Christian by the Episcopal Church, but a close inspection reveals otherwise. In the area of the north wall there is a small frieze depicting the crucifixion; but closer examination shows that this is not the crucifixion of Jesus Christ, but the torture of the last Grand Master of the Knights Templar, Jacques de Molay. The characters are clearly dressed in medieval garb including hooded members of the Inquisition. Another section shows Templars with an executioner next to them and remarkably, there is a carving depicting figures holding up the Shroud of Turin with the face of Jacques de Molay clearly visible. Clearly William Sinclair was aware of the Templar belief that the figure on the Shroud was that of their Grand Master de Molay and not of Christ as many Christians are wont to believe.

It took forty-five years to complete the chapel, the first four years being involved in the excavations for the foundation alone, an unusual amount of time considering the "chapel" is a relatively small single room with a very tiny crypt at a lower level in the east. The mission of William Sinclair was to recreate the underground vaults of Herod's Temple exactly as Hugues de Payen and the other eight knights had found them over three hundred years earlier. The underground system is far larger than everything above ground.

It now seems certain that the beginning place for Freemasonry was the construction of Rosslyn Chapel in the fifteenth century. The Sinclair family of Rosslyn became the hereditary Grand Masters of the Crafts and Guilds and Orders of Scotland, and later held the post of the Master of Masons of Scotland until the late 1700s.

Two types of treasure were deposited beneath the Rosslyn Chapel in the warrens and vaults so carefully excavated by Sinclair. The bulk of the treasure came from the immense treasury of the Templars that had been saved from the vaults of the Paris Preceptory upon the death of Jacques de Molay. Not only the relics and hoards from beneath Herod's Temple (Solomon's treasure) but gold, silver and precious gems that were part of the Templar's banking system, estimated to be the wealthiest accumulation in world history—possibly twelve shiploads. More than this, in addition to the treasure of Solomon, it is believed that the Templar treasure included relics from Herod's Temple, carried away by the Romans in 70 A.D. Altogether, the wealth exceeds the imagination.

The second type of treasure secreted in Rosslyn's vaults may have been the most valuable of all—scrolls.

It has long been speculated that the Jerusalem Essenes were some kind of proto-Christians, and that Jesus may have been one of them. Evidence of this was scant until numerous writings were unearthed at the ancient settlement at Qumran. Soon afterwards the site was extensively excavated by the Jordan Department of Antiquities, L'erole Archeologique Francaise and the Palestine Archaeological Museum under G.L. Harding and Pere R. de Vaux between 1951 and 1956. What they found was the theologian's equivalent to a ticking time-bomb. The world of Christianity could blow up if the lid could not be kept on it. Those in charge of the research were not independent scholars, but members of various Christian establishments with a faith to protect. Other scholars saw evidence that appeared to change the view of Christ and the New Testament, but they were effectively silenced or discredited.

Accusations of scandal, cover-up and deliberate withholding of the truth were met by denials and counter accusations. Nevertheless, the fact is that for more than forty years after their discovery, over half of the 800 scrolls discovered have not been published. The academic community was outraged by this unprecedented secrecy. After widespread protests, led by the Huntington Library of San Marino, California, the Israeli authorities removed restrictions on public access to the contents of the scrolls in October 1991.

Various versions of biblical texts were found, all of them more than a thousand years older than the oldest surviving Hebrew texts that were produced by Aaron ben Moses ben Asher in 1008 A.D. Prior to the discovery of the scrolls the Christian world did not know for sure how accurate the current Old Testament was. From the texts carefully stored in the caves of Qumran, it soon became apparent that there were a large number of different texts and that the one translated into the Greek Septuagint was just one of them. There is no "correct" version of the Bible after all.

It also soon became apparent that the story of Jesus in the Four Gospels—especially in the Gospels of Mark and

Luke—had been tampered with. The events as they describe them simply could not have happened. An example is in the way King Herod is linked with Roman taxation under Quirinius—when Herod had been dead since 4 B.C., at least ten years before Quirinius came on the scene.

The Qumran scrolls identify that there was a secret tradition that members had to swear never to divulge. These secrets were written down and preserved in readiness for the day when God would visit his people in the last times. Scholars such as Morton Smith (author of *The Secret Gospel*) have detected the existence of a secret gospel, believed to predate the gospel of Mark, with elements running beneath the Four Gospels.

The Qumranians were all but destroyed in the war with the Romans in 66-70 A.D. and the Christians were left to tell the story as they saw it. The facts are clear. The Nasoreans/Qumranians were instructed (by the Assumption of Moses) to put their most treasured scrolls under the Holy of Holies in about 69 A.D. Other documents, somewhat more mundane, such as the Community Rule, were deposited around Judaea in places such as the caves at Qumran. The scrolls deposited beneath the Temple by the Qumranians have come to be known as the Nasorean Scrolls, and may be the famous lost gospel of "Q" (from the German word "quelle" for "source"). They ostensibly tell us about the life of Jesus.

The Rosslyn Chapel appears to be a replica of Solomon's Temple, including the replicas of the pillars Boaz and Jachin. The original Temple did not have a middle chamber; but the Rosslyn shrine does. The crypt of the chapel lies in the southeast, with steps going down to it immediately to the right of the kingly pillar. These steep steps are considerably worn with deeply arched risers making ascent and descent difficult. The official guidebook says of them:

These well worn steps indicate that

many pilgrims visited this chapel in the ninety or one hundred years between its completion and the Reformation. The exact reasons for this pilgrimage are, as yet, unclear, but it is possible that Templar knights had deposited some holy relic of ancient veneration here....

Halfway down is a door leading into a small lower chamber with an even smaller room to the north and a fireplace with a chimney that was built into the main southern wall of the building. The presence of the fireplace indicates that the room was designed to be used for reasonably extended periods by the knights.

Next to this fireplace there is a figure that resembles St. Peter, because he carries a key. The figure is obviously not the Catholic saint, which does not even remotely represent Templar belief, and the key in the guardian's hand has a handle in a perfect square—"a true and certain sign to recognize a Freemason." This is believed to mark the entrance to the scroll vaults.

The room, which is now referred to as the crypt, was the middle room of the reconstructed Temple, because it linked the main upper room with the underground vault that housed the holy scrolls. Before the vaults were sealed off at the completion of the building, several of the Templars were granted the right to be buried alongside the holy scrolls. It is a matter of historical record that there are knights buried here who are not in coffins, but repose in their full suits of armor, a privilege normally reserved for kings alone. Sir Walter Scott, himself a Master Mason, immortalized this in his poem, *The Lay of The Last Minstrel*:

Seemed all on fire that chapel proud,

Where Roslin's chiefs uncoffined lie:

Each baron, for a sable shroud,

Sheathed in his iron panoply...

There are twenty of Roslin's barons bold

Lie burid within that proud chapelle.

Here in the crypt is found the Gunn coat-of-arms, signifying that at least one of the knights there entombed was a member of that clan. It may signify more than this.

A guidebook to Rosslyn Chapel hints at the truths we have mentioned:

The vaults themselves may yet be far more than a simple tomb, other important artefacts may be contained therein. The one recorded action of the Lords Sinclair that apparently contradicts their well earned reputation for chivalry and loyalty may also be explained if the vaults are opened, for it is just possible that some clue as to the whereabouts of certain treasures of great historical interest may also be discovered. We must acknowledge this when we attempt to understand the motivation of both the builder of this unique and magnificent chapel and of the gifted artists and craftsmen who executed its design. The fruits of this open-minded approach will inevitably lead us to hypotheses which will direct us in further study to locate evidence that, at present at least, may be hidden or have been overlooked for any one of a variety of reasons...[*An Illustrated Guide to Rosslyn Chapel*, Tim Wallace-Murphy]

How do we know there are four trunks of scrolls? This came to light with the discovery of an account of a fire that occurred in 1447, one year after the foundation stone was laid for Rosslyn Chapel. The fire occurred in a portion of Rosslyn Castle where William Sinclair was storing items while awaiting completion of the shrine. In the following account, William Sinclair is referred to by his title "Prince of Orkney":

About this time [1447] there was a fire in the square keep [of Roslyn Castle] by occasion of which the occupants were forced to flee the building. The Prince's chaplain seeing this, and remembering all of his master's writings, passed to the head of the dungeon where they all were, and threw out four great trunks where they were. The news of the fire coming to the Prince through the lamentable cries of the ladies and gentle-women, and the sight thereof coming to his view in the place where he stood upon Colledge Hill, he was sorry for nothing but the loss of his Charters and other writings; but when the chaplain who had saved himself by coming down the bell rope tied to a beam, declared how his Charters and Writts were all saved, he became cheerful and went to recomfort his Princess and the Ladys. [Ibid.]

What could have been so important in those four trunks that William Sinclair was more concerned for them than for his own wife and her ladies? The answer is self-evident: the Nasorean Scrolls, the greatest historical treasure in the history of the Christian world. Certainly he would not have been so heartless had the trunks contained mere land deeds and charters, all of which were replaceable.

Perhaps the strongest evidence that Rosslyn Chapel was a Templar shrine is the fact that it still exists at all. During the English Civil War, Oliver Cromwell and his Parliamentary forces sought out all Royalist and Catholic property in England, Ireland, Wales and Scotland to destroy it off the face of the Earth. Cromwell himself visited Rosslyn and while he destroyed every Papist church he encountered, he left Rosslyn Chapel completely intact. Oliver Cromwell was a Freemason of high standing and was aware that Rosslyn was a Masonic shrine, and thereby preserved it.

The Sinclairs were, of course, staunch Royalists, and even when Rosslyn castle was utterly destroyed by General Monk in 1650 the Rosslyn shrine emerged unscathed. Had it been viewed as a Catholic chapel, it would not have survived the purge.

The guide book to Rosslyn Chapel lists among William Sinclair's numerous titles that of "the Knight of the Cockle and Golden Fleece." This title we found highly significant inasmuch as Freemasonry describes itself as being "more ancient than the Golden Fleece or Roman Eagle." More-over, in light of our discoveries as to the importance of the Golden Fleece as a source of Solomon's treasure, it comes as no surprise that Sinclair should have been a Knight of the Golden Fleece, a Templar order.

———

Shortly after Robert the Bruce had himself crowned as King Robert by Bishop Wishat (weeks after the murder of John Red Comyn and six years before the victory at Bannockburn), his army suffered a serious loss to the English at the Battle of Methuen in June of 1306. Bruce was forced into hiding throughout the long winter. A rival earl captured Bruce's wife, and his daughter, Marjorie, was also taken captive. His brother Nigel, also on the run, was caught and beheaded.

The tragedies continued even after Bruce came out of hiding. The Earl of Atholl was hanged for supporting him. Simon Fraser, who had joined with Sir William Wallace in revolt, was impaled on London Bridge. Bishop Wishart and Bishop Lamberton, who gave moral support to the Scottish cause, were put in chains. Isabel of Buchan and a sister of Robert the Bruce were exposed in lattice cages in the city of Berwick for public ridicule.

In France, in the same year, the Templars saw the writing on the wall. Only a delay by the pope to King Philip's orders prevented immediate arrests. The Templars negotiated with the Sinclairs, who had been instrumental in the creation of the Templar order, and the Templar fleet sailed with the Templar treasury to the isles of Scotland. The death of the English King Edward on his way to Scotland provided temporary respite for Bruce; the money and arms that the Templars brought to Scotland would save the day.

Templar legend says that the fleet, now devoid of the treasure, sailed to the support of Scotland. The English king complained that the Templars were funding weapons purchases for Scotland through neutral

Ireland. Bruce suddenly made an amazing come back. He marched through Scotland punishing his enemies and seizing their lands. By 1313 Bruce was raiding England itself and captured the Isle of Man by virtue of a seaborne attack aided by the Templar fleet.

In 1314 Bannockburn decided the issue of Scottish independence which also secured the place of the Templars in Scotland, for within weeks of Bannockburn, Jacques de Molay, Grand Master, was burned to death in France. This followed the mass executions of Templars. Before succumbing to the flames, Molay cursed the Pope and King of France, promising that neither would live a year after his death. Neither did.

The Order survived Molay's death. In Spain the orders of Calatrava and Montesa permitted the Templars to continue their work. In Portugal, Templars were admitted to the newly formed Knights of Christ, from whose ranks came the intrepid Prince Henry the Navigator and Vasco da Gama. Even the father-in-law of Christopher Columbus was a Templar. In England King Edward continued persecution of the Templars because they supported the Scots against him. He ordered that Scotland must arrest all Templars within her borders, but the order was received as a joke as the Templars were the saving force behind Scottish independence.

Robert the Bruce died in 1329. His last request was that his heart be buried in Jerusalem. On crusades against the Moors, Sir William Sinclair, Sir James Douglas of the Black Douglas clan, and Sir William Keith rode together into battle. Believing that all was lost, Sir James Douglas threw Bruce's heart into the fray, asking the brave heart to lead them, as before. The Moors defeated the Scottish contingent badly, and Sir William Sinclair and Sir James Douglas were killed. Keith, the only one of the three to survive, recovered the heart and brought it home to Scotland, where it was buried at Melrose Abbey.

From Bannockburn forward the powerful and wealthy Sinclairs met their responsibilities as guardians of the Templar treasure. They were the patrons of the Freemason trade guilds wherein the Knights Templars survived. James II of Scotland named them the guardian family of Freemasonry, a role through which they preserved the secrets and the wealth of the Templars. As the hereditary Grand Masters of Scottish Freemasonry, they furthered the exploration for which the family is renowned, and all from behind the scenes.

By 1545, however, the Sinclairs could no longer remain in the background of history. Oliver Sinclair was the military might behind King James IV. But King James died at the Battle of Flodden and the new king, James V, was only two years old when he was crowned. Oliver Sinclair became his guardian and guardian to the country of Scotland. James V later married Mary of Guise, of French nobility, to whom the Sinclairs were allied both by marriage and the politics of their secretive elite group.

The marriage united France and Scotland, but it threatened the English and was a catalyst of the battle at Solway, where the Scots were badly defeated, and Oliver Sinclair was taken captive. James V, who had depended on Oliver Sinclair since childhood, died in despair within days of hearing of Sinclair's capture. Six days earlier his daughter Mary had been born— Mary Queen of Scots.

After his release, Oliver Sinclair felt his own despair, with his king dead and an infant female on the throne. The French failed to come to his aid in battling the English. Granted a short release from prison, Oliver Sinclair, guardian of the Templar treasure, disappeared from Scotland and history.

The Rosslyn Sinclairs continued to rule as the hidden overseers of a turbulent Scotland. They lived at Rosslyn and enjoyed great wealth. William, grandson of Henry, the first earl, as Earl of Orkney and Caithness, lived in lavish splendor. Among the members of his court were Lord Dirleton, Lord Barthwick, Lord Fleming, and others. His wife Elizabeth, who was called a "princess" of the great Douglas clan [co-author Lisa Lee Boren is a Douglas clan descendant], had seventy-five servants—fifty-three "of noble birth"—and two hundred "riding women" to attend her. Vessels of gold, clothes of silk, and an entourage greater than most kings, made the Sinclairs legendary. But their greatest legacy remains their guardianship of the great Templar treasure, which remained their sacred inviolate trust; and so great was their devotion to duty that to this very day the secret of the treasure has remained intact.

Rosslyn Chapel—Scotland
Courtesy: Rosslyn Chapel Trust

Rosslyn Chapel—Scotland
Courtesy: Rosslyn Chapel Trust

Chapter Seven

The Sea Kings—The Earls of Orkney

Only some 250 miles (400 km) separate the southwestern coast of Norway from the shores of Orkney. For centuries its fertile soil had nourished the simple farming folk known as the Picts. Then, in 793 AD the Viking Age began with the attack on the monastery at Lindisfarne on the east coast of England. A monk at Lindisfarne recorded the event in these words:

...we and our forefathers have inhabited this most lovely land, and never before has such a terror appeared in Britain as we have now suffered from a pagan race, nor was it thought possible that such an inroad from the sea could be made. [*Orkney Inga Sagas*: 1139-1148, Rolls Series (no. 88) "*Icelandic Sagas*", Vol. 1 ed. Gudbrand Vigfusson, 1887; *Orkney Inga Sagas*, IV, 34; *Icelandic Sagas*, Sir GW Dasent, H.M.S.O., trans., Vol. 3, 1894]

Hostile, violent and sudden, the Norwegians poured out of Norway and made the North Sea a Norse sea. The evolution of the Gokstad-type ship and the broad-breasted knorr made it possible to make continuous voyages of unimagined rapidity along the whole of the European seaboard. In 794 "all the islands of Britain" were attacked, by which was meant also the Hebrides and Orkney, and in the following year Vikings were active in Skye and Iona. By 796 attacks had spread southwards to Ireland, and in 798 attacks were further recorded in the Hebrides and Ulster, and again on Iona in 802 and 806.

It was natural that Orkney and Shetland were colonized first, as they were the closest. Orkney became a base for Viking expeditions further west to Ireland and Man, and for the new land taking in the Faeroes and Iceland. It is possible that the attack on the monastery at Lindisfarne came from Orkney.

From the *Orkneyinga Saga*, written in the thirteenth century, we learn about the political history of the islands from the time the earldom was established some time in the ninth century. The saga describes the earldom under the great earls Thorfinn the Mighty and Rognvald Kali Kolsson, and ends with the death of Harald Maddadarson in 1206.

The *Orkneyinga Saga* is also called the *Earl's Saga*, a more appropriate name for it, for it deals almost exclusively on the earls and their family—the powerful family of Möre. The story of Orkney is more a family saga than the saga of kings.

Sigurd Eysteinsson from Giske, the brother of Rognvald, Earl of Möre, is known as the first Earl of Orkney. He started the expansion southwards on the Scottish mainland, conquering Caithness, Sutherland, Ross and parts of what is now Moray.

Earl Einar taught the islanders to use peat for fuel and thus he became known to posterity as Turf-Einar. He was considered to be a "good earl," and had the distinction of having been one of the few who died in bed. He had three sons, the two elder sons, Arnkell and Erlend, fell with Erik Blood-Axe in the Battle of Stanesmoor in England in 950, and so the younger son, Thorfinn the Skull-Splitter, inherited the earldom from his father.

Thorfinn the Skull-Splitter left five sons when he died in 963 AD: Arnfinn, Havard Harvest-Happy, Ljot (Liot), Hlodver and

Skuli. Odal law, which decreed equal shares for all heirs, also applied to the earldom, and led to disastrous family feuds with brother against brother. Three of Thorfinn's sons let themselves be charmed by Ragnhild, daughter of Erik Blood-Axe, King of Norway and York, by his wife Gunnhild. She had been taught well by her parents in the ways of intrigue. Ragnhild married all three in turn, and managed to kill off two of them. In the end, Hlodvir Thorfinnsson was the sole surviving brother. The saga calls him a great chieftain. He married Eithne (Audna), daughter of Kjarval, an Irish king. She was said to have had "the sight," a gift attributed to the Celts. Their son was Sigurd Hlodvisson, who was also called Sigurd the Stout.

Sigurd is one of the great earls of the *Orkneyinga Saga*. He inherited the earldom from his father in 980 A.D., and fought against the Scots who were threatening Caithness from the south. A Scottish earl named Finnleik challenged Sigurd to a fight, and since Sigurd was the weaker of the two, he sought his mother's advice. Eithne made her son a raven banner and, according to the *Orkneyinga Saga*, told him:

Had I thought you might live for ever, I'd have reared you in my wool-basket. But lifetimes are shaped by what will be, not by where you are. Now, take this banner, I've made it for you with all the skill I have, and my belief is this: that it will bring victory to the man it's carried before, but death to the one who carries it.

Eithne was proved right. Three standard bearers fell, but the battle was won.

Sigurd was a powerful earl and a troublesome neighbor. He married Plantula, daughter of Malcolm II, King of Scots, and they had a son, Thorfinn. This child was fostered by King Malcolm, his maternal grandfather.

Earl Sigurd joined King Sigtrygg Silk-Beard, a Norse King of Ireland, in a campaign against Brian Boru, King of the Irish. The Battle of Clontarf outside Dublin on Good Friday 1014 was won by the Irish, giving a blow to Norse colonization in Ireland from which it never recovered. Both Brian and Sigurd fell in the battle. The saga explains Sigurd's death by the fact that he himself carried the raven banner when he could find no one else to do so.

When Sigurd died, his son Thorfinn, who was still living with his grandfather in Scotland, was only five years old. But Sigurd had three older sons from an earlier marriage: Sumarlidi, Brusi and Einar Wry-Mouth. These three brothers divided the islands among themselves after their father's death. Sumarlidi and Brusi were peaceable men, but Einar was obstinate, as his nickname suggests.

Sumarlidi died, and Einar was killed in an underhanded attack by Thorfinn's friends. King Olaf Haraldsson used this struggle for power to his own advantage by quickly approaching the islands and gave the half-brothers a share each in fee, causing them to swear an oath of fealty to him. The brothers became reluctantly reconciled and shared the earldom, but Thorfinn, who had the support of the King of Scots, retained the greater authority overall.

However, King Olaf brought Brusi's ten year-old son, Rognvald Brusason, to Norway as a hostage to insure Brusi's loyalty. Rognvald grew up in King Olaf's court and went with him when he fled to Russia in 1028. Only nineteen years old, Rognvald led a contingent of the King's army in the Battle of Stiklestad, where Olaf was killed. He rescued the badly wounded Harold Sigurdsson from the battlefield and carried him across the border into Sweden. This was King Olaf's young half-brother, later known as King Harold Hardrada, who was killed at Stamford Bridge in 1066, trying to invade England. Together with other survivors from the Battle of Stiklestad, Rognvald and Harold made it back to King Yaroslav in Russia. When it became known that Earl Brusi was dead, Rognvald was installed as Earl of two-thirds of Orkney by King Magnus the Good in 1035. Thorfinn ruled the other third, but also large parts of Scotland.

For ten years Rognvald and Thorfinn ruled Orkney jointly in peace; Rognvald even went along on raiding expeditions in the south to safeguard Thorfinn's land. But eventually Thorfinn demanded a greater share of the earldom and they clashed in conflict. It ended when Rognvald was killed in Papa Stronsay where he had gone to get malt for the Christmas ale. About Rognvald Brusason the *Orkneyinga Saga* says that "of all the Earls of Orkney he was the most popular and gifted, and his death was mourned by many."

When Rognvald died there was nobody left to challenge Thorfinn's absolute control of Orkney, but the saga says "Thorfinn spent most of his time in Caithness and Scotland, leaving his stewards to look after the islands...." Thorfinn's territories were large: nine earldoms in Scotland, apart from the Sudreys and parts of Ireland.

Thorfinn married Ingibjorg, daughter of Finn Arnason, a Norwegian chieftain, and thus became part of one of Norway's most influential families, the Arnmodlings. It was also a turbulent family. It had been Finn's brother Kalf Arnason who led the peasant army against King Olaf in the Battle of Stiklestad.

Thorfinn's grandfather, King Malcolm II, had no sons, but his daughter's son Duncan I ruled Scotland until he was killed in battle by the unknown Macbeth in 1040. Macbeth appears to have been a good king who ruled for seventeen years until he fell in battle against Duncan's son, who became King Malcolm III, nicknamed Canmore, which means Big Head in Gaelic. Malcolm Canmore married Thorfinn's widow, Ingibjorg. Their son Duncan became King of Scots after his father.

A recent theory suggests that Macbeth and Thorfinn are one and the same person. In the north he was Norse Earl of Orkney and Macbeth, "son of life," in Gaelic Scotland, where the name Thorfinn would sound pagan. Though it can hardly be proved, it answers many contradictions. Both Thorfinn and Macbeth went on a pilgrimage to Rome circa 1050, and one source mentions a visit by "Malbeatha, King of Orkney." Thorfinn died circa 1064, aged eighty.

King Harald Hardrada stayed in Orkney while he recruited an army for his campaign against England. Thorfinn had since died, and his sons Paul and Erlend joined King Harald, and survived the Battle of Stamford Bridge. They ruled together well and it was not until their sons were grown that there was friction between them.

Paul's son Hakon and Erlend's elder son Erling were both quick-tempered and proud. Magnus, Erlend's younger son, was more peaceful by nature, but the saga says that in his youth he took part in Viking raids, and "he seemed for some winters like wicked men." Hakon and Erling fought against each other and prominent men tried to reconcile them. But the arrogant and stubborn Hakon Paulsson urged his father to take more share of his power, and the conflict flared up again. The chieftains then asked Hakon to leave the islands and he went to Norway.

Magnus Erlendsson was born circa 1075. The sagas tell us that "many men leaned towards the sons of Erlend and would not let them bear a lower lot there in the islands, for they were better friends of the people and more beloved of men." But "Hakon harboured many a grudge for this all his day."

Hakon, aware that the people of Orkney would not support him, persuaded the new King of Norway, Magnus Bare-Legs, to make a western expedition. Magnus Bare-Legs invaded in 1098, took Orkney without a fight, removed the two earls and sent them as prisoners to Norway. King Magnus installed his eight year-old son, Sigurd, as overlord of the islands. Instead of rewarding Hakon with the power he sought, the King took the earls' sons along on his further expedition to the Sudreys. (The Orkneys were called the Nordreys and the Hebrides the Sudreys.)

Magnus Erlendsson was made the King's cup-bearer and "used to serve at the King's table," a position of honor. Then there occurred an event which changed this. Off the coast of Wales, in the Menai Strait, King Magnus fought a hard battle against two local earls, Hugh the Stout and Hugh the Proud. Then, the saga tells us:

When the troops were getting their weapons ready for battle, Magnus Erlendsson settled down in the main cabin and refused to arm himself. The King asked him why he was sitting around and his answer was that he had no quarrel with anyone there. "That's why I've no intention of fighting," he said. "If you haven't the guts to fight," said the King, "and in my opinion this has nothing to do with your Faith, get below. Don't lie there under everybody's feet." [Orkney Inga Sagas VI, 77]

Magnus Erlendsson had embraced Christianity and the saga states that Magnus took a psalter and sang as long as the battle lasted. It is not surprising that Magnus fell out of grace with the King after this battle, and when they were anchored off the coast of Scotland he escaped from the King's ship. He made his way to Scotland and stayed with the King of Scotland, never returning to Orkney while Magnus Bare-Legs was king.

Magnus Bare-Legs fell in Ulster in 1103. His sons Sigurd, Olaf, and Eystein became kings after him. The Orkney earls Paul and Erlend died in exile in Norway, and Erling Erlendsson fell in Ulster with Magnus Bare-Legs. The two cousins Hakon Paulsson and Magnus Erlendsson again claimed power in Orkney. Hakon resented sharing that power, but was compelled to bear it by the Norwegian kings, who realized that control was better kept by division—the divide and conquer principle. The breach between them was inevitable.

Then one year Magnus went to England and spent a year at the court of King Henry I. Hakon seized this opportunity to wrest power from his cousin; but Magnus returned with five warships to demand his share of power once again. The Thing (Viking council of chieftains) decided that the two earls reach a final solution, and arranged for them to meet on the small green island of Egilsay for peace and good will in Easter Week of 1117.

Hakon's men found him the next morning down by the shore. Holdbodi, a farmer from the Sudreys, who was one of the two men who stayed with Magnus until the end, reported what was said between the two earls. Magnus offered Hakon three choices:

First, that I should go on a pilgrimage to Rome, or even as far as the Holy Land, to visit sacred places. I'd take two ships with me to carry all we need, do penance for both our souls, and swear never to return to Orkney.

Hakon rejected this choice at once. The second choice, exile in Scotland, was also rejected. To the third choice, for Magnus to let himself be mutilated and blinded, Hakon said, "I'll accept these terms, and make no further conditions." The chieftains present objected to this, saying that one of them must die, for they tired of the earls' joint rule. Hakon haughtily replied, "Better kill him then, I don't want an early death; I much prefer ruling over people and places."

Hakon wanted his standard bearer to kill Magnus, but he refused. Hakon then ordered his cook, Lifolf, to kill Magnus, but the cook began to cry. Magnus comforted him. After having prayed and received the sacrament, Magnus said to Lifolf, "Stand in front of me and strike me hard on the head, it's not fitting for a chieftain to be beheaded like a thief. Take heart, poor fellow, I've prayed that God grant you his mercy." And the saga says he then "crossed himself and stooped to receive the blow."

At first Hakon refused to allow Magnus' body to be taken to the church; but Thora, Earl Magnus' mother, pleaded with him and at last he relented and allowed Magnus' body to be buried in consecrated ground. He was buried at Christ Church, the church Thorfinn had built. Christ Church was at that time the seat of the Bishop of Orkney. There were tales of miracles at the grave and before the end of the first year after Magnus' death people were making pilgrimages to the gravesite and leaving cured of illness. Hakon ruled Orkney alone, and alone he ruled well and was much liked. He died in 1123.

Magnus' body was tried in consecrated fire in 1135 and the Church canonized him as a saint. He became the patron saint of Orkney. In June every year to this day there is a St. Magnus Festival in Orkney.

We have mentioned Rognvald Brusason, who was stabbed to death when he innocently sought malt for Christmas ale. His body was deposited in the Cathedral of St. Magnus, and like Magnus he was made a saint. He left only one daughter, Ingigerde, who married Eric Stagbreller, to whom she bore three sons and three daughters. Of all of these, the son Harold came into possession of the whole earldom of Caithness. The power and success of this Earl against his rivals was due primarily to the exertions of Sweyn Asleifson, the "Pirate of Freswick."

We have also mentioned Thorfinn Sigurdsson, grandson of King Malcolm II of Scotland who, in addition to having shared the earldom of Orkney with his half-brothers, was created Earl of Caithness by his maternal grandfather. Having refused to pay tribute to his successor on the Scottish throne, he was supplanted in the earldom of Caithness by one Moddan who, with a body of troops, had established his headquarters in Thurso. Highly resenting the indignity, Thorfinn surprised his rival by night, set fire to his house, and slew him as he attempted to escape the flames through a window. Sweyn, the Pirate of Freswick, and Moddan were related by marriage, and we will learn more of them in a subsequent chapter.

The Orkney Islands were not yet the property of the Sinclair clan in 1307; they belonged to Malise, a descendant of the fighting earls, whose daughter, Isabel, William Sinclair later married. The Sinclairs themselves were descendants of the same Norse family, the Möres, who sent a branch to France in the tenth century which, as we have seen, became the St. Clairs and later the Scottish Sinclairs.

William Sinclair, Earl of Orkney, obtained a grant of the Earldom of Caithness in 1455 from King James II, bringing together the two great earldoms in one house. In personal appearance he is described as having been "a very fair man, of great stature, broad bodied, yellow haired, and well proportioned."

The Sinclairs were important and powerful, but they owed most of that acclaim to their alliance by marriage to the greatest sea kings in Norse history—the clan Gunn.

Chapter Eight

The Sea Kings—The Gunns of Caithness

Geoffrey of Monmouth, writing in 1136, is among the earliest historians to compile a history of the British Isles. He names a certain King Gunhpar (Latinized as Gunuasius) as the regent of Orcadum (Orkney) in his list of six kings who fought alongside King Arthur against the Saxons. This King "Gunn" is the first of the name to be mentioned, predating the arrival of the Norse by nearly 300 years. The realm of this ancient sea king would necessarily include a fleet of ships adept at navigating the turbulent and icy North Atlantic seas.

In the popular pursuit of genealogy and heraldry, the prevalent belief is that all families descend from one famous ancestor who lends his name to the line. In *Clans and Tartans of Scotland*, Robert Bain claims that members of the clan Gunn were all descended from Olave the Black, a Norse invader who sailed to the "Sutherlands" (Southlands) after the fifth century. Bain maintains that it was a son of Olave, named Gunnar, who became the first of the Gunn clan. The name Gunnar derives from the word *gunn*, which means "a long, strong reed," most often referring to a spear.

However, other scholars agree with Geoffrey of Monmouth. In *Scottish Clans and Tartans*, Ian Grimble maintains that the Gunn name was already ancient when the Norse arrived in the Orkneys. In fact, the name was Pictish. The origin of the Picts in uncertain. They were first called by that name in 279 A.D. when Eumenius records them as among the warlike tribes which Julius Caesar attempted to subdue in Scotland. In 305 A.D. Constantius Chlorus, father of Constantine the Great, campaigned against them. In 343 A.D., even the famed Roman legions were put to flight by the fierce blue-painted diminutive Pict warriors. The fact that they painted their bodies blue for battle indicates some connection to the Celts.

The "Scotti" (descendants of Scota) came over from Ireland and colonized Scotland, and the Picts and Scots coexisted with other tribes, extinct to history not long afterwards, such as the Attacotti and Verturiones. In time the Picts were assimilated by the Scots. It was their ability to assimilate that has made their history so difficult to trace. The Picts were renowned for their silver work and adopted chariots after capturing some of them from the Roman legions. They were also skilled sailors, inventing skin boats that would travel great distances. It seems certain that Picts and the Norse had contact with each other from very early times. Whether Pictish or Norse, the clan Gunn was the greatest sea power in the north.

In her well-researched book *Guinevere* (Harper Collins, New York, 1991, pp.5, 50-58), Norma Lorre Goodrich makes the case that Guinevere was a Pictish queen. The matriarchal Picts granted women equal status with men (as did the Celts), and they often rode into battle. Women also had the prerogative of choosing and discarding a husband at will. Such behavior on the part of Guinevere was viewed in Grail literature as immoral, a later Christian addition, but Goodrich sees it simply as custom. The early Gunns were often recorded as "Guin," and "Guinevere" was originally "Guin-hyfer," which means literally "daughter of Guin." It is a short step from this to accepting that Queen Guinevere of Pictish Orkney, was daughter of the Pictish King Gunn, allied with Arthur against the

Saxons, Geoffrey's Gunuasius of Ordcadum. This seems further substantiated by the fact that the Sinclairs and all other earls of Orkney and Caithness could not rule without the consent of the clan Gunn, who were the title crowners of Caithness. When the Norman Sinclairs made Scotland and the northern isles their demesne, the Norse chieftain Malise was already related to the clan Gunn, and the Gunns continued to intermarry with the Sinclairs for generations. It was this powerful sea going alliance that admitted the Templars into their realm and embraced their secret.

Simply because the Gunns were earlier Picts does not preclude them from also being Norse, due to their proclivity for assimilation. All evidence seems to indicate that the Gunns, though originally Pictish, became full-blown Norse through heavy intermarriage. It was in fact quite natural for such marriages to be made in royal families to secure alliances. Thus by the time Olave the Black descended upon the isles in the fifth century, the clan Gunn was already firmly entrenched, and his son Gunnar was likely a product of an allied marriage; Olave himself may have been a Gunn descendant. The Gunns of the fifth century were Kings of Orkney, Caithness and the Isle of Man. By the tenth century they were virtually totally Norse, by virtue of assimilation, and the coat of arms of the Gunns from all three places show them to be not only the same family, but Vikings.

There is further evidence that the Gunns, among the greatest sailors the world has ever known, had voyaged to America at least by the tenth century, and possibly as early as the ninth. This is known because the Norse trader Gunnbiorn (Gunn), who was blown off course in 920 A.D., reached Greenland, and his description of it led Eric the Red to make a settlement in that inhospitable land (*The Norse Discovery of America*, Arthur M. Reeves, p.31). Leif Ericsson, son of Eric the Red, using the same descriptions, "discov-ered" America in 1001 AD. Because of its importance to our text, Leif Ericsson's story is worth recounting.

The oldest of the sagas that record the journeys of the Norse to America was written in 1137, more than 350 years before Columbus, and is entitled *Islendinabok*. The book calls North America "Vinland the Good" and recalls the travels of Ari Thorgilsson. Thorgilsson is mentioned again in another Norse saga, the *Landanamabok*, which tells of his having been driven off course to a place called Hvitramannaland, meaning "Greater Ireland." Irish monks had preceded the Vikings to America. They had also preceded them to Iceland, and they had a monastery on an island off Iceland called Papays (the Norse name for Catholics), and had sailed even farther west.

Another Norseman, Gudleif Gudlaugson, was also described as having sailed to a place in Greater Ireland called Eyrbyggja, where he met people who spoke the Irish language. Gudlaugson was a trader and one of his ports of call was Dublin.

The most well-known Norseman, of course, is Leif Ericsson. He was a member of one of the more colorful Norse families. His father, Eric (or Erik) the Red, had been exiled from his home in Iceland as a result of having committed several murders, and he settled in Greenland. While Eric is credited with naming Greenland, it has always remained a mystery why he should have chosen such a name, for Greenland is desolate and forbidding while Iceland, a more appropriate name for Greenland, is greener and more inviting. We have our own hypothesis: we believe that Eric the Red named the place "Gunnarland," after its discoverer, and the name was corrupted in language changes to "Greenland." While many of the Norse were farmers, those who could trade prospered, and among the traders were the Ericssons and the Herjolf-sons.

Bjarni Herjolfson, a trader, regularly traveled the icy North Atlantic between Iceland and Scandinavia. One year he landed in Iceland only to find that his father had moved west to Greenland. On his way to Greenland a storm blew his ship west and south of his destination, to a foreign shore. Afraid to land, Herjolfson sought only to return to Greenland, and for this perceived lack of adventurous spirit, Leif Ericsson later rebuked him.

Ericsson decided to see the lands that Herjolfson had described. He bought Herjolfson's ship and sailed to Labrador in 1001 A.D., which the Norse called Helluland ("Flat Rock Land"), and from there to Nova Scotia, calling it Mark Land ("Forest Land"). Turning south he arrived at Vinland, which may have been as far south as Virginia but more likely modern day Massachusetts. Leif's brother, Thorvald, also made a voyage to Vinland in 1002 A.D., and landed certainly at Massachusetts, where he named a cape Kiarlanes, which means "Keel-Cape" in old Norse. This was almost certainly keel-shaped Cape Cod. At another promontory Thorvald and his men were attacked by natives; eight natives were killed but so was Thorvald, who was buried under a cross and the Norsemen named the place Krossanes in his memory.

Other than L'Anse aux Meadows, a settlement in Newfoundland, no other permanent Norse settlements have been found in the New World. The Norse sagas report several trips to Vinland, but all had lasted three years or less. Nevertheless, the Norse maintained a presence in North America for three centuries, though Leif Ericsson remained only three years. During his stay, a son was born to Gudrid, Leif's sister, and her husband, Thorfinn Karlsefn. The child named Snorri is the first recorded birth of a European in America.

Adam of Bremen, in his *Descriptio Insularum Aquilonis*, written in 1070 AD, told of a land called Vinland where wild grapes were found, and also self-sown wheat. The Roman Catholic Church also has records of their far-flung outposts in Greenland and Vinland. Thirteen bishops had served in Greenland beginning in 1112 A.D., and at least one, Erik Gnupsson (known as Henricus), was sent to Christianize the Norse settlers in America. In 1112, Henricus traveled three hundred miles across land from Maine to Rhode Island as a missionary. Another bishop, Olav, traveled to the Arctic lands to administer to the Christian converts there.

Several hundred years later, Catholic missionaries were still visiting these remote climes. The Pope became concerned for the missionaries in Norse lands because of piracy and instructed King Magnus to send an expedition westward to seek them out. He offered the king half the tithes collected in Norway and Sweden for his efforts. The king dispatched Sir Paul Knutson in 1354, but he never returned. The next year, King Haakon, successor to Magnus, sent out another expedition, which encountered piracy among the Inuit peoples in Greenland. This second expedition returned with two kayaks, which the bishop of Oslo hung in the cathedral of that city. With the Norse outposts in Greenland gone, trade ceased, and the New World was all but forgotten.

———

The official version of the Gunn descent and family history has been summarized by the *Clan Gunn Society of North America* in the following manner:

The Clan Gunn claims descent from the Norse Jarls or Earls of Orkney and from the ancient Celtic Moraers of Caithness through Ragnhild, daughter of Moddan in Dale, son of Moddan, Mormaer (High Steward) of Caithness, who was killed in 1040, and granddaughter of Saint Rognvald, Jarl of Orkney, who married Gunni, the reputed name-father of the Clan. Gunni was himself a grandson of Sweyn Asleif's-son, the 'Ultimate Viking' and hero of the Orkneyinga Saga.

Sweyn Asleif's-son had his long hall on the island of Gairsay, off the east coast of the Mainland of Orkney and lands in Caithness at Freswick, a few miles south of Duncansbay. The principal Gunn lands were, however, acquired through Ragnhild, who inherited great estates in Caithness and Sutherland on the death of her brother, Harold Ungi, Jarl in Orkney and Earl of Caithness in 1198.

At this time the Clan Gunn were at the height of their power. They appeared to possess virtually the whole of Caithness, which was then passing from the influence of the Norse Earldom to that of the King of Scots. Snaekoll Gunnisson is reputed to have built Castle Gunn at Bruan, on the east coast of Caithness south of Wick. There is a tradition that Castle Gunn was destroyed by the King of Norway, whose daughter one of the Gunn chiefs had married, though he already had a wife at Castle Gunn. When the second wife sailed to Caithness to join her husband, the Gunn clan arranged for the beacon to be placed on a dangerous rock at Ulbster and so wrecked the ship and all aboard were drowned. The castle was destroyed in revenge and the Gunn chief and his retainers were slain.

Little is known of the history of the Clan during the 13th and 14th century and it is not until the 15th century that history records the exploits of the Clan and its chiefs. Nonetheless, it is clear that during the 14th and 15th centuries the Gunns were gradually dispossessed of their lands in the fertile parts of Caithness by the Sinclairs, Keiths and others, who obtained grants of land from the Scottish kings, anxious to increase their influence over the fringes of their kingdom. Consequently by the mid 15th century George Gunn of Ulbster, Chief of Clan Gunn and Crowner of Caithness, held his main lands at Ulbster and Clyth on the rocky coast of Caithness, and the majority of the Clan by then occupied the highland regions of Caithness in what are now the Parishes of Latheron, Halkirk and Reay.

It was George Gunn, the Crowner, also known as "Am Braisdeach Mor," or "Big Broochy" from the insignia worn by the Gunn Chiefs, as Crowners of Caithness, who after many skirmishes with the Clan Keith over rival land claims sought to reach a conciliation with the Keiths at St. Tayre's Chapel, near Ackergill Tower, the seat of Keith of Ackergill in 1478 (other say 1464) and was killed in the unequal battle at the chapel where the Keiths arrived for the twelve-aside Parlay with two men to each horse. In 1978 the Earl of Kintore, Chief of Clan Keith and Iain Gunn of Banniskirk, the Commander of Clan Gunn, signed a Treaty of Friendship between the two clans at the site of the chapel, bringing to end the 500 year old feud.

After the death of George, the Crowner, and his sons at Ackergill, the Clan split into three distinct families—James or Seumas, the Crowner's eldest son who survived the battle, moved with his family to Kildonan in Sutherland, subsequently known as Gleann na Guineach or Gunn's Glen, where he obtained lands from the Earls of Sutherland; Robert, the second surviving son established his line in Braemore, in the southern heights of Caithness as the Robson Gunns, and John, the third surviving son settled in Cattaig or Bregual in Strathmore, in the higher reaches of the River Thurso above Westerdale. [From *The Clan Gunn and Its Country*, published by the Clan Gunn Heritage Center, Latheron, Caithness.]

While the Earls of Orkney possessed Caithness they chiefly managed the affairs of the county by deputies or governors who resided at Duncansbay, in the parish of Canisbay, under the title of "Prefecturae de Dungaldsbeis." At the beginning of the twelfth century the resident governor was Olaus Rolfi, who came from the island of Gairsay in Orkney, and was in high estimation with the Earl because of his bravery. His wife, whose maiden name was Asleif, was descended of a noble Norwegian family. Her father was Moddan of Dale, whose father was Moddan the Mormaer. Her maternal grandfather was the great St.

Rognvald, Earl of Orkney.

Frakirk, the relict of a powerful chieftain in Sutherland had conceived a mortal grudge against Olaus, and she sent her grandson, Aulver Rosti, with a party of men, to destroy him. They arrived at Duncansbay about Christmas (a season which the Norsemen, from whom the festival of Yule had originated, particularly devoted to festivity) and surrounded the governor's house. After plundering it of everything valuable, they set fire to the house and burnt him to death with most of his attendants. His wife, with her two sons, Sweyn and Gunn, happened to be away from home on a visit, and thus fortunately survived. As soon as she learned of the death of her husband she took a boat and sailed across with her sons to Orkney.

Frakirk, the instigator of this atrocious outrage, was in fact a near relation of Asleif. It seems possible that they were sisters, or half-sisters, for she was the daughter of Moddan, a Norwegian nobleman, who resided in that part of the parish of Bower which is said to have been named for him—Bowermadden. This Moddan had another daughter, Helga, who in wickedness was equal to her sister, and was married to Haco, Earl of Orkney. Frakirk was living with them at this time.

Earl Haco had a son by Helga, named Harold, and by a former marriage had a son named Paul. The two boys were of opposite disposition and had disagreed since boyhood. On the death of their father, the earldom was partitioned between them. From the moment the title came into their hands they began to quarrel. Helga, supported by her sister, did everything within her power to widen the breach between them, naturally wishing her son to have the earldom.

Harold agreed to give a sumptuous banquet for his brother at Christmas in his palace at Ophir with the view of reconciliation. Near the end of the feast, Harold entered his mother's apartment and found his aunt Frakirk finishing an exquisite embroidered shirt of fine linen, spangled with gold thread. Struck with its beauty, he inquired for whom the shirt was being made, and with some reluctance his mother told him it was for his brother Paul. Harold, drunk with wine, upbraided his mother for her partiality and demanded the shirt for himself. On bended knees Helga implored him not to touch it, assuring him that if he did so it would cost him his life. But Harold jerked it from her hands and put it on. But the fatal garment was impregnated with deadly poison, and no sooner did it come into contact with his body, then he was seized with a trembling fit and excruciating pain. He was carried to bed and died soon after in extreme agony.

Paul, who saw that his own death was intended, immediately banished the wicked sisters from Orkney. They went over to Caithness, and thence to Kildonan, in Sutherlandshire, where Frakirk's castle and land was situated. After the death of Harold, the earldom of Orkney and Caithness was jointly ruled over by his half-brother Paul, and by Rognvald, nephew of Magnus, who was assassinated in the isle of Eaglesay in 1110.

As mentioned previously, on the death of Olaus Rolf, the late governor of Duncansbay, his widow, with her two sons Sweyn and Gunn had retired to Orkney. The two boys were born, it is believed, in Canisbay. Sweyn took his mother's name and was afterwards called Sweyn Asleifson. He became the celebrated "Pirate of Freswick," and was a most extraordinary character. He had two castles, one on the island of Gairsay, about four miles north of Kirkwall, and the other in Freswick, in the county of Caithness. The ruins of his castle at Freswick can still be seen, consisting of a small dilapidated tower on a wild peninsular rock rising abruptly from the sea, some fifty or sixty yards from the main precipices at the shore. A more foreboding place to live can hardly be imagined, with barren rocks on one side and the interminable ocean on the other. In the winter season, when eastern storms pounded the shores, with winds and waves in tremendous fury all around, it must have been a frightful residence. Torfaeus, the chronicler, gives it the strange name of "Lambaburgum," and says that the castle was strong and well built, and from its peculiar situation could not be easily taken. It was, in fact, a regular pirate's keep, and there is no doubt that it was originally built by Sweyn.

Sweyn sometimes spent the winter in this castle, and sometimes in his other castle on the island of Gairsay, with a retinue of about eighty followers, during which time there was "one continued round of revelry and wassail." As soon as spring arrived, he equipped his galleys and set out on his marauding expeditions.

Haco, the Earl of Orkney's son, often accompanied Sweyn on his piratical expeditions, and the young nobleman could not have had a more able tutor. Sweyn not only plied along the coast of Scotland, but he plundered as far as Cornwall, the Isle of Man, and Ireland. The Gunns were long acquainted with the Isle of Man, for Olave was king of the Isle of Man, and his son Guin founded another branch of the Gunn family.

Sweyn was on intimate and friendly terms with Earl Paul, but in a drunken brawl on Christmas he killed one of the Earl's retainers, and fled for safety to Perthshire where he lived for some time with the Earl and Countess of Atholl (Haco [Hakon] Paulsson married the above-mentioned Helga Maddansdatter; their daughter Margaret married Maddad, Earl of Atholl). Magaret, the countess, was a beautiful woman, but unscrupulous and a profligate. At her instigation a plot was hatched to seize her half-brother Paul and convey him to Atholl, the object being to make her own son Earl of Orkney. Sweyn, who was ever ready for any plot, no matter how perilous, at once agreed to execute her intention.

Being furnished with a large galley and a crew of thirty desperate vagabonds, Sweyn set sail for Orkney. He found Earl Paul on the island of Rousay, where he was amusing himself with catching seals, and after a severe struggle during the course of which nineteen of the Earl's attendants and six of Sweyn's men were killed, Earl Paul was seized and carried captive to the residence of his sister in Perthshire. The place where the Earl was abducted is still called Sweyndroog. Earl Paul was kept closely confined until he was forced to convey to young Harold, his nephew, all his rights and titles to the earldom of Orkney. Afterwards Paul disappeared, and it is believed that he was put to death by the orders of his unnatural sister.

Young Harold, the protegé of Sweyn, was brought to Orkney where, under the supervision of Rognvald, he received an education and as soon as he came of age was admitted to a share of the earldom. Not long afterwards, Rognvald set out on his pious pilgrimage to Jerusalem, and Harold began to exhibit in his absence all of the bad qualities of his nature which earned him the sobriquet of Harold the Wicked. He oppressed the people to such a degree that Eystein, King of Norway, set sail for Orkney to bring down Harold's lofty pretensions and bring to an end his tyranny. Harold was seized and thrown into prison, and was later released after agreeing to stringent restrictions on his fiefdom. The chronicler Torfaeus assures us that Harold might have escaped this humiliation had he obtained the able counsel and assistance of his friend Sweyn, but the latter was away at the time on a piratical excursion.

Subsequent to kidnaping the Earl of Orkney, Sweyn inflicted a summary vengeance on Frakirk for her part in the death of his father at Duncansbay. He landed in Sutherlandshire with a select band of his pirates, first plundered her house, then set it on fire and burnt Frakirk with her sister Helga and all their domestics. This was done with the aid of

Margaret, Countess of Atholl, who furnished guides to the locality in Sutherland where Frakirk resided. There are few instances in history more barbarous than this woman who, after first putting her brother, Earl Paul, to death, next consented and aided the burning death of her mother and aunt.

Sweyn himself was no respecter of persons. One day he sallied forth from his castle at Freswick to the Pentland Firth, and attacked and robbed a vessel with Earl Harold's rents from Shetland, on its way to Wick, where the Earl was sojourning.

On another occasion, while cruising in the Irish Channel, he attacked two merchant ships bound for the Isle of Man, and seized a large quantity of scarlet cloth and other commodities of great value. On his way home, Sweyn did something peculiar, perhaps a product of his ego. "When near the Orkney Islands with his fleet," says Torfaeus, "he caused sew some of the cloth on the sails, so that they appeared like sails of scarlet, for which reason that expedition was called the 'scarlet cruise.'"

Along the east side of Elwick Bay, in the island of Shapinshay, lies an uninhabited islet called Elgarholm, forming a natural breakwater. The Earl of Orkney, with the large and well-manned galley, here gave chase to Sweyn, who was cruising about Shapinshay in a small boat with only two or three of his followers. As soon as he saw that he was pursued, Sweyn applied the oars with vigor, and turning one of the points of Elgarholm, he ran his skiff into a cave. On rounding the same point only moments later, the Earl was amazed to see that Sweyn and his boat had seemingly disappeared. Sweyn knew his waters well.

A Norseman named Arne had obtained some goods from one of Sweyn's tenants, and when the man afterwards demanded payment Arne beat him severely, and told him he should go and seek the aid of the pirate of whose prowess he boasted so much. The peasant went directly to Sweyn,

who after being informed of the slight, immediately seized an axe with a short handle, and taking four men with him crossed over in an eight-oared boat to the island where Arne lived. He left his crew with the boat and proceeded alone to Arne's residence where he found him in a storeroom with four of his companions. Sweyn demanded that Arne make immediate payment to his tenant, and when Arne refused, Sweyn drove his axe into his skull, so that, as the saga says, "the iron was buried therein." Losing hold of the weapon, Sweyn charged out of the room and ran for the shore pursued closely by Arne's four companions. One of the men had nearly overtaken him, when Sweyn grabbed up a handful of seaweed mixed with mud and dashed it in the man's face. Sweyn leaped into his boat and safely escaped to the island of Gairsay.

Again, when his castle at Freswick was besieged by the Earl, Sweyn encouraged his men to surrender rather than die from famine, while Sweyn himself and his agent Margad let themselves down long ropes to the sea, and miraculously swam to safety, though wearing full armor.

Sweyn at length surprised and plundered Dublin and carried off to his ships some of the principal men of the city, and agreed to return them for a ransom, which was called "Danegelt." Next day, when he went ashore to receive his money, he was ambushed by the inhabitants, and he and his entire party were slain. This event occurred in the autumn of the year 1160. So ended the career of the man credited with being ancestor of the Clan Gunn.

———

The Clan Gunn seems to have occupied chiefly the highland portions of Caithness, although their burial-place was at Spittal (Sinclair territory). Their connection with Caithness as a distinct clan ended about 1619. Until the middle of the seventeenth century, we find no written evidence of their tenure of land. Probably, as in the case of Donald Gunn of Braemore, noted in "Ministers and Men in the Far North" (as quoted in *Caithness Family History*, John Henderson, C.S., David Douglas, Edinburgh, 1934, p.319 "The Gunns"), what possessions they had were "gained by the sword" and retained by the same means while they were a power in Caithness.

George Gunn was chief of the clan in the fifteenth century and lived at the castle of Hagberry in Clyth. He was popularly styled the "Cruner Gunn" (i.e. Crouner, Crowner), from his holding the office of "Crowner" of the district, an ancient office which empowered the holder to attach the persons of offenders against the Crown. This also entitled him to summarily approve or disapprove of those appointed to royal offices, including the earls. By his clansmen and other highlanders he was known as the "Nin Braistack-more," from the great silver brooch worn by him as a badge of office.

He is reputed to have had seven sons, four of whom fell along with himself in 1464 (or 1478) in a combat with the Keiths, their hereditary foes. Of these sons, James succeeded to the chieftainship; Robert, the second son, is ancestor of the Gunns of Braemore; from John, the third surviving son, are descended the Gunns of Dalmore and Dale.

James, the successor, settled with his brothers William, Henry and Alexander in Sutherlandshire, where we find mention of the two latter in an ancient document entitled "Inventar of the Gudes of Alexander Sutherland, 1456" (father-in-law of William Sinclair, first Earl of Caithness). There are entries proving the "Crouner" to have had sons Henry and Alexander, thus: "Item, Alexander the Crouner's son an (owing) me for the Teind of Dael, Thurno, and the begyn, with uther geeds that he tuk of myn that comes to 24 of Marks and mair;" and, "Item, Henry the Crounars son an me for tends and ky (teinds and cattle) that he tuk of myn 40 merks and mar, as vitail (Victual) was sold in the countrie that tym."

The Gunns and Sinclairs continued a long association. The quartered arms of the Sinclairs contain the arms of the Gunns, indicating that the Sinclairs had intermarried with the Clan Gunn and owed title as earls of Caithness to them. As late as 1732 George Gunn, son and successor of John of Braemore, got a wadset for 17,000 merks from Sir James Sinclair of Dunbeath. Sir James acquired Braemore in 1729 as part of the Caithness estate purchased by him and Ulster from Lord Glenorchy.

The Gunns and Sinclairs were, in addition to being related through marriage, cousins and descendants of the same family —the ancient Earls of Möre (More og Romsdal), Norway. Gunns and Sinclairs are entombed side by side in the catacombs beneath Rosslyn Chapel. And the Gunns and Sinclairs were together in an epic making voyage to the New World nearly a hundred years before the voyage of Christopher Columbus.

Gunn coat-of-arms
(Translation: Either Peace or War)

Chapter Nine

The Westford Knight

Henry Sinclair was the Earl of the Orkneys. He inherited the title by virtue of his mother Isabel, daughter of Malise II, 40th Jarl of Orkney. These windswept islands that lie off the northernmost point of Scotland had been inhabited by Scots, Picts, and Norse settlers before the advent of the Sinclairs. The Gunns had been the ancient Kings of Orkney, as well as the Hebrides and the Isle of Man.

The Sinclairs already owned large stretches of land in the Scottish northlands and other strategic property near Edinburgh, granted to their ancestor Walderne de St. Clair for his support of William the Conqueror. In 1390 Henry Sinclair sailed with his fleet throughout the Orkneys in a show of strength to survey his earldom. It was a timely voyage for some Italians who owed their lives to Henry's arrival.

Niccolo Zeno was an Italian of royal blood who had sailed north in search of adventure. His father was a nobleman descended from one of the wealthiest and most influential families of Venice. His brother Carlo, a naval war hero, had saved Venice from a Genoese invasion. The only member of his family not to have made a name for himself, Niccolo set out on a northern voyage in search of fame and fortune.

He had sailed from Venice across the Mediterranean Sea and north up the Atlantic along the coast of Britain and even farther north. On tiny Fer Island, between the Shetlands and the Orkneys, Zeno's ship ran aground on a reef and he almost lost his life. The islanders there still have a custom called "grindadrap," which means whale hunt, but it is a far more gruesome practice

than that. As many as a hundred pilot whales at a time will swim close to the shore in the narrows, and with the war cry "grint" the islanders rush into the surf with ten-inch knives and harpoons, and the ensuing slaughter turns the water pink with blood.

The islanders were ready to "grindadrap" Zeno and his crew when the Earl of Orkney arrived at the last minute. Henry Sinclair dispersed the islanders and spared the sailors' lives. It was a fortuitous meeting for both men. Sinclair had heard of Niccolo's famous brother Carlo, known as the "Lion of Venice." In the course of swapping stories of their experiences they discovered that their not-too-distant ancestors had been acquainted—during the Crusades, Sinclair knights had been transported by Venetian ships owned by the Zeno family on the last leg of travel to the Holy Land.

Sinclair was impressed with Niccolo Zeno's naval experience enough to appoint him as admiral of the Sinclair fleet. Niccolo, happy with the appointment, wrote home to another brother, Antonio, to join him in Scotland in the employ of "Prince" Henry Sinclair. Sinclair and Zeno joined forces to assert the Sinclair claim to the islands off the coast of Scotland, and Zeno even made a trip to Greenland on his patron's behalf, where he mapped the coastline.

Henry Sinclair was aware that lands existed west of Greenland. His Gunn relatives had visited these strange lands for centuries and had brought back amazing accounts of their adventures and discoveries. But Henry had also learned more recent details from a Faeroese fisherman who had been captured during a voyage to the Grand Banks. He described his capture by natives in this strange land and claimed to have met there a man living with his captors who spoke Latin and had books. He had been taken south in the new land with six other fishermen who had been shipwrecked with him, and they had fallen victim to cannibals, who murdered his companions but spared his life when he taught them how to catch fish with a net. He was allowed to return to the north through a land called Drogio and finally made his way back to Estotiland where he built a vessel large enough to return to Europe.

The fisherman described Estotiland as being smaller than Iceland, that it had a great mountain in the center with four rivers, and that the people there traded with "Engroveland" (Greenland), taking trade goods for the furs and pitch they brought from their own country. Henry Sinclair heard this story in 1397, and by the next year he was ready to set sail to see these lands for himself.

Sinclair was well acquainted with Greenland. Gunnar (Gunn) had first discovered it in 920 A.D. and the Gunns had sailed there often since. In 1394 Pope Boniface IX had sent the bishop of Orkney to Greenland in one of Sinclair's ships. The Church outpost of Greenland was in Gardar, a settlement on the west coast of the island. Notably, it is no farther from western Greenland to Canada than it is from there to Iceland, where the Norse had settled early in considerable numbers.

By the time Henry Sinclair had made the preparations for his intended voyage, Niccolo's brother Antonio had joined the expedition; and timely too, as it proved, because Niccolo Zeno died before they could start, and so it was Antonio Zeno who accompanied Sinclair to America and recorded the entire account of the voyage. Unlike his brother, Antonio was not appointed admiral. Although he had inherited his brother's titles and wealth, the most important part of his inheritance included the maps and reports compiled by Niccolo, who had spent his last few years exploring and charting the coast on a three-ship expedition. The account of the voyage was preserved for posterity in the maps and letters that Antonio sent to Venice, which were published in 1558. It was the first recorded expedition since the Norse crossed the Atlantic, and included a map of the New World.

The expedition of Henry Sinclair and Antonio Zeno was ready to sail in 1398, but just three days before they were scheduled to embark, the fisherman—who was to be their guide—suddenly died. But he had managed to convey directions in sailors' terms and with the aid of an astrolabe, which helped them to calculate latitude, the journey could go on.

The expedition began in Scotland and was made by hopping from one island to the next: from Scotland to the Orkneys, past tiny Fer Island. On Antonio Zeno's map, Fer Island—where Sinclair had rescued Niccolo—was noted as "FerIslanda," and later as "Frisland." Fer Island is only one day away from the Orkneys, and two days north they stopped at the Faeroes. Because of bad weather they stayed in the Shetlands for a week before proceeding north, but no sooner were they underway than a storm intervened. Their plan had been to follow the Viking route westward, with a stop at Iceland for supplies, then onward to Greenland; but the storm altered their course and they by-passed Iceland and made one unscheduled stop at an island called Icaria, which place has never been found, casting some doubt on the voyage by certain scholars. Either the island no longer exists (as in the case of Gunnar's Skerries) or they have not been located. Their description matches the location of Gunnar's Skerries (or Gunnbiorn) and there is no doubt that they existed. They are still shown on United States Hydrographic Office maps; the problem is that they have sunk (by 1456) and now form an underwater plateau. In 1456, when most of the main island was underwater, it was still sixty-five miles long and twenty-five miles wide and was called Gombar Skaare.

The Zeno narrative states that Icaria (there is a Greek island of the same name) was ruled by a king, and there was only one man among the Icarians, an Icelander, who could speak a language that Sinclair could understand. The Icarians were openly hostile and through the Icelander they forbade Sinclair's ships to land. The king of that place stated that Icaria was a refuge for those who had fled religious persecution and Viking plundering, and they were ready to fight to the death rather than to flee again. The king would allow only one man to set foot on the island to converse with the Icelander and convey the words of the king.

Sinclair feigned sailing away and instructed his ships to circle the island to avoid the hostile inhabitants and finding a small harbor attempted to land, but the Icarians had followed the ships as they circled the island. Sinclair was forced to sail onward without supplies. They sailed past Cape Race on the coast of Greenland, a noted port for the Norse, but Zeno reports that they hoped to find a safer landfall. It was risky, but it worked.

Two days later they reached the coast of Newfoundland, but because of stormy conditions they decided not to risk a landing, and after two more days they reached Nova Scotia. Based on the descriptions in Zeno's letters, Tor Bay seems to be their most likely landing place. On entering the harbor they saw a hill in the distance, since Nova Scotia is very flat with one high hill in what is now Antigonish, in Picctou County, which can be seen from the bay. After landing they gathered bird eggs from the extensive rookeries and went fishing to replenish their supplies. Sinclair dispatched one hundred men to cross the "island," where they reported sighting another sea (the Northumberland Strait) and a spring where pitch ran into the sea (rare asphalt, which is found in Stellarton, Nova Scotia). Zeno also described a

"smoking hole," perhaps a lightning caused or manmade fire that had smoldered for some time.

The soldiers also reported that very short natives ran from them and hid in caves. These were the Micmacs, who were known to be timid. The Micmac name derives from their term "nikmaq," meaning "my kin friends." They were a nomadic people, wintering inland and summering along the Atlantic Coast where they became skilled at fishing. By the eighteenth century they had developed a writing system.

Frederick Pohl, who wrote extensively on early European discoveries in the New World, had been able to determine Sinclair's landing date. Recognizing that sailors often gave place-names taken from the religious day celebrated on their day of discovery, he noted that according to Zeno's letters the harbor was named "Trin," and the month was June. The eighth Sunday Easter is called Trinity Sunday, and so the Sinclair-Zeno landing can be calculated as 2 June 1398.

Henry Sinclair was very taken with Nova Scotia. The climate was moderate, fish and game were abundant, and the harbors were suitable for shipping. He declared that he would one day build a city there and leave Scotland to make Nova Scotia ("New Scotland") his home. This did not sit well with his crew who were anxious to return home before the seasons changed and the Atlantic became even more dangerous. Sinclair was not ready to leave. He appointed Zeno as captain of a return expedition and all who wished to return could do so, while he and a smaller group would stay on and continue their explorations.

Zeno sailed for Scotland, first stopping in the Faeroes. He sent his account of the voyage to his brother in Venice and thus recorded the event for history. Apart from these letters, we have no further account of these expeditions, except that one of Zeno's letters states that Sinclair did explore the

New World further and that he built a "town in the port of the island newly discovered by him." Fortunately, there is other evidence of Sinclair's explorations.

Sinclair either marched or sailed along a coastal route southward to explore as far as the region which would later be called New England. His route took him along coastal New Brunswick past what is now the border between Canada and the United States at Saint Stephen, and just beyond he entered Maine in the vicinity of Machias Bay. Here, on a ledge that juts into Machias Bay at Clark's Point, Maine, there is a "petroglyph of a cross incised beside one of a European ship of the late fourteenth century." Andrew Sinclair, a distant descendant, in his book *The Sword and The Grail* (Crown Pub., New York, 1992, p.147), maintains that this stone confirms the voyage. Farther south, there is even more compelling evidence.

———

On a granite pedestal in the small Massachusetts town of Westford lies a carved rock memorial to a Scottish Knight. The rock has been known to exist since colonial times, but it lay unnoticed, covered by brush. Frank Glynn, an amateur archaeologist from Connecticut, became interested in the rock carving and set about uncovering it. He cleared away the brush, exposed the carving, and sparked an instant debate. The rock ledge, which is now on Depot Street in Westford, was faded with time and difficult to discern. Glynn highlighted the carving by pouring chalk into the punched holes and incised lines. It clearly revealed the figure of a knight complete with chain mail and a coat-of-arms.

Glynn made a rubbing of the stone and sent it to T.C. Lethbridge, a British archaeologist and curator of the University of Archaeology and Ethnology at Cambridge, England. Beginning in 1954 Lethbridge researched the coat-of-arms and the figure itself in Scotland and Wales. He concluded that it was a depiction of a knight of consid-

erable importance.

The memorial carving of the depicted knight is six feet. It shows a "basinet" helmet, which came into use in the 1360s and continued in usage until the fifteenth century, helping to date the carving. Lethbridge also determined that such effigies in stone were common during that time period in Ireland and the western isles of Britain. The carvings would be made at the place where the knight had fallen, usually the site of a battle. The detailed carving included the hilt of a sword held over the knight's breast and a shield bearing a coat-of-arms, the latter of which depicted a buckle, a crescent, a five-pointed star, and a ship.

In 1956 Lethbridge wrote to Glynn that he had discovered the origin of the armor and crest as coming from the outer islands of Scotland circa 1350. The buckle (which is actually a brooch) on the shield was an emblem possessed by only a few families, which Lethbridge was able to trace by consulting early Orkney medals. The coat-of-arms, he declared, were "clearly the arms of some maternal relation of the Sinclairs." The incidence of galley portrayals on Scottish coats-of-arms indicated that those bearing this heraldic emblem were either from Norse kings of the isles, or from the "Norse Jarls" of Orkney—the Sinclairs. In medieval Scotland families under the protection of a ruling family might take their surname from the clan of their protector. The shield and coat-of-arms proved to be those of a branch of the Sinclair group, the Clan Gunn, and more specifically to a knight who was the principal lieutenant of Henry Sinclair—Sir James Gunn. In 1973, Sir Ian Moncreiffe, one of heraldry's foremost authorities, verified Lethbridge's conclusions.

Confirmation of the Gunn coat-of-arms was found in another stone carving of the ship, the crescent, and the star, on a ledge of rock at Oak Island, Nova Scotia. In the crypt below Rosslyn Chapel in Scotland one can still see a small coat-of-arms on the wall, which shows on its left-hand side, above the "Engrailed Cross" of the Sinclair family, a single-masted, twin-sailed ship identical to the one found on the shield of the Westford knight. It is shown pointing to the west, but instead of furled sails under a western star this vessel is under full sail. There is no longer any doubt that the arms belonged to Sir James Gunn, and that the Gunns and Sinclairs were allied by marriage.

The importance of the Westford stone carving is not only to prove the close link between the Gunn and Sinclair class in Scotland, but to link them with the "Crowners of Caithness," and according to Steven Sora, in his informative book *The Lost Treasure of the Knights Templar* (Destiny Books, Rochester, Vermont, 1999, pp.58-59): "In the north the Gunns were the 'Crowners of Caithness,' and tradition held that without their consent, no one could rule over their province in the Scottish northlands. This right was affirmed by the insignia of the buckle on their coat of arms. The Sinclairs gained the lands through inheritance, but still they ruled with the consent of the Gunn clan." It is clear that the Gunns were, in essence, the "power behind the throne." It is also clear that Sir James Gunn was ancestor of George Gunn, the "Crowner of Caithness." Only "Crowners" were entitled to carry the buckle.

In the 1960s a farmer discovered a second marker in his field not far from the Westford carving, but not knowing its significance he left it in his barn. The stone was inscribed with the same punched style as the stone depicting Sir James Gunn, the depths of the holes as well as their diameter being identical. The carving on this stone portrays again the galley design that appears on the Gunn coat-of-arms, and a mysterious "184" with an arrow, which might have been some kind of instruction to the finder, but unfortunately because the stone had been removed, any such instruc-

tions would be meaningless. This stone was eventually placed in the lobby of the Fletcher Library in Westford, not far from the Depot Road granite memorial to Sir James Gunn.

Near Fall River, Massachusetts, the Taunton River empties into Assonct Bay. On the east side of the bay there is a large rock with a 7 x 11 foot surface inscribed with symbols described as runic. Called "Dighton Rock," its existence was first recorded by the colonial preacher-mystic-historian-scientist Cotton Mather in 1690. Both Glynn and Lethbridge describe it as being of the same "punch" style as the Westford inscription.

In 1831 the skeleton of a man wearing heavy metal plate armor was dug up at the corner of Fifth Street and Harley in Fall River. Henry Wadsworth Longfellow wrote a poem about this mysterious "Skeleton in Armor," and it was his opinion that he built the nearby Norse Tower for his "fair lady." A fire in the museum in 1843 deprived posterity of any further opportunity to examine the skeleton of the knight. Anthropologists connected to Harvard's Peabody Museum, without being able to examine the remains, made what amounted to a ridiculous "guess," that the armor was probably that of a Wampanoag Indian! Such armor was typical of a fourteenth century knight, however, and it seems likely that the skeleton was that of Sir James Gunn. It would appear that Sir James was killed in battle with the natives at Westford and taken to Fall River, near the bay, for burial.

In Newport, Rhode Island, there stands a rounded gray stone tower set above arches that are ten feet above ground, with a floor built above the arches. On this floor was the remnants of a fireplace that may have been used as a signal light for Newport Harbor. The inner diameter of the tower is eighteen feet, while the outside is twenty-four feet, attesting to the thickness of the stone walls. N. Ludlow Beamish, in his book *The Norse Discovery of America* (London, 1906, p.239), believed that early

Norse explorers built it and that it is related to nearby Dighton Rock. Hjalmar R. Holand believes the tower was a church dedicated to Henricus, one of the last Norse Catholics to be sent to the New World (*Explorations in America before Columbus*, Twayne Pub., New York, 1958, pp.218-25).

The first map on which it appeared was made by the Verranzano expedition (1524), which recorded it as a "Norman Villa," and further stated that the natives of this region are inclined "more to whiteness" than other New England natives.

Andrew Sinclair sees in the tower an indication of a second Sinclair settlement in the New World (op.cit., pp.144-47). Its construction is identical with the round churches and temples of the Knights Templar, which are circular and complete with eight arches. The only one in Scotland was constructed in Orkney, the home of Henry Sinclair, and the Sinclair family were the protectors of the Templars and Freemasonry, which grew out of Templarism. Hjalmar Holand traces the construction of the tower to the Cistercian monastic order, the same order that was instrumental in founding the Templars. The tower appears to have been part of a Templar temple, and Henry Sinclair was its probable builder.

While Sinclair's base of operations in North America was probably situated in Nova Scotia, he explored southward to Massachusetts and probably as far as Virginia or farther. He may have brought as many as 300 men to America; his fleet was larger than that of the Norse king of Norway. How long he remained in the New World is unknown, and he may have made a second voyage. Even the date of his death is unsettled. Father Hay, an early Scottish genealogist, maintains that Henry died in 1400 during an English raid. The English chronicler Raphael Holinshed states that the fatal raid took place in 1404. Frederick Pohl [as quoted by Steven Sora, op.cit.] wrote that nearly all of Sinclair's life can be accounted for except the years 1400 to

1404, but he concludes that Sinclair remained in America until 1400 and came home to Scotland to be killed in a raid that same year. It is also possible that Sinclair came home in 1400, made a second trip to the New World, and then returned to Scotland to meet his death in 1404. Antonio Zeno did not return to Venice until 1404, leading to the conclusion that Sinclair's death in that year freed him from his obligations.

In 1558 a descendant of Antonio Zeno's turned the old maps and letters into a published narrative. Some historians question why the discovery set off no shock waves in Europe. The answer is that Henry Sinclair wanted his discovery kept secret, for the Sinclairs had another motive for establishing themselves in the New World, far from the English king and the Roman Church.

The Micmac tribe of Nova Scotia have a legend that tells of a "Great Prince" who brought his people to their country "on the backs of whales." This prince remained with them for half a year, only to leave, but to return again a second time. The Micmacs claim the prince lived in a wigwam he called "Winter." In the Micmac language this prince's name was translated as "Glooskap" which literally means "deceiver," but this was a title given in respect. The Norse god Loki was the trickster god who stole fire from the gods and gave it to ordinary humans. Glooskap had the knowledge to make fire, and the Micmac regarded the prince as "wasteful" because he put his fire out at night. Frederick Pohl identifies Glooskap as Sinclair.

According to the Micmac, Glooskap built a town, probably in a place the Micmacs called Piktook, now Pictou. Glooskap taught the Micmac games that are similar to existing Scottish children's games, and Micmac songs are very similar to Scottish sailing songs. Numerous words in the Micmac dialect correspond with equivalent Gaelic: Gaelic *Mor-riomach* means "from the deep place," and Algonquin (Micmac) *Merrimack* means "deep fishing place." Norse equivalents are also found: The Iroquois (from which Micmacs derive) word for "stones" is ariesta, which is also their word for "testicles"; the Norse also called both stones and testicles by the same name—*eista*, etc.

Perhaps the most telling evidence is to be found in the Micmac's name for Nova Scotia, i.e. the New World. When Henry Sinclair asked the Micmacs of Nova Scotia where he was, they answered "Fertile Land." In Micmac this is "Acadie." To the Templars, "Arcadia" was the equivalent to the "Promised Land." The early name of Orkney was "Orcadum," a form of "Arcadia." The theme of Arcadia, which to the esoteric Templars meant an idyllic place, an unspoiled land, an Eden—the Promised Land—was to have profound significance later.

Future Sinclairs would come back to the Promised Land in the years to come; for them, Arcadia held an even greater significance than just new lands—it became a sanctuary and a hiding place for a family with something very important to hide.

The Westford Knight

the Westland Knight

Chapter Ten

The Oak Island Mystery

On a summer afternoon in the year 1795, three young men decided to go digging for pirate treasure on uninhabited Oak Island, one of 350 islands in Mahone Bay off mainland Nova Scotia. Stories of buried loot hidden by the pirate Captain William Kidd were prevalent all along the cold waters of the Canadian Atlantic.

One of the boys, Daniel McGinnis, had been exploring Oak Island when he noticed a spot in the woods that appeared to have recently been cleared and planted with red clover and other plants foreign to the island. A ship's tackle was also hanging from a sawed-off tree branch, fifteen feet above the ground. In the middle of the clearing was a depression in the ground that indicated something might be buried there. The nearby tree with the tackle hanging from it had strange symbols carved into the trunk.

Sixteen year-old Daniel McGinnis persuaded two of his friends, teenager Anthony Vaughn, and twenty year-old John Smith, to accompany him back to the 128-acre island with shovels and pickaxes. They set to work excavating the soft ground in the center of the depression.

After only two feet they reached a layer of carefully laid flagstones that were not indigenous to the island; it was later determined that they came from Golden River on mainland Nova Scotia, two miles away. When they had removed the layer of stones they realized they had uncovered a previously dug shaft. Hollowing out the shaft, after ten feet, they came to a platform made of oak logs, carefully fitted and imbedded into the sides of the thirteen foot-wide shaft. The logs were rotted with age and

easy to remove. At twenty feet a second platform of oak logs impeded their progress, but they were convinced that whoever went to so much trouble must have something important to hide, so they removed those logs and continued to excavate. They reached another platform at the thirty foot level, and at last realized that they needed help. They would require more man-power and machinery if they were to continue, so they returned to the mainland to secure assistance.

Local farmers were not enthusiastic about leaving their chores to aid impressionable youth in a quest for pirate treasure. Besides, to the superstitious locals Oak Island was haunted. Years earlier, mysterious lights had been seen moving around on the island at night, and when some local men rowed out to investigate, they were never heard from again. For some years after the boys' discovery, no work was done on the pit excavation.

Daniel McGinnis farmed a small piece of property on the island. Before the year was out, John Smith also bought a farm there, and when he married, he moved there to work it. When Smith's wife became pregnant with their first child, he took her to the mainland to visit the family physician, Dr. Simeon Lynds, who happened to be related to fellow treasure hunter Anthony Vaughn. Dr. Lynds became interested in what was by then being referred to as the "money pit," and decided to invest money into excavating the shaft.

In 1801 Dr. Lynds formed a syndicate, raising capital from thirty other prominent Nova Scotians, and the excavations began. Using ropes and pulleys, hired workers removed a layer of mud that had settled into the shaft, then continued digging. Again they encountered oak platforms at ten-foot intervals, together with layers of charcoal, putty, and a brown fibrous material.

At ninety feet, directly above the next oak platform, they encountered a flagstone with an inscription. In time, they showed the symbols to a professor of languages at nearby Halifax, who said the inscription told of treasure buried another "forty feet below." It was a common code, one used by Edgar Allan Poe in his story "The Gold Bug," in which a simple cipher is used in a search for a buried treasure. The key was substituting the most frequently used symbol for the most commonly used letter in the English language—an E. The inscribed stone was made a part of the mantel of John Smith's fireplace and in time found its way to a bookstore in Halifax, where another syndicate used it to raise money. When the store closed, the stone disappeared.

At ninety-three feet, below the next platform, the workers ran into a booby-trap —water flooded the shaft. A pump was brought in, but it soon burst, and work was discontinued. The next year the Onslow Syndicate (as Dr. Lynd's group was called) dug the second of what would be many shafts. After reaching 110 feet, they started to tunnel over to the first shaft, but water soon flooded this tunnel also. Funds were soon exhausted and work would not resume again for forty years.

A new company was formed in 1845 that included a second Dr. Lynd, of Truro, Nova Scotia, and a mining engineer, James Pitbaldo. Anthony Vaughn and John Smith were involved in this renewed search, though both were nearing seventy years of age.

Both of the other pits had caved in and it took twelve days to reach sixty-eight feet. They stopped on a Saturday, attended church on Sunday morning, and when they returned Sunday afternoon the pit was again flooded. This time, however, they had prepared for this contingency. They erected a platform for a horse-driven drill. At ninety-eight feet the drill went through a platform made of five inch-thick spruce, and another foot farther was another platform of oak. After going through twenty-two inches of metal, they encountered still another oak platform.

After another level of spruce, they reached clay, then more oak, and the drill brought up more of the brown fibrous material (which turned out to be coconut husks). Jotham McCully, who was in charge of the drilling, said these fragments resembled "links of watch chain." One of the workers noticed the foreman, James Pitbaldo, slip something into his pocket. When confronted, he would not reveal it to the others. When threatened, he said he would reveal it at the next meeting of syndicate directors, but he did not. Later he approached another businessman, Charles Archibald, of Acadia Iron Works, and attempted to buy the pit from the other directors, but they refused. Shortly thereafter, Pitbaldo was killed in another mining accident, and the secret of what he found died with him.

In 1850 the syndicate drilled another shaft to 109 feet in another attempt to reach the original tunnel, and although it too was flooded, it led to a significant discovery. By watching the water in the pit and the seawater offshore, they discovered that the water level in the pit was rising and falling with the tides of the bay. At Smith's Cove they discovered a channel surrounded by more of the brown fibrous material. Under a layer of eelgrass they found a mass of beach rock, indicating to their utter disbelief that the channel was manmade!

During ensuing weeks the syndicate built dams and discovered that the original builders had built an artificial beach and a 500-foot tunnel from the sea inland to lay the pit trap, channeling 600 gallons of ocean water per minute. The tunnel was complete with a filter system that prevented clogging, and the artificial beach protected the workings of the whole system. The entire operation was an engineering marvel and only served as further proof that something very important indeed was concealed under Oak Island.

Just when they recovered from the shock of this discovery, the syndicate discovered that there were five drains, each constructed of twin rows of rock, eight inches apart, covered with stone slabs. Then, shortly after they dismantled the five drains, an Atlantic storm hit and broke their coffer dam that had held back the waters. They hurriedly dug one shaft, then another, to absorb any water from the destroyed drain system. Then their new shaft collapsed into a cave and then was flooded. The collapse occurred during a break in the work, so no one was killed, but the workers refused to return to the shaft and all work was suspended.

By 1859 the Truro Syndicate raised enough money to resume work. Sixty-three men were hired, manual pumps were replaced by steam pumps, and more shafts were dug. A boiler explosion killed one man and the work stopped again. Then, most of Oak Island was sold to Anthony Graves, a local farmer, who leased search rights to a different syndicate, but this group failed to raise enough funds.

In 1866 another company was formed with an emphasis on building a larger dam, but the wild Atlantic soon flooded this project. They sunk a few more shafts which caused complications for later ventures, but in the meantime the land reverted back to Anthony Graves and work ceased again. In 1880, when farmer Graves was plowing eighty feet from the original pit, the earth gave way into a tunnel. It was said that a coin dated 1317 A.D. was discovered, but the coin disappeared before it could be examined by a numismatist.

In 1881 twenty-four year-old Frederick Blair of Amherst, Nova Scotia, formed the Oak Island Treasure Company with sixty thousand dollars of capital, half of which went to lease the land. With modern technology at their disposal, this group managed to prevent water from flooding the shafts, but when they exploded 160 pounds of dynamite, the shafts again flooded. By using red dye, it was discovered that another water tunnel system existed, this time extending 600 feet from a beach on the other side of the island. There had been a second trap to protect whatever was concealed in the Money Pit.

During the 1890s a number of discoveries were made. A drill was deflected at a depth of 151 feet which Blair decided must be a chest. When it was penetrated the drill brought up a piece of parchment. The parchment was mangled and only the letters "V.I." could be read. In time they brought up a pick, a seal-oil lamp, and an axe head, all of which Blair dated to at least the 1680s. Then the Blair expedition suffered the second fatality of the search, when a worker fell to his death from a hoisting platform.

In 1909 Franklin Delano Roosevelt, then a budding young attorney with the law firm of Carter, Ledyard and Milburn, was vacationing off the coast of New Brunswick. Learning of the activity in Nova Scotia, he invested in Blair's syndicate and brought in other wealthy investors, including Duncan Harris, Albert Gallatin and John Shields. Roosevelt not only visited the site but participated in the work. As early as 1896 he had spent four days digging on Grand Manan Island for Captain Kidd's treasure, and even as President of the United States he had a navy cruiser land on Cocos Island, 350 miles southwest of Costa Rica, where the pirate Edward Davis reputedly stashed some of his loot.

Franklin Delano Roosevelt was not the only celebrity to become involved in the search for the Oak Island treasure. Investors for future syndicates included John Wayne, Errol Flynn, Vincent Astor and Admiral Richard Byrd.

In 1922 a major investor was found in the person of William Chappell of Sydney, Nova Scotia, and his son, Mel, who joined Blair in the search. Mel Chappell was an engineer, and they utilized the latest equipment and technology without success, though they did find an anchor flute and more concrete. The greatest discovery was made by Chappell, not at the pit, but elsewhere on the island—a stone triangle set up as a marker. It is believed to hold the key to the location of the treasure, but no one has been able to solve the puzzle.

In 1934 Gilbert Hedden, another wealthy investor, was brought in. Hedden had been manager of a family-owned steel business in New Jersey, an auto dealer, and mayor of Chatham, New Jersey. Chappel, who died in 1946, was sixty-seven and realized that he hadn't much time. Hedden brought electricity to the island and a professional drilling team from the coal mines of Pennsylvania, but after three years with no success, Hedden backed out.

Hedden found no treasure, but he did find other monuments, including two boulders with mooring holes similar to those made by Norse sailors in Norway. Hedden brought in a surveyor who determined that the stones had been placed to form an arrowhead. Mel Chappell, who was ten years old when he first came to Oak Island in 1895, continued as owner until 1975.

A number of others continued the search; another engineer, Edwin Hamilton; George Green, a petroleum engineer from Texas, with John Lewis, a gold miner with a new ten thousand dollar drill; Bob Dumfield, a California geologist, and a Miami contractor, Dan Blankenship, and others. In 1960 a stunt motorcycle rider, Robert Restall, his son, and two workers lost their lives in the search, succumbing to carbon monoxide in the shaft.

In 1970, David C. Tobias of Montreal incorporated the last syndicate called the Triton Alliance, which still runs the Oak Island excavation today. Tobias, Blankenship and Nolan all still own lots. The Triton Alliance is now a consortium of fifty-two American and Canadian investors, including George Jennison, past president of the Toronto Stock Exchange; Charles Brown, a Boston developer; Donald Webster, a Toronto financier; Bill Sobey, of Canada's largest supermarket chain; Bill Parkin, a weapon systems designer for the Pentagon; and Gordon Coles, Nova Scotia's deputy attorney general. Triton Alliance has been joined by a group called Oak Island Discoveries, a partnership between a Boston millionaire, David Mugar, and film director William Cosel.

Together, Triton and Oak Island Discoveries have funded testing by the prestigious Woods Hole Oceanographic Institute on the shafts with technological equipment similar to that used in exploring the Titanic in 1991. Efforts are underway to raise an additional ten million dollars. The National Museum of Natural Science in Ottawa confirmed that the fibrous material was coconut fiber, and the Steel Company of Canada analyzed the iron spikes in the coffer dam and determined that they had been forged prior to 1790.

David Tobias believes that the elusive Money Pit was constructed by the English navigator and privateer Sir Francis Drake. Drake had raided the Spanish Main for Queen Elizabeth I, and Tobias thinks he needed to preserve a portion of his gains outside of England.

———

Sir Francis Drake began his career young, capturing small ships in American waters. In 1572 he was ready for bigger things and joined forces with William Le Testu, a French pirate who was later hung for his complicity with Drake. Drake was not only never charged with piracy but returned home a wealthy man.

According to Drake's biographer, James A. Williamson, in 1576 Drake had a meeting with Queen Elizabeth I, presenting a secret plan within a secret plan (*Sir Francis*

Drake, Crief, Lives-Collins, London, 1951, pp.49-59). His cover story was that he was going to sail to the Pacific to discover lands to claim for his queen, while in reality he was going to privateer with an arrangement to split the proceeds of his piracy with the crown. Because England was not at war with Spain at the time, his acts against Spanish ships and territories could not be openly sponsored by Queen Elizabeth. Nevertheless, on Drake's voyage, his ship, the *Golden Hind*, circumnavigated the globe after taking on twenty-six tons of Spanish gold. He returned home a hero, and wealthy. This particular aspect of Drake's career has always held particular interest to me because my ancestor, Francis Bryan II, was with Drake on this voyage, and on subsequent voyages as well.

When at last England went to war with Spain, Drake put to sea with the blessing of the queen. Throughout 1585 he raided ports and looted ships from the Caribbean to the Azores. Ten years later Drake made his last voyage; he died of dysentery in Panama. Bryan wrote a famous poem eulogizing the great explorer. David Tobias claims that after one of Drake's raids he employed a crew of Cornish miners to construct the treasure depository on Oak Island.

Queen Elizabeth I was something of a mystic. One reason for her excommunication from the Church was her belief that kings and queens could hear with their touch. She did nothing without consulting her astrologer, Dr. John Dee, who even fixed the date of her coronation. Dee later wrote a book entitled *The Perfect Art of Navigation*, with an aim to convincing Elizabeth to sponsor foreign navigation, and which did convince Drake of the possibility of circumnavigating the globe. Author Steven Sora has written:

While she lived her intellectual life through magicians and alchemists like Dr. Dee and Dr. Philip Sidney, Elizabeth lived a life of adventure through her privateers Sir Francis Drake and Sir Walter Raleigh.

Raleigh, however, fell out of the queen's favor and was banished from her court.

Under James I, Raleigh was imprisoned for conspiracy against the Crown and languished in prison until 1616. There he wrote his own history of the world. In it he declared the sea god of the Philistines, Dagon, to be the same god as the Greek Triton. Just why this was important to him is unknown, but the god of Greek mythology has some significance to the Oak Island mystery. Triton was the god who came to the aid of the Argonauts in their search for the Golden Fleece. Raleigh also wrote of his belief that the philosopher's stone, the hypothetical substance that medieval alchemists believed would convert base metals to gold, was the Golden Fleece sought by Jason and his Argonauts. Both Raleigh and Drake had pushed Elizabeth to pursue her rights to land in the New World. Since the Elizabethan court included magicians and alchemists like Dr. Dee, was there a prevalent belief that the philosopher's stone, or the Golden Fleece, was in America? The Elizabethan court was a whirlwind of intrigue, and with the likes of the mysterious Dr. Dee and plotters like Sir Francis Bacon pushing Elizabeth to take her rightful place as Queen of America, we cannot rule out agents of the court as the catalyst for Oak Island's construction. [*The Lost Treasure of the Knights Templar*, Steven Sora, op.cit. P.29]

Inscription found at Oak Island. The chalk-filled grooves reveal Gunn Clan heraldry.

Replica of an inscribed stone found at ninety feet that allegedly tells of a treasure buried forty feet below. The original stone, once a part of John Smith's fireplace, has disappeared.

Chapter Eleven

Arcadia

The Sinclair family achieved significant prominence in the years after Robert the Bruce secured independence for Scotland. They had signed the Declaration of Arboath in 1320 (akin to being a signer of the American Declaration of Independence), an unusual document inasmuch as it claimed an Asian ancestry for the Scots and calls Robert the Bruce a second Maccabeus, who was an early Jewish freedom fighter.

The Sinclairs became renowned as champions of the Knights Templar in Scotland. The pope attempted to acquire all Templar lands in Scotland to grant to the Hospitalers, but the Sinclairs denied that Templars owned land in Scotland, although they did own more than 500 individual properties. As each property was discovered, the Sinclairs took steps to defend them. And it was the Sinclairs who held and protected the Templar order's treasures.

Thirty years after the last Viking expedition to America, Henry Sinclair and the Venetian Antonio Zeno made their first voyage to the New World. Between 1398 and 1400 Henry Sinclair made perhaps two trips to America and laid plans for a colony. He controlled the largest fleet in the world and was guardian of the largest treasure in the world.

When Sinclair returned to Scotland, he found the clans warring among themselves and the English, seizing this advantage, attacked both Edinburgh and Kirkwall, the latter being a chief Sinclair property in the Orkneys. Henry Sinclair rushed to defend this stronghold, which was a castle with a walled harbor, and there lost his life.

Scotland's independence was in jeopardy, and Henry Sinclair the younger, son of the deceased explorer, was appointed guardian of Crown Prince James of Scotland by King Robert III. Henry Sinclair sailed with the Crown Prince for France and safety, but both were taken captive and later released for ransom.

Next came a threat from the northern clans. The Clan Donald made a violent bid to rule the northern islands, believing themselves to be more powerful than the Sinclairs and other allied clans. They managed to raise the largest army ever to fight in a clan war in the Highlands. After defeating the McKay clan (traditional enemy of the Gunns), these wild Donalds marched south toward Aberdeen, ravaging and plundering everything in their path.

In 1411 the Earl of Mar defended his lands at Harlaw against them, bringing about the bloodiest battle ever fought in the Highlands. When it was over, 9,000 of the invaders lay dead, and an equal number of defenders. The wars raged for years until King James I (the prince who had been imprisoned with Henry Sinclair) ordered the heads of forty clans to come before him in 1428. He arrested most of them, tossed them into his dungeon, and executed three of the instigators.

King James made an even bolder move: he denied the pope's powers, declaring the pope corrupt. But in standing up to Rome, he made deadly enemies. In 1436 he was assassinated in his bedchamber by Robert Graham. He died with twenty-eight dagger wounds. His queen sought revenge, torturing and executing Graham and Robert Stewart, the son of the Earl of Atholl who allowed access to the bedchamber. That same year, Prince Henry's grandson,

William Sinclair, was appointed admiral; he was already inheritor of the world's largest fleet and the Templar treasure. The designation of admiral seems to have belonged to the Sinclairs as a birthright.

With the assassination of King James, the fortunes of the Sinclairs declined. James I had married Lady Joan Beaufort, granddaughter of John of Gaunt. Lady Joan had married secondly to James Stewart, the Black Knight of Lorne, and their son, John Stewart of Balveny, first Earl of Atholl, married Elizabeth Sinclair, daughter of William, Earl of Orkney. Upon the death of James I, the country was in charge of a child king and a warring regent. The Douglas clan, allied with the Livingstons, were at war with the Crichton clan in the region around Stirling and the Sinclair base of power at Rosslyn. The English seized the advantage of these internecine conflicts to march north to Edinburgh and the Sinclair ancestral home. William Sinclair was imprisoned for the unpaid part of his father's ransom. Henry Sinclair (the younger) had been confined in the Tower of London, but had been set free when he agreed to pay a ransom—a ransom he never paid once he was free.

William Sinclair was already engaged in construction of the Rosslyn Chapel as a safeguard for the Templar treasure, but the threat from the English and uncertainty of Scotland's continued independence showed him the writing on the wall. He needed a secondary place to hide the treasure. Along with the role of guardian of the Templar wealth and the surviving Freemasons, the secret of lands across the Atlantic had been inherited by him. About this time, William Sinclair made his first voyage from Scotland to Nova Scotia. The voyage could be made in three weeks and an expedition probably took three months.

William Sinclair began importing workers in 1441, five years before he began the work on Rosslyn Chapel that took forty years to complete. While he was building a warren of tunnels and secret depositories

beneath Rosslyn Chapel, he was also constructing a vault to guard the Templar treasure in Nova Scotia. Sometime between 1436 and 1441, Sinclair's ships took miners from the home borough of Rosslyn and began a settlement near Oak Island, Nova Scotia.

In the midst of all of these preparations, Sinclair also formed an elite group of fighting men called the Scots Guard. The Scots Guard was composed of young men from wealthy and noble families (like the Templars before them). It was pledged not to Scotland but to the King of France, and more directly to the Valois rulers and the House of Guise. Additionally, William Sinclair was appointed—or rather reappointed—as grand master of the crafts and guilds and orders of Scotland by James II. This office remained hereditary until the Lodge was formed three hundred years later. Sinclair also appointed himself protector of the gypsies. Annually, from May to June, gypsies from all over Great Britain would migrate to Rosslyn where they were given land to camp on and granted license to perform their summer pageant, a play about Robin Hood and the May Queen. The Protestant Calvinists believed this to be nothing short of paganism and protested fiercely.

The Douglas clan rebellion raged on, and though the king defeated the Douglas armies, King James II was also fighting the English. In one of the skirmishes with the English in 1460, a cannon exploded, killing James II. His son, James III, succeeded to the throne. In the midst of these escalating conflicts, William Sinclair began moving the family inheritance to the New World.

Young James III was kidnapped shortly after ascending the throne, but managed to escape. Not long after his escape he married Margaret, the daughter of King Christian of Norway and Denmark. The following year he purchased the earldom of Orkney from another William Sinclair, Prince Henry's great-grandson. The Sinclair castle at Kirkwall was traded for Ravenscraig in

Edinburgh, though several Orkney estates were retained. This William came to be known as "William the Waster" for trading off the family property.

In 1488 the Douglas rebellion was rekindled, and James III went to battle, carrying the sword of Robert the Bruce; but it failed him and he was killed. Thirteen year-old James IV became king. In 1503 he married the twelve year-old Margaret Tudor, daughter of Henry VII of England and sister of the future King Henry VIII. Protestant Henry VIII went to war with Catholic France and Scotland, loyal to France, invaded England in 1513. At the Battle of Flodden the Scots were beaten badly, and the Sinclairs lost a great deal personally. Forty Sinclairs had marched to Flodden; only one survived. Since that day, no Sinclair has ever worn the color green— the battle color worn that day—to battle again. James IV allegedly died at Flodden as well, although the body identified as his own was missing the ever present chain of expiation, leading many to believe he had survived.

Oliver Sinclair was a favorite of King James V. James' protection of Sinclair and his marriage to Mary of Guise ensured his loyalty to the Catholics, even though Henry VIII tried to convert him to the Protestant side; James refused to repudiate his faith. In 1542 the Battle of Solway brought defeat to Scotland and Oliver Sinclair was captured. James V lamented that all was lost with the capture of Oliver. Simultaneous with the defeat at Solway, James heard of the birth of his daughter, Mary, and he predicted the dynasty was over. He died shortly afterward. His daughter became known as Mary, Queen of Scots.

In 1545, while the new queen was under the protection of the Sinclairs, Oliver Sinclair was released from prison in England for a short visit home. He disappeared from Scotland and history—forever. In the same year, the Reformation bishops ordered the Sinclair family to turn over the treasures of the Scottish Catholic Church which were under their protection. This also included relics the Sinclairs had brought back from the Crusades, including a piece of the True Cross. The Reformation mobs everywhere were looting Catholic churches and stealing and destroying all such relics, and the Sinclairs were not about to allow this to happen at Rosslyn. In the same year that Oliver Sinclair disappeared, so did the sacred objects under the care and protection of the Sinclair family.

William Sinclair revealed the secret of Rosslyn to the Guise family. Mary of Guise proclaimed a "bond of obligation" to William Sinclair, stating, "We shall be loyal and true masters to him. ...His counsel and secret shown to us, we shall keep secret." [Steven Sora, op.cit.] William Sinclair and Sir Oliver Sinclair harbored an even greater secret—Oak Island. Sir Oliver, commander of both the army and the navy, had already set sail for the New World in 1545, never to return.

The fortunes of the Sinclairs continued to decline. William Sinclair was made Lord Justice General by Queen Mary of Scotland and served as ambassador to France. Mary of Guise died in 1560. Francois, Duke of Guise, was assassinated in 1563. Mary, Queen of Scots, was executed by Queen Elizabeth I in 1587. Her son James became King James VI of Scotland and eventually, after the death of Elizabeth I, King James I of England. During the year following Mary's execution, Francois of Guise's son and heir, with his brother, the Cardinal Guise, were both assassinated on the orders of Henry III of France. In 1589 the Guise family had Henry III assassinated. In 1615 the head of the family, William Sinclair, was condemned to death for allowing a Jesuit priest to conduct the Catholic Mass at Rosslyn. The priest was hung and William Sinclair was pardoned with exile to Ireland. Mobs destroyed the Sinclair home and chapel. They excavated some underground chambers, found stairways leading nowhere, and discovered nothing. The Sinclairs had been transferring the objects in their care to the vault in Nova Scotia for more than half a century, and that transfer had been completed by 1545; Oliver Sinclair apparently left to permanently guard the treasure in the New World.

———

In 1188 a group split away from the Templars in what is known as the "cutting of the Elm," and formed an elite secret society known as the Prieuré de Sion. The first Grand Master of that group was Jean de Gisors. The second was Marie de St. Clair, a descendant of the Rosslyn branch of Sinclairs. Her maiden name was Levis, indicating a marriage connection between the Sinclairs and the royal line of David.

The third Grand Master was Guillaume de Gisors, who had founded another secret society, the Order of the Ship and the Double Crescent. He was related to the St. Clairs and connected to the temple at Paris from which the Templar treasure had disappeared into history. His sister married into the des Plantard family, who gave their name to the Plantagenet dynasty, and the Plantards claimed descent from David. The word "plantard" is French for "flowering shoot" or "ardent branch," and was symbolic of a special bloodline.

Two members of the de Bar family were the next Grand Masters of the Prieuré de Sion. The de Bars were related to the family of René d'Anjou. The sixth Grand Master was another St. Clair, this time from the French branch of the family.

The ninth Grand Master was René d'Anjou, arguably the greatest figure of medieval history, whose multitude of titles included Count of Guise; Mary, Queen of Scots, was his great granddaughter. He almost single handedly ushered in the Renaissance and effectively altered world history. He was married at the age of twelve to Isabella of Lorraine, and though it was a political alliance, the marriage lasted thirty-eight years until her death. "Good King René," as he was known, composed music, learned numerous languages, studied mathematics and geology, learned the law, and reformed the lands he governed. With Cosimo de Medici, he acquired books and manuscripts from around the world, and assembled them into one of the greatest libraries in history. He also collected relics, his prize possession being a cup that had been used at the marriage at Cana, a marriage incidentally that René and the Templars believed united Jesus with Mary Magdalene. He claimed to have obtained the cup in Marseilles.

René d'Anjou belonged to a number of secret societies, many of which he founded, including a revival of the de Gisors' Order of the Ship. One member of that order was a Sforza, father of Leonardo da Vinci's patron. Da Vinci, too, became a Grand Master of the Prieuré de Sion. René was also a promoter of the pageantry and chivalric pursuits of his times, and wrote the handbook of rules for jousting that governed that art for several hundred years. He participated in the festival at Tarascon, in which the town celebrated Martha's driving away the dragon that had plagued that town (and the Prieuré de Sion believed that Martha was sister of Mary Magdalene). He further staged the *pas d'armes*, medieval combinations of plays and tournaments. The theme most often revolved around the concept of Arcadia, an earthly Garden of Eden, and an underground stream. The Arcadia theme was important to d'Anjou, and each year his mistress played the role of shepherdess.

The great medieval painter Nicolas Poussin captured the ideals of the Arcadia theme in his painting *Les Bergers d'Arcadie* (The Shepherds of Arcadia). Research by Father Saunière, a Catholic priest in the little village of Rennes-le-Chateau, convinced him that this painting was the clue to part of the Templar treasure near the village. The clue led him to a tomb that he deemed so important he obliterated the engraving on it. The key was a pentagonal geometric code (which was frequently employed by the Templars) which was used to conceal the directions to the treasure. The lines forming the pentagon had a center on the forehead of the shepherdess in the painting. Why was the shepherdess so important to Poussin and René d'Anjou?

The painting depicts three shepherds and a shepherdess examining an ancient tomb. Two of the shepherds are pointing to an engraving on the tomb which reads "Et in Arcadia ego" (loosely translated it means "I too was in Arcadia," although other possible meanings might be made). The shepherdess is believed to be Mary Magdalene (the wife of the shepherd Jesus). Mary showed the apostles the tomb in Jerusalem after discovering Jesus was not there. Now, in Poussin's painting, she seems to be saying: he is here, and he is dead. The tomb depicted in Poussin's painting is located six miles from Rennes-le-Chateau, and it held further secret codes and clues to the mystery of the Templar treasure. [For further information on this topic, see: *Holy Blood, Holy Grail*, Michael Baigent, Richard Leigh, Henry Lincoln, Dell Pub. Co., New York, 1982].

In 1448, when René d'Anjou established the Order of the Crescent, the revival of the Order of the Ship and the Double Crescent, William Sinclair was in the process of building Rosslyn and the "Money Pit" at Oak Island. Steven Sora writes: "Related by marriage, brought together by the secret societies in which they both participated, united by a religion under siege, it is tempting to speculate that there might have been correspondence from William Sinclair to D'Anjou, telling him of the land the natives call 'Acadie.'" (p. 195)

The supposition is not so far-fetched. It is known that Christopher Columbus was provided with a map to the New World prior to his voyage, and that the man who provided it was none other than René d'Anjou! Columbus was a privateer in the employ of King René, whose navy rivaled that of the Sinclair fleet. William Sinclair may have provided René with a copy of the map of his family's explorations to

America, though as we shall see later, it might also have come from another source. But the connections seem more than mere coincidence.

René d'Anjou's daughter, Iolande de Bar, succeeded her father as Grand Master of the Prieuré de Sion. She employed George Antoine Vespucci as tutor to her son, and Georges' brother, Amerigo Vespucci, gave his name to America—or so the story goes. Iolande's son, also named René, was Duke of Lorraine, and with the Vespucci family became patron to both Leonardo da Vinci, and the artist Botticelli (Sandro Filipepi). Other patrons of Botticelli included the Medicis, Gonzagas, and Estes, who were all contemporaries and peers of the Zeno family in Venice. Botticelli incorporated the theme of Arcadia into his own work and became Grand Master of the Prieuré de Sion.

Leonard da Vinci also counted the Estes and Medicis among his patrons. As a struggling painter he had become acquainted with the wealthy Vespucci family of Florence. He had followed Amerigo's grandfather through the streets to sketch his face. Vespucci introduced him to Ludovico Sforza, whose father was a member of René d'Anjou's Order of the Crescent. Da Vinci was Grand Master of the Prieuré de Sion from 1510 until his death in 1519.

While Da Vinci started his career as an artist, he was also an inventor, physicist, geologist and engineer. As a military engineer, he designed an underwater suit and was adept in the science of hydraulics. He devised plans for harnessing water both for agricultural purposes and as a potential for weaponry. He was also a student of botany. One of his inventions was what he called the "cogged bracket," a movable sluice. He claimed that by grouping these sluices together, he could make a barrier to the current which could cause water to rise and fall. A series of sluices and dams could control the widest bodies of water. He also invented a portable dredger that floated on two rafts.

Steven Sora asks the question whether Leonardo da Vinci's blueprints might have been used to construct the complicated vault and protective hydraulic trap, and perhaps the bay of Mahone in Nova Scotia could be held back by a sluice of his design.

Lynn Picknett and Clive Prince, in their book *Turin Shroud* (Harper Collins, New York, 1994, pp.148-151), believe that Da Vinci had invented a sort of proto-camera and captured his own image. They propose also that he was the artist who painted or otherwise imprinted the image on the Turin Shroud, which many venerate as the burial cloth and image of the crucified Jesus. It seems more likely that it is the image of Jacques de Molay, martyred Grand Master of the Knights Templars (who died in 1314, some two hundred years before Da Vinci).

An alchemist and a necromancer, Da Vinci was also a devotee of the goddess Isis, the Black Madonna, and was accused of heresy together with a group of young men; his connection to the Medici family saved him. The Medicis were among a handful of elite families heavily intermarried and strongly allied, who moved Europe from behind the scenes. The Italian families shared control of northern Italy with the Zeno family.

In 1524 an Italian banker in the circle of the Medicis, Bonacorso Rucellai, backed another expedition to the New World. Rucellai hired a captain from another noble family to take charge of his exploratory voyage—Giovanni da Verrazano. The family crest of the Verrazanos was, coincidentally, the six-pointed Star of David, the symbol of those descendants of that royal bloodline.

Verrazano took with him the Prieuré de Sions' passion for the theme of Arcadia to the New World. Sailing along the coast covered with stands of stately trees, he said that it reminded him of Jacopo Sannazaro's idyllic Greek land, and called the place Arcadia. The harbor now known as Newport he named Rhodes after the harbor in Greece. Sinclair's "Viking Tower" Verrazano labeled as a "Norman Villa" on his map.

When Oliver Sinclair set sail in 1545, the Grand Master of the Prieuré de Sion was Ferrante de Gonzaga, son of the Duke of Mantua and Isabella d'Este, Leonardo da Vinci's patron. Both Ferrante and Leonardo assisted Charles de Montpensier in military operations in France. France and England were at war and Scotland was trapped in the middle. After Oliver Sinclair's departure, the Duke of Somerset attacked Scotland on the River Esk, slaughtering ten thousand Scots and nobles and clansmen.

William Sinclair, as emissary for Mary Stuart, asked France to send help, but the nation that claimed Scotland was part of France failed to support her ally. Queen Elizabeth did not want a French queen on the Scottish throne, and King James IV of Scotland allowed his mother to be executed without protest. He was also no friend of the Catholic Sinclairs. He began to grant land in the New World to Protestant members who came to the support of Elizabeth in England. Sir William Alexander was given a charter for Nova Scotia. Even Sir Francis Bacon was granted land in the New World.

Sir Francis Bacon was the Lord Chancellor and Keeper of the Great Seal of England. He was also a member of the "Invisible College," a collection of scientists and alchemists, physicians and writers, a group resembling the Prieuré de Sion, but having its roots in Rosicrucianism with Isaac Newton, Robert Boyle, Dr. John Dee, Sir Francis Bryan, and even Christopher Columbus. But this group had no Catholic leanings. Bacon hid his esoteric connections well. It was not until he left government service that hints of his criticism of the divine right of kings and the government in general surfaced. Under his own name he published a book entitled *The New Atlantis*.

Bacon's New Atlantis was very much

like the Arcadia of the Catholic d'Anjous and Sinclairs—a utopia where the true Renaissance man could be free to publish and study science and philosophy without fears of government censorship or a church inquisition. The name of this utopia was Bensalem. Jerusalem means "Foundation of Salem," and Bensalem means the "Son of Salem," a New Jerusalem. Here in "New Salem," said Bacon, a secret society resided, to which few were admitted and even fewer were privy to the secrets. This secret society had as its founder a wise king, and the order founded by this wise king was called Solomon's House. Bacon accentuated the point that on this secret island Jews were allowed to reside and practice their arts and sciences.

In his voluminous writings Bacon discussed flasks of mercury as a means for preserving and hiding documents. On Oak Island such empty mercury flasks have been found. Did Sir Francis Bacon and Sir Francis Drake formulate a joint undertaking to bring an expedition to the New World, to the Money Pit on Oak Island, to hide treasure and documents relating to the Invisible College?

Giovanni Verrazano, who was Italian, sailed to the New World in 1524 under the French flag. He is credited with giving Nova Scotia one of its earliest names—Arcadia. Verrazano's family crest, as we have noted, was the six-pointed Star of David, which has given rise to speculation that he might not have been the Christian he was purported to be. Even the religion of Columbus has been the cause of speculation, for his family were Spanish Jews; but due to the Inquisition, a non-Catholic would be disqualified from leading a mission to the New World. It was common to mask one's religion in those times to prevent torture and even death.

Verrazano derived the name from a very popular piece of literature by Jacobo Sannazaro called *Arcadia*, set in Greece, and printed fifteen separate times before Verrazano arrived in America. Arcadia, as defined by Sannazaro, was the idyllic world, a Garden of Eden lost to the medieval world, where thought and deed were free to blossom away from official punishment by church and state. The secret societies which fostered these utopian ideals believed in a new country, outside of Europe, where freedoms would be guaranteed and all religions would be tolerated.

Verrazano's trip to America had been short compared to other such European voyages. He departed the Madeira Islands off the coast of Africa on January 17th (a mystic date of importance to the Prieuré de Sion) and was back in France by mid-June of the same year. The only place he had lingered for any amount of time was the area now known as Rhode Island, where he described the natives as "the most civilized in customs" and "inclining more to whiteness," indicating previous contact and later marriage with earlier European explorers.

In the tight-knit circle of Bacon's associates in the Invisible College were such figures as Sir Walter Raleigh and his half-brother, Sir Humphrey Gilbert; both had sailed to the New World. Raleigh had sailed to South America in search of El Dorado, the fabled source of gold reputed to be the greatest in the world (which corresponds to the Golden Fleece and Solomon's Mines), with which he hoped to ransom himself from a death sentence. Failing to discover it, he was summarily beheaded.

Sir Humphrey Gilbert hoped to claim the New World for Queen Elizabeth I, and sailed to Newfoundland to establish a colony. My own ancestor, Francis Bryan II, who was the son of Sir Francis Bryan, Grand Master of the Rosicrucians in England, accompanied Gilbert on this voyage (as he had also accompanied Sir. Francis Drake). Francis Bryan II was himself a member of the Invisible College. Sir Humphrey Gilbert was lost at sea off the coast of Nova Scotia, and nothing further came of his colony.

The Invisible College also included Dr.

Robert Fludd, who headed the group of learned men who made the King James Translation of the Bible. Dr. Fludd was a Rosicrucian. In fact, he was Grand Master of both the English Rosicrucians and the French Prieuré de Sion. Fludd became Grand Master of the Rosicrucians succeeding Dr. John Dee, and was himself succeeded by none other than Sir Francis Bacon. Laurence Gardner, in his monumental work *Bloodline of the Holy Grail*, outlines the connections as follows:

Among the notable Rosicrucian Grand Masters was the Italian poet and philosopher Dante Alighieri, author of *The Divine Comedy* in around 1307. One of Dante's most avid students was Christopher Columbus who, in addition to his patronage by the Spanish court, was sponsored by Leonardo da Vinci, a member of René d'Anjou's Order of the Crescent (a revival of an earlier crusading Order established by Louis IX). Another prominent Grand Master was Dr. John Dee, the astrologer, mathematician, Secret Service operative, and personal advisor to Queen Elizabeth I.

Also the lawyer and philosopher writer Sir Francis Bacon, Viscount St. Albans, was Grand Master in the early 1600s. Under James VI (1) Stuart, Bacon became Attorney General and Lord Chancellor. Because of the continuing Catholic Inquisition, he was greatly troubled by the prospect of large scale Spanish settlement in America, and so he became particularly involved with Britain's own transatlantic colonization, including the famous *Mayflower* voyage of 1620. Among Bacon's Rosicrucian colleagues was the noted Oxford physician and theological philosopher Robert Fludd, who assisted with the English translation of the King James (Authorized Version of the) Bible....

Sir Philip Sydney, another member of the Invisible College, was a known esotericist, the author of the masterful work *Arcadia*, and a close friend of Dr. John Dee. Both Sydney and Dee had hosted the appearance of Giordano Bruno and Louis de Nevers (Grand Master of the Prieuré de Sion) at Oxford.

John Dee (1527-1608) was one of the most enigmatic and eccentric characters of his or any age. His origins are, like a great deal else about him, obscure. Dr. John David Rhys asserted that he was descended from the ancient family of Dee of Nant-yr-Groes, Radnorshire. Dee himself, a collector of ancient genealogies, drew up a genealogical table in which he claimed to be "Roderick, Prince of Wales," implying thereby that he was a descendant of the house of Gwynedd, a fact which would become very important, as we shall see.

Dee attended Cambridge University, where it is said he studied eighteen hours a day, becoming a fellow of Trinity College, after which he made a pilgrimage to the Low Countries. On his return he brought back with him an astronomer's staff of brass from the great Gerard Mercator (to whom all modern maps of the world are indebted).

While on his pilgrimage to the Continent, Dee procured copies of famous manuscripts and old maps from the archives of the Vatican, Florence and Vienna. Upon his return he steeped himself in astrology, alchemy and magic and was nearly all of his life suspected of being a black magician. Two informers accused him of conspiring to take the life of Queen Mary by poison or magic, inspired in part perhaps by his (accurate) prophecy that she would die childless.

Dee was, on the other hand, popular with Queen Elizabeth and at her command wrote an astrological calculation respecting "a fit day for Coronation." In 1580 Dee drew up a hydro-graphical and geographical description of all her countries in all parts of the world, on two large rolls. He traveled extensively, usually accompanied by his Irish associate, Edward Kelly, visiting St. Helena, Prague and Russia, where the Emperor offered him £2,000 a year for his services (nearly a quarter-million dollars at today's values).

"But Dee had a passion for secrecy," author Richard Deacon tells us, "and kept a great deal of his knowledge to himself, committed only to his 'Secret Book,' which he is said to have shown to Queen Elizabeth when she visited his library at Mortlake. But, alas, a mob, inflamed by stories of his black magic and incited by his enemies, broke into his house and looted many of his books and manuscripts."

Dee was a pioneer in the field of navigation and developed his theories with mathematical precision; yet his own definition of navigation was simplicity itself: "the art which demonstrateth how by the shortest way, and in the shortest time, a sufficient ship....be conducted."

Dr. Dee collected maps, navigational data and information from travelers and every other possible source. His cartographical notes suggest that he based many of his claims upon a mysterious chart called the *Fortunata* map. Precisely what this map was, and whether there was more than one version of it, remains a mystery. Benjamin F. de Costa delivered an address on this subject to the American Geographical Society in 1890 in which he attributed two works to the Carmelite monk, Nicholas of Lynne, who is said to have a made a voyage to lands near the North Pole in about 1360. One work was an astronomical calendar, adapted for use in navigation, and the other, which is lost, was the *Inventio Fortunatae* map and book, a copy of which he presented to King Edward III. The earliest allusion to this map was contained on the margin of John Ruysch's Rome Map of 1508, which read: "It is written in the Book of Fortunate Discovery that, under the Arctic Pole, there is a high magnetic rock, thirty-three German miles in circumference. This is surrounded by the fluid surgenum sea, that, as a vase, pours out water by four mouths from below."

In the early Middle Ages there was a strong fear of magnetic rocks, as witnessed by the fact that wooden or horn nails were used in ships. But the same theme emerges as the source of some form of magnetic compass, rumored to have been in the possession of Columbus, and we could not help but recall the "marvelous directors" which guided the discoveries of America in the Book of Mormon.

Dee claimed to have obtained much of his information from James Cnoyen, of Bois-le-Duc, a renowned Dutch explorer. Cnoyen's book, *Belgica Lingua*, is also lost, though both Dee and Mercator made extracts from it, and Dee seemed to possess other information obtained through Cnoyen. He asserted, for example, that Cnoyen had in his possession a map dating back prior to 1400, based on information from Nicholas of Lynne, Willem of Ghent and "a priest of Brittany who had an astrolabe." The statements of Gerardus Mercator offer some interesting background:

Touching the description of the north partes I have taken the same out of the voyage of Iames Cnoyen, of hartzeman Buske, which allegeth among the rest he learned of a certaine priest in the King of Norwaye's Court in the yeere 1364. This priest was descended from them which King Arthur had sent to inhabit those islands. He sayd that those foure indraughts were drawne into an inwarde gulfe or whirlpoole, with so great a force, that the ships which once entered therein could by no meanes be driven back againe and that there is never in those partes so much winde blowing as might be sufficient to drive a corn mill. [As quoted in *The Diaries of John Dee*, Edward Fenton ed., Day Books, Oxfordshire, 1998, notes]

In fact, however, Cnoyen's actual statement was as follows: "...a certain priest who came of that race famed in legend by King Arthur and who knew of his countrymen's voyage to a strange sea filled with weed." Dee was quick to pick up on this statement and avowed that it must therefore have been either "Bermoothes or an islande in the Bahamas." Dee's "Bermoothes" were, of course, Bermuda, "the still-vexed Bermoothes" which Shakespeare refers to in *The Tempest*. The "sea of weed" was correctly surmised by Dee as being the Sargasso Sea, which became the graveyard of numerous ships caught in its miles of floating seaweed. Dee's familiarity with the "Bermoothes" and the Sargasso Sea, and his vast knowledge of navigation, indicates a strong possibility that Dee himself had been to sea.

Even more fascinating is the revelation that King Arthur commissioned an expedition which apparently reached America—or at least as far as Bermuda and the Bahamas. One account states that the expedition was led by Arthur's father, Aidan, King of Dalriada (Scotland), known in the Arthurian romances as Uther Pendragon. It is from Aidan that Edinburgh is named. This expedition must have taken place in about the 6th century A.D.

It should be stated that the long-held view that the legends of Arthur were fictitious is slowly being eroded. As recently as 1965 a fifteenth-century chronicle of King Arthur and his knights was discovered in the library of Alnwick Castle, Northumberland, shedding much new light on the origins of Arthur. Arthur was certainly a true sixth century military leader, fighting for the Britons against the Saxons.

One of the first to record the story of Arthur as history was Geoffrey of Monmouth, who was Bishop of St. Asaph, which was in the kingdom of Gwynedd. In the latter part of the twelfth century he wrote his *Historia Britonium* in which he claimed that King Arthur went to Iceland and conquered that country.

Dr. John Dee was one of the "invisible superiors" of the Rosicrucian establishment, and was the reputed author of the Rosicrucian Manifestos and *The Chemical Wedding of Christian Rosenkreutz*, which contained elements of the Grail romances

and the Knight's Templar, which was promulgated after his death by Johann Valentin Andrea (1586-1654). Andrea had succeeded Robert Fludd as Grand Master of the Prieuré de Sion.

Iolo Morganwg was a Welsh historian (real name Edward Williams, 1740-1826) who wrote a series of triads in the *Myvyrian Archaiology*. The tenth of these triads claims to be a record of three great mysteries of the sea: the first, that of Gafran ab Aeddan (brother of King Arthur) and his followers who set out in search of the Isles of Llion (which Dee placed somewhere near the Sargasso Sea, i.e. America) and were never heard of again; the second, that of Merlin, the bard of Aurelius Ambrosius, and his nine Cylfeirdd, who sailed away in the Glass House into oblivion; and the third, that of Madoc ab Owain Gwynedd who "went to sea with three hundred men in ten ships and nobody knows where they went to."

—from the binding of a presentation copy of *Novum Organum*, 1620

-the Sir Francis Bacon boar

NOTE: The boar represents a map of America with the symbol of the

Ark of the Covenant represented

Chapter Twelve

Prince Madoc—Man of the Sea

At Fort Morgan, Mobile Bay, Alabama, there is a commemorative marker, erected by the Virginia Cavalier Chapter of the Daughters of the American Revolution (10 Nov. 1953), which reads:

In memory of Prince Madoc, a Welsh explorer,

who landed on the shores of Mobile Bay in 1170

and left behind, with the Indians, the Welsh language.

The identification of Madoc is well established. Dr. David Powel, in his landmark work *The Historie of Cambria* (1584), drawing upon even earlier sources, describes Owain Gwynedd as the son of Gruffyth ap Conan, Prince of North Wales. Powel writes that Owain died in 1169 "after he had governed his countrie well and worthilie thirty-two yeares. This prince was fortunate and victorious in all his affaires, he never took any enterprise in hand but he achieve it. He left behind him manie children gotten by diverse women which were not esteemed by their mothers and birth, but by their prowes and valiantnesse." [*The Historie of Cambria*, Dr. David Powel, London, 1584]

Powel lists all of Owain's sons, adding that Madoc was one of those "by diverse women." He further describes Madoc, the illegitimate son, as being loved by many but caring nothing for power, who "left the land in contention between his brethren and prepared certain ships with men and munition, and sought adventures by seas, sailing west."

Owain's first wife, Gwladys, daughter of Llywarch ap Trahaiarn, died in 1162; she is generally accepted as the mother of Iowerth, eldest son and heir [ancestor of author Kerry Ross Boren]. Owain's second wife, Chrisiant, daughter of Goronwy ab Owain ab Edwina, was Owain's first cousin, so the marriage was considered illegal and incestuous by the Church. Owain's defiance of the Church's ban resulted in his excommunication by Thomas à Beckett, Archbishop of Canterbury. Chrisiant was the mother of Madoc ap Owain Gwynedd.

According to Ievan Brechfa, a contemporary Welsh chronicler, "Madoc was the outcast son of Owain, and commanded by his father to be slain at birth." [cited by J. Morgan Lewis: Brechfa: *First Critic of the Bards*, Cincinnati Cymmordorion Society, 1887] The account is plausible, for Owain was more bloodthirsty than most of his age, and he demanded fierce and brutal penalties for disloyalty. He imprisoned his son Cynan in 1150, and two years later he sentenced his nephew, Canedda, to be blinded and castrated on suspicion of intriguing for the succession.

Brechfa's version states that Madoc was smuggled away from the court through the connivance of his mother and the appointed executioner. Brechfa also wrote:

Madoc, alive in truth, but slain in name,

A name that could be whispered on the waves,

But never uttered on the land.

Madoc was probably born in Dolwyddelan Castle in the Lledr Valley of Wales. A fifteenth century Welsh poem alleges that Madoc, like Moses, was set adrift in a skin bag shaped into a boat (a coracle). Richard Deacon, in his book *Madoc and The*

Discovery of America (George Braziller, pub., New York, 1966), says: "The suggestion is that Madoc as a tiny baby was cast adrift in a coracle, that his affinity with water enabled him to survive to manhood. It could be that a coracle fisherman was paid to ferry Madoc away from the castle of Owain Gwynedd when his mother saved him from execution."

The formative years of Madoc are unknown, except that he was allegedly the suppositious child of a foster family. At the age of sixteen Madoc returned to his father's court disguised as a wandering minstrel, in order to see his mother again. Madoc was embracing his mother when Owain surprised them and, not knowing that his son still lived, assumed the pair to be lovers. Once more Madoc was forced to flee into exile.

The Welsh chronicler Meiron quotes the poet-historian Llywarch as saying that "Owain Gwynedd was wrathful with his son and jealous of [Chrisiant's] love for the boy; he wrongfully suspected them of an incestuous relationship. Not for many years was Owain's suspicion of this completely allayed and then only on his mother's death-bed."

While at court Madoc met and fell in love with Amnesta, his mother's hand-maiden, and they eventually married. During the internecine battles between Owain's numerous sons, Amnesta was murdered by Madoc's brother, Dafydd. An ode by Llywarch tells of "Madoc, the lonely one, robbed of his love; forced to find consolation on the great ocean." At this time Madoc appears to have been living on Lundy Island in the Bristol Channel, some fifteen miles off the coast of Devon.

The anonymous fifteenth century poet describes Madoc as "a skilled handler of the coracle, both on river and sea, learning much from his experience among the Irish curraghs in his long exile." [Anonymous: cited by Richard Deacon, op.cit.] In another place he refers to Madoc as "the magician of Bardsey, the creator of a magic ship that could not sink, wise in his knowledge of the seas, their tempers and deceits." [ibid.]

In a prose work by Roger Morris, at Coed y Talwrn, dated 12 March 1582, he asserts that "the son of Owain Gwynedd was a great sailor, much given to voyaging far afield," and that he constructed "a ship without nails, but fastened with stag horns so that the sea would not swallow it." Madoc named his ship *Gwennan Gorn* (Horn Gwennan) and, writes Morris, he "traversed the seas in it and visited many foreign lands without fear of misadventure."

The Irish antiquarian, G.D. Burtchaell, in his investigations into the Kavanagh family of Co. Carlow, referred to "Madoc, a Welsh-Irish sailor-prince, a friend of Caomhinach (Kavanagh), son of Dermot McMurrough, King of Leinster, descended from the Scandinavian Kings of Ireland."

T. Gwynn Jones has related that Madoc was so wretched at the strife of his native Wales that he consulted an Irish priest named Mabon, who told him of a fair land in the west where all was peace and offered to sail with Madoc to find it. Madoc's brother Riryd, who was Lord of Clochran in Ireland, was also reputed to have been a great sailor.

A detailed account of the feats of Madoc are to be found in Powel's *Historie of Cambria*. It is worth recounting in its entirety:

Madoc...left the land in contention betwixt his brethren and prepared certain shipps with men and munition, and sought adventures by seas, sailing west, leaving the coast of Ireland so farre north, that he came to a land unknown where he saw manie strange things. This land must needs be some part of that countrie of which the Spaniardes affirme themselves to be the first founders since Haunoe's time; for, by reason and order of cosmogrophie, this land to which Madoc came, must needs be some part of Nova Hispania, or Florida.

Of the viage and returne of this Madoc there be manie fables faimed, as the common people do use in distance of place and length of time, rathcr to augment than diminish; but sure it is that there he was. And after he had returned home, and declared the pleasant and fruitfulle countries that he had seen without inhabitants, and upon the contrarie part, for what barren and wilde ground his brethren and nepheues did murther one another, he prepared a number of shipps, and got with him such men and women as were desirous to live in quietnesse, and taking leave of his freends tooke his journie thitheraward againe. Therefore it was to be presupposed that he and his people inhabited part of those countries; for it appeareth by Francis Lopez de Gomara, that in Acuzamil, and other places, the people honoreth the crosse: Whereby it may be gathered, that christians had beene there before the comming of Spaniardes. But because this people were not manie, they followed the manners of the land and used the language found there. This Madoc arriving in the countrie, into the which he came in the yeare 1170, left most of his people there, and returning back for more of his own nation, acquaintance, and freends to inhabit that fayre and large countrie, went thither againe. [Powel, op.cit.]

Dr. Powel specifically cites Gutyn Owen, a pre-Columbian historian and genealogist, as stating that in the year 1170 Madoc "went thither...with ten sailes, as I find noted by my friend, Gutyn Owen."

Powel further allows that Mexico was the probable landing place of Madoc because of "A common report of the inhabitants of that countrie, which affirme that theyr rulers descended from a strange nation that came thither from a farre countrie: which thing is confessed by Montezuma, king of that countrie, in an oration made for quieting his people, as his submission to the king of Castille, Hernando Curteis (Cortes) being present, which is laid downe in the Spanish chroni-cles of the conquest of the West Indies."

The reports of Cortes do clearly show that he supported the accounts of Mexico having been settled by a strange race from across the ocean, and he further mentioned the speech by Montezuma. The speech by Montezuma was discovered in an ancient Spanish manuscript found in Mexico in 1748, and was as follows:

Kinsmen, friends and fellow-countrymen, you must know that I have reigned as a King over you for eighteen years, as a descendant of my ancestors, who reigned before me. We came from a generation very far, in a little island in the north; the language and religion continue here to this day. I have been an affectionate Father and Prince, and you have been my faithful subjects and willing servants. Let it be remembered that you have a claim to illustrious blood and that you are worthy of your kindred, because you are a free, manly race.

Sir Thomas Herbert (1597-1692), a noted historian of his age, has left a lengthy account of Madoc's voyages, drawing upon earlier sources, some of which are no longer extant. Herbert wrote:

Anno 1170 he left his countrie, and after long saile and no less patience, blest with some happy winds, at last described land in the Gulph of Mexico not farre from Florida. ....Madoc was overjoyed and had reason to account his happy estate superior to that his brothers strive for, so early emulating with ambitious hate and bloud each other from a little Territory, incomparable to that good destiny alloted him, being a vast and weal Kingdome, obtained in some part without opposition, and able to satiate the most covetous. There he planted, fortified some advantagious places, left a hundred and twenty men to finish what he had begun and returned home after some bad windes, guided by supremme providence and the benefit of the Pole-Starre gave him in the night.

When he had landed and had accounted

his happy and miraculous voyage, told the hopes of succeeding Conquests, and other motives of persuasion and admiration, these and the words of Madoc himselfe drew so many willing minds and purses to returne, that he attempted it with ten good Barques, loaded with all necessary provisions, a matter that confidence required.

At his arrivall he found many of his Britaines dead, caused by the Natives' Villainy, or alternation of the clime, which notwithstanding he digested patiently, and with Edwoll and Eneon, his brothers, bettered the first attention, living with content and dying in no less distance from Heaven, than when at home, unhappiest in this that their own Nation forgot them quite, either judging them lost, because never after hearing from them, or because their own Beings were turned topsie turvy by the fatall end of the last unhappy Prince Llwellyn ap Griffith....[*A Relation of Some Yeares' Travaile*, Sir Thomas Herbert, William Stansby, London, 1634]

Meiron's version is a follows:

The country became embroiled in civil war. Influenced by disgust, Madoc, who is represented as a very mild disposition, resolved upon the matchless enterprise of exploring the ocean westwards, in search of more tranquil scenes. The event was, according to various old documents, the discovering of a new world, from which he affected his return to inform his country of his good fortune. The consequence of which was the fitting out of a second expedition, and Madoc, with his brother Riryd, Lord of Clochran in Ireland, prevailed upon so many to accompany them as to fill seven ships and, sailing from the Isle of Lundy, they took an eternal leave of Wales. [*Welch Histories & Poets* (1796) Cottonian Manuscripts, Oxford, England]

Meiron mentions Riryd as accompanying his brother, whereas Herbert states that it was Edwal and Einion. Einion may have been present, but Herbert must have been misinformed about Edwal, for Pennant states that Edwal was murdered at Llyn Idwal by Dunawt, son of Nefydd Hardd, to whom Owain had entrusted Edwal as a youth. Riryd seems to be confirmed, however, for Irish sources say that "the Lord of Clochran sailed away from Ireland and was never seen again." It is equally feasible that Einion accompanied Madoc on the first voyage and that Riryd joined him on the second.

The number of ships for the second expedition are reported variously from seven to ten. Similarly, the number of men mentioned by various accounts range from one hundred and twenty to three hundred men. The late Rector of Iden, in Kent, the Reverend E. F. Synnott, discovered in a sale-room at Rye in Sussex a collection of old books and an assortment of moldy manuscripts dating from the twelfth and thirteenth centuries. Many of these appeared to be lists of ships lost or unaccounted for, and one of these is most significant:

ABER-KERRIK-GUIGNON:

non sunt

Guignon Gorn, Madauc.

Pedr Sant, Riryd,

filius Ouen; Gueneti an.1171.

Here was a clear association of Madoc with the legendary ship *Gwennan Gorn*, and his brother Riryd with a second ship, *Pedr Sant* (Saint Peter). Both are listed clearly as sons of Owain Gwynedd. This is contemporary proof that Madoc had a ship named *Gwennan Gorn* and that in 1171 this ship was missing, or her whereabouts unknown.

———

Some of the strongest evidence in support of the claim that Madoc reached America stems from reports by later explorers of encounters with relics and Welsh-speaking "white" Indians claiming descent from Madoc and his colony (we are reminded of Verrazano's encounter with the natives of Rhode Island who were "the most civilized in customs" and "inclining more to whiteness.") Hernando de Soto, in his reports after his voyages to Mexico and Alabama, relates the discovery at Mobile Bay of the remains of ancient fortifications which he said could not have been erected by Indians. Captain John Smith, of Jamestown, Virginia, in 1621, gave a report of the confirmation of the Madoc story. The first mention of the presence of "Welsh" Indians in America came from Spanish and English explorers, but it was left to the Welsh themselves to gather detailed accounts of such tribes, having better knowledge of Welsh customs and language.

One of the earliest accounts by a Welshman is contained in a letter written on 10 March 1686 by the Rev. Morgan Jones, the minister of a New York church, to Dr. Thomas Lloyd of New York. This letter was eventually presented by Dr. Lloyd to Edward Llwyd, keeper of the Ashmolean Museum at Oxford. In the letter Morgan Jones described how in the year 1666, when he was chaplain to Major General Bennett, the Governor of Virginia, he was dispatched by ship to Carolina, landing at Oyster Point. While traveling overland with five companions to Virginia, they were captured by Tuscarora Indians and sentenced to die. Jones lamented aloud in his native Welsh tongue, whereby an Indian who was "War Captain belonging to the Sachem of the Doegs, whose origin I find is from the old British, and took me and told me in the British tongue that I should not die, and thereupon went to the Emperor and agreed for my ransom." Jones remained with these Indians for four months, during which time he preached to them in the Welsh language "and they would confer with me about anything that was difficult therein."

Confirmation of the Doeg Indians can be found in the *Letters writ by a Turkish Spy*, published in 1673 by Paul Morana, a native of Italy, in which he refers not only to the Doegs being an Indian tribe reputedly descended from the Welsh, but mentions the Satchem as well.

At a date between 1660 and 1665 a Welsh sailor named Stedman from Brecon was shipwrecked in the Atlantic and washed ashore somewhere between Florida and Virginia. He was found by Indians who spoke a language akin to Welsh, and when he replied to them in that language they expressed astonishment, treated him extremely well and "supplied him with the best things they had. They told Stedman that their ancestors came from a country name *Gwynedd in Prydain Fawr* (Great Britain)."

Sir Walter Raleigh was a strong advocate of the Madoc story and repeated it in his monumental *History of the World* (written while he was imprisoned in the Tower of London). He produced a list of Indian words that were identical with Welsh words of the same meaning, and he reported that some of his colonists were greeted by Indians shouting "Hao, houi, iach" and "Yachi Tha", which are phonetically equivalent to Welsh.

Many Europeans were surprised to encounter the "white Indians" in their travels. Father Chalevfoix, a Catholic priest, traveled from Canada to the Mississippi in 1721 to make a study of the history, religion, language and customs of various Indian tribes. A certain tribe he called Aiouaz (Iowas) informed him "that the Omans, three days journey from them, had white skins and fair hair, especially the women." We were reminded that Joseph Smith expressed special interest in the Iowas and sent missionaries among them (D&C Sec. 32), and even commanded them to marry women of that tribe. Moreover, Smith called for a settlement to be made in Iowa and named it Zarahemla, after a city named in the Book of Mormon (D&C Sec.125). The name seems obviously connected to Zarah, brother of Pharez, of the special bloodline so revered by the Templars. The number of reports of Welsh Indians by European explorers and others are far too numerous to recount here.

But it is with the Mandans that we finally encounter a bonafide tribe of Welsh Indians. In 1735 the Sieur de la Verendrye, a French explorer, set out on an expedition to the Missouri River to find a strange tribe he had been told lived in earth-covered lodges. Verendrye, a cultured man and a competent observer, eventually encountered the Mandans and remained among the tribe as a guest. In 1738 Verendrye gave us the first authentic account of this then almost unknown mysterious tribe of "white Indians."

Verendrye was surprised to discover that in their customs and mode of living the Mandans differed from every other Indian tribe he had encountered. They had fair skins and many of them had blond hair and blue eyes. They lived in villages which were laid out in streets and squares, and kept scrupulously clean. Lodges were made of a framework of logs covered with earth several feet thick, rounded into shapes like domes, with a hole in the roof that allowed smoke to escape. They lived more by cultivating their land than by hunting, raising large crops of beans, corn, fruits and vegetables. A Mandan chief told Verendrye that his people used to live far to the south, but had been driven north by their enemies. Verendrye felt certain that the Mandans must have some trace of European ancestry as one of the tribe wore a cross and spoke the names of Jesus and Mary. His men found "a few words not unlike the dialect of Brittany." The Welsh language has affinities with that of Brittany and certain Welsh words resemble those of the same meaning in French, e.g. eglwys and église (both meaning "church").

Daniel Boone (1735-1820) was another explorer who, from first-hand experience in Kentucky and Tennessee, testified to the existence of the Welsh Indians. He was especially impressed by a tribe of "Blue-Eyed Indians" and thought these might be "of the same kith and kin as the Welsh, though I have no means of assessing their language." [*History of Kentucky*, John Filson; Filson Papers, Kentucky Historical Society, Frankfort. Filsons' interview with Daniel Boone]

George Catlin, renowned artist, was so moved by the beauty of the Mandans that he lived among them and used them as models for numerous portraits, each picture emphasized by the blue eyes. Catlin was a remarkable man in every respect, a trained observer with a flair for detail and a picturesque style of writing, and he left an unsurpassable record of the Mandan people. He set out on his quest to record the Mandans in 1832 and lived among them for eight years.

"They continued to make the repeated moves," Catlin wrote, "until they arrived at the place of their residence on the upper Missouri. Ancient fortifications on the Missouri, some of which being built on the banks of the rivers with walls in some places twenty or thirty feet in height, with covered ways to the water, evince a knowledge of the science of fortifications, apparently not a century behind that of the present day and present incontestable proof of the former existence of a people far advanced in the arts of civilization, who have for some cause or other disappeared and left these imperishable proofs of their former existence."

The Mandans, as well as other tribes of "white Indians," claimed to have ancient books and scraps of records sometimes referred to as "Welsh Bibles." Richard Deacon has commented, "the mysterious books recur so frequently in the reports of the Welsh Indians that one wonders whether there is some strange psychological explanation for the phenomena."

The phrase "Welsh Bibles" is misleading. Madoc's arrival in America predated not only the translation of the Bible into Welsh but also the first printing, and so the mysterious "books" of the Welsh

Indians must be some other ancient manuscript writing. Yet, reports of the books are too numerous to be discounted.

There was the case of an aged man who had been held prisoner by the Cherokee Indians and who obtained from them "an old manuscript on vellum, very dingy, which appeared to be an old Roman missal."

Zella Armstrong, who has written extensively on Madoc, has proposed the theory that the "sacred books" may have been similar to manuscripts mentioned by Giraldus Cambrensis as existing in Wales before the defeat of Boadicea, and that there was a manuscript Bible (in Latin) in that country before 300 A.D.

In the *Gentleman's Magazine*, Iolo Morganwg (Edward Williams) related the account of Mr. Binon, of Coyty in Glamorganshire, who had been a trader among the Indians for more than thirty years. Binon reported that in about the year 1750 he and five or six others penetrated far westward of the Mississippi and there discovered a tribe who spoke the Welsh tongue.

"They lived in stone-built villages, and were better clothed than the other tribes. There were ruined buildings; one among them appeared very like an old Welsh castle, another like a ruined church." In his continuation, Iolo reveals even more:

They showed Mr. Binon a book, in manuscript, which they had carefully kept, believing it to contain *the mystery of Religion*. They told Mr. Binon that it was not very long since a man had come among them who understood it. This man, *whom they esteemed as a prophet*, told them a people would some time visit them, and explain to them the mysteries in their book which would make them completely happy.

When they informed Mr. Binon that they could not read it, they appeared very concerned. They conducted him and his companions for many days through vast deserts, and plentifully supplied them with provisions which the woods afforded, until

they brought them to a place they knew well; and at parting they wept bitterly and urgently entreated Mr. Binon to send a person to them who could interpret their book.

A gentleman in company with Mr. Binon at that time, in a letter, confirms the above statement. He says that Mr. Binon declared that these Indians worshiped their book as God, but could not read it. When Mr. Binon said that he came from Wales, they replied: "It was from thence that our ancestors came, but we do not know in what part of the world Wales is."

Charles Beatty encountered a man named Benjamin Sutton in 1755 who had spent his youth among the Indians. Beatty, a missionary from New York, recorded the details in his journal. Sutton related his encounter with the Welsh Indians who lived on the west side of the Missouri River, and further reported that they had in their keeping a book, wrapped in an otter skin, and which he supposed was a "Welsh Bible." He further observed that both men and women of the tribe kept the rites of Mosaic law; the former "observed the feats of the first fruits" and the latter "separated seven days from the men" during menstruation. They claimed that these rites had been handed down to them by their founder "who had escaped from a land far off after a battle between his brothers for possession of his father's lands."

Verendrye had noted that whereas all other Indians were clean-shaven, some of the Mandans grew beards. He also noted the "grey hair" of the older Indians, which is significant because full-blood Indians do not have grey hair.

Reuben Thwaite recorded that "a tradition of white bearded Indians was rife among the French traders and explorers in the eighteenth century. ...The variation of colour of complexion, hair and eyes among the Mandans led to various theories of their origin, among them that of Welsh derivation gained much currency. ...The colour of these Indians is sometimes reddish, sometimes a less dark copper color. In some it is grayish brown, in others yellowish. After a thorough ablution the skin of some of them appears almost white and even shows colour in the cheeks. There are whole families among them with gray hair."

————

We have shown that Columbus, himself a Spanish Jew, was a pirate in the service of René d'Anjou, and allegedly possessed a map which he utilized to "discover" the New World. We have shown a connection of Colombus to the Templars, and we were about to learn that Columbus may have known of Madoc prior to his own voyage of discovery.

Dr. John Williams, in his early treatment of the case for Madoc, cited the Dutch writer, Hornius, as saying that he believed the Americans were descended from Jews, Canaanites, Phoenicians, Carthaginians, Greeks and Scythians, augmented later by the Chinese, Swedes, Norwegians, Welsh and Spaniards, in that precise order.

In Hornius' work entitled *De Originibus Americanis*, published at the Hague in 1652, Hornius observed that "Madoc, a Prince of Cambria, with some of his nation, discovered and inhabited some lands in the west, and that his name and memory are still retained among the people living there scarcely any doubt remains."

Hornius lists as his primary source Peter Martyr's *Decades*. Martyr, a celebrated scholar of Anghiera, was invited to the Spanish Court by Ferdinand V, and his first *Decade* was issued *ex-Hispana Curia* on 6 November 1493. Inasmuch as Columbus returned from his first voyage of discovery in March of that same year, we can conclude that Peter Martyr was at the Spanish Court when the great explorer came back, and so obtained his evidence from Columbus himself. Martyr testified that "some of the inhabitants of the land (America) honoreth the memory of one Matec (or Mateo) when Columbus arrived

on the coast" and that "the nations of Virginia and Gautimale (Guatemala) celebrate the memory of one of their ancient heroes whom they call Matec."

Hornius claimed that Madoc probably made two landings, once in "Chicimeeccas Indian territory and again in Mexico." He further maintained that there was in existence a map showing the New World, or "parts thereof," based on the explorations of the Norsemen and probably known to Madoc due to his Danish ancestry. Hornius believed that this map had at some time been copied by the Belgian, Cnoyen, and that Nicholas of Lynne, the Carmelite monk from Oxford, also had access to the map when he made a voyage to lands near the North Pole in 1360. We were reminded of the map possessed by Columbus through the auspices of René d'Anjou, and wondered whether it was the same.

There is other evidence of Columbus' probable knowledge of Madoc. In 1490, when the Spanish Commission rejected Columbus' proposal for an exploration of the Atlantic Ocean, he dispatched his brother Bartolomé to London to seek financial aid from King Henry VII. Near this same time, Gutyn Owen, a genealogist and compiler of pedigrees, a historian and historiographer at Basingwerk Monastery in Flintshire (author of *Llyfr du Basing* and the memorable poems *Cywyddau*), was named as one of the heralds consulted by the Royal Commission appointed to trace Henry VII's descent from the "ancient Brytish Kings" (notably Arthur). Dates for Gutyn Owen are scant, but inasmuch as he is known to have attended the "Great Carmarthen Eisteddfod of 1451," it is clear that most of all of his writings are before the voyage of Columbus. If Bartolomé did not meet Owen at this time, he was certainly acquainted with his writings about Madoc's voyages. The English King expressed great interest in Columbus' proposed exploration and requested that Bartolomé urge his brother to bring his plans and charts to London. But

Bartolomé's ship was seized by pirates on his return to Spain and he was held prisoner for an extended period of time, during which time his brother had already sailed for the New World.

Professor Isypernik, of the Uzbec Academy, a Russian historian, discovered in 1959 a secret letter written by Columbus, revealing that he was well aware of the existence of the West Indies when he set off on his first expedition and, more importantly, that *he even had a map of the islands provided by earlier navigators*. The letter was written to Queen Isabella of Spain, and contained the quote of Isaiah 11:1-5. He told of great wealth in the New World, of gold mines, pearls, precious stones, spices and perfumes. "As the countries of Asia were fabulous for such wealth," Professor Isypernik declares, "it was declared that the new lands were in fact the blessed lands of Asia. Later research workers decided on the basis of these reports that Columbus had discovered America by accident and that Asia had been the real goal of his voyage."

Peter Martyr asserted that Columbus had marked on one of his charts at a place "in the direction of" the West Indies the words "Questo he mar de Cambrio" ("These are Welsh waters.")

The picture which emerges of Madoc from bardic legend is of a man passionately in love with the sea, who dreamed of exploring unknown lands, and he emerges too as an almost magical, mystical being of mythological proportions. We were soon to discover he was much more than this.

Chapter Thirteen

Madoc - The Mormon Templar

We had found ample evidence that Madoc ap Owain Gwynedd was a real historical figure who had left his native Wales to avoid the internecine wars between his numerous brothers, a strife which had seen his beloved wife Amnesta murdered by his own brother, Dafydd.

Madoc sailed to the New World in 1170 A.D., establishing a colony at Mobile Bay, Alabama. He returned to Wales in 1171 where he outfitted another expedition to America that same year, never to be heard of again in Wales. According to tradition, the second voyage was blown off course during a storm in the Gulf of Mexico, eventually landing somewhere along the Yucatan coast of Mexico where he established a second colony.

The earliest chronicles of Madoc were written by his contemporaries, or near-contemporaries, such as Willem the Minstrel, Jacob of Maerlant, Robert de Boron, Wolfram von Eschenbach, Walter Map, Chrètien de Troyes, Guiot de Provins, and others, all of whom were in some fashion connected to the Knights Templars. These chroniclers of Madoc were also the chroniclers of the Templars, and of Joseph of Arimathea and the Arthurian cycle. All of them equated Madoc in importance to the Templars and, without actually making the claim, insinuated that Madoc himself was a Templar. Chrètien de Troyes, for example, subtly refers to the fact that Madoc's ship, the *Gwennan Gorn*, had "a sail of square cloth, and banner'd cross the red." These early Templar chroniclers constituted an early hermetic society which was the precursor of the Rosicrucians.

During the Tudor/Elizabethan era, Dr.

John Dee was the catalyst for still another arcane society based in part upon the Madoc legend. Dee, author of the Rosicrucian Manifestos and "*The Secret Book of Madog*" (a history and writings of Madoc), organized an elite group of Madoc cultists that included Christopher Llwyd, Dr. David Powel, Richard Hakluyt, Thomas Harriot (cartographer, alchemist, astrologer and scientist who had himself sailed to America at the head of an expedition for his friend Raleigh), Sir Walter Raleigh, Christopher Marlowe, Robert Fludd, and others, all of whom perpetuated the Madoc legend. They promulgated the premise, shrouded in mystery, that Madoc was someone very special and significant, someone whose story protected some secret unobtainable to the world at large.

Dee and his society passed on the mantle to another group which, some two hundred years later, established a Madoc cult which met at the Gentlemen's Club of Spalding in London, which had long been the seat of esoteric and arcane pursuits. In the past it had hosted such members as Sir Isaac Newton, Benjamin Franklin, and two of Joseph Smith's ancestors, Robert Smith and Thomas French. The latter was an alchemist and a Scot, with ties to the Sinclair family of Rosslyn.

The Madoc cult included such notables as the poet Robert Southey (with ties to Harmony, Pennsylvania, where the gold plates of Joseph Smith were translated into the Book of Mormon), Edward Williams (a.k.a. Iolo Morganwg), Dr. Samuel Johnson, Dr. W. Owen-Pughe, Owen Jones, John Evans (who came to America in search of Welsh Indian descendants of Madoc), and John Hoppner (with ties to the Egyptian mummies purchased by Joseph Smith), to name only a few. We also found connections to Robert Owen, who not only had ties to Harmony, Pennsylvania, but directly to the Mormon Church, through his association with Isaac Morley and Sidney Rigdon.

There were emerging in our research strong associations between the Madoc legend and the Book of Mormon. We are not the first to recognize these parallels. Richard Deacon, author of *Madoc and the Discovery of America*, wrote:

There are extravagant accounts that Madoc and his companions reached Mexico and established the Aztec Empire, and then traveled on their all-conquering way to found the Mayan civilization and the Empire of the Incas in Peru.

F.W. Hodge wrote in his *Handbook of American Indians North of Mexico*, "the myth of a tribe of Welsh Indians...placed them first on the Atlantic coast, where they were identified with the Tuscarora, and then farther and farther west until about 1776 we find 'Welsh' or 'white' Indians on the Missouri, where they appeared as the Mandan, and later on Red River. Later still they were identified with the Hopi of Arizona (of which the Moquis derive), and finally with the Modoc of Oregon, after which they vanish."

We have the testimony of Cortez, Peter Martyr, Hornius, Biud de Haro, and even Prescott in his *History of Mexico*, that long before Columbus there was the arrival on Mexican shores of a people from far across the ocean. Cortez maintained that Madoc had made himself an Aztec King, and that Montezuma was his direct descendant.

Mormons generally equate Quetzalcoatl of Aztec legend and worship with Jesus Christ, as recounted in the *Book of Mormon*. John P. Brown, however, claimed that Quetzalcoatl was in fact Madoc:

The god was white and he had a beard. He was certainly no Indian. How would the Indians have known of such a person unless he existed? The legend contributed largely to the comparative ease with which Cortez conquered Mexico.

...The god really existed and he may have been Madoc, who arrived in Mexico on the second of his voyages, earned the affection of the Indians, taught them, and eventually left them, but promising to return. ...The Indians thought that the Fair God, Quetzalcoatl, had returned to them when Cortez came. The winged serpent of Mexico also has never been explained. It may have derived from the Griffin of Wales. [*Old Frontier*, John P. Brown, as quoted in *Madoc and The Discovery of America*, Richard Deacon, George Braziller pub., New York, 1966]

Torquemada testified that the Spaniards learned that Quetzalcoatl was honored as the memory of the white man who came out of the far north. He said that Quetzalcoatl urged the Mexicans to stop blood sacrifices, and taught them to offer bread and flowers and burn incense instead. Other Spaniards, as we have mentioned, reported finding traces of Christianity and such relics as the Cross of Mexico when they arrived there. Samuel Purchas mentioned that the Pueblos on the Rio del Norte (Colorado) might have originated with Madoc and his followers.

Mormon scholars are quick to point out that the Indians of Mexico and Central America are descendants of Book of Mormon voyagers from across the sea, and place most of the events recounted in that book in the same setting. Once again we found that writer Richard Deacon recognized, as we did, the parallels between the Madoc legend and the Book of Mormon.

Thomas Jefferson's ancestors came from Snowdonia and some of his co-signatories to the Declaration of Independence were of Welsh origin. Among them were William Williams, Lewis Morris and Francis Lewis. The last-named was a native of Llandaff and sat as a member of the Committee of One Hundred; his son,

Morgan Lewis, became Governor of New York in 1804.

The vast majority of these mighty Welshmen were from the villages and remote country places of Wales, and they naturally sought similar territories in America, setting prolifically in Indiana, Illinois, Wisconsin and Minnesota. A few centuries later they joined the great trek of the Mormons to Utah, and it is interesting to note that incidents of the Madoc legend and of the supposed migrations of his colony are paralleled in The Book of Mormon, published by Joseph Smith at Palmyra in 1830. The Brigham Young University at Provo, forty miles distant from Salt Lake City, has a collection of Welsh Americans and intends ultimately to set up a Department of Welsh American studies... [ibid.]

When we examined the Book of Mormon for a passage which might refer directly to Madoc, we found what we were looking for, in a passage which the Mormon Church frequently points to as an allusion to Christopher Columbus, but which could, in our opinion, equally apply to Madoc, who preceded Columbus to America by 322 years. The passage reads:

And I looked and beheld a man among the Gentiles, who was separated from the seed of my brethren by the many waters; and I beheld the Spirit of God, that it came down and wrought upon the man; and he went forth upon the many waters, even unto the seed of my brethren, who were in the promised land. (1 Nephi 13:12)

Madoc was one of the primary discoverers of America, and himself a Templar (as we shall see). Madoc laid claim to the New World as his kingdom and thus set a royal precedent. His descendants were, therefore, heirs to his kingdom, and the Templars thereby had sovereign claim upon America. This explains the Rosicrucian-Freemason influence in the founding of the new nation, and their efforts to establish their own king at its head.

John Dee showed his *Secret Book of Madog* to Queen Elizabeth I. His purpose for doing so seems to have been related to her desire to establish an English colony in America. Madoc's discovery of America in 1170 pre-dated that of Columbus by 322 years, giving England's claim precedence over that of Spain.

Evidence of this can be found in a pamphlet entitled *A True Reporte*, written by Sir George Peckham, a member of Dee's society, and dedicated to Sir Francis Walsingham (the Queen's head of Secret Service), published in 1583. This pamphlet set out "to prove Queen Elizabeth's lawful title to the New Worlde, based on not onlie upon Sir Humphrey Gilbert's discoveries, but also those of Madoc." It referred to David Ingram, of Barking, who had sailed with Sir John Hawkins (a cousin of Sir Walter Raleigh), as one source, and to "an ancient Welsh chronicle" as the other, which could only have been Dee's *Secret Book of Madog*, allegedly based upon Madoc's own written account of his explorations. Ingram confirmed the story, claiming to be the first of many travelers to hear Welsh words spoken by Indians in America.

If John Dee possessed actual writings by Madoc, the question remains how did he obtain them? Dee lived at least 400 years after Madoc. The answer lies in the person of one Willem the Minstrel, a Fleming who lived in Wales contemporary with Madoc and who was likely acquainted with him personally.

Willem has been variously described as minstrel, poet, priest and scholar, whose origins are vague and shadowy. He certainly lived in Wales for a lengthy period, probably along the Welsh borders adjoining Herefordshire, inasmuch as his friend, Walter Map, was himself a Hereford man. Willem's best known work was *Van den Vos Reinaerde* (Reynard the Fox), in which prologue he introduces himself as "Willem, die Madocke makede" (Willem, the author of Madoc).

Professor J.W. Muller, in his introduction to his critique of *Vos Reinaerde*, asks: "To whom do we owe this masterpiece? When and where was it written?...a certain Willem in the first line of the prologue called himself a poet who had earlier written a work about one Madoc, a work which has often been mentioned by more recent authors, and seems to have been very popular at one time, but now, alas, is lost." [*Van den Voss Reinaerde*, Prof. Doctor J.W. Muller, Leiden, 1939 issued by the Mij. der Ned. Letterkund]

Walter map tells us that Willem went to the court of Marie of Champagne, daughter of the wife of Henry II. This places Willem in France at the time when it was a hot-bed of esoteric Templar revivalism. Thus it is no surprise to discover Willem in association with the Templar writers Audefroi le Bâtard, Gace Brûlie, and most importantly Chrétien de Troyes. M. Edouard Duvivier, of Poitiers, recognized this connection, and insists that it was not *Reinaerde* that was best known for centuries, but it was instead his lost work of *Madoc*. "It is said to have been obtained originally through Willem's knowledge of Welsh, to have been translated first into Latin, then into French, and probably not at all into Flemish. A reputed copy of a French manuscript of the work was found in Poitiers in the seventeenth century, and, having inspected this closely, I am convinced that it must have been translated not later than the end of the fourteenth century and quite possibly much earlier." [Letter, *M. Edwourd Duvivier to Richard Deacon*, dated 20 Dec. 1965, cited in Madoc, Deacon, op.cit., p168]

The manuscript is written in medieval French, and the author describes himself as "Guillaume qui fait Reynaud" (Willem, author of Reynard). An autobiographical postscript in the text explains that the narrator, Willem, had been both a minstrel and a soldier, originally attached to the Flemish mercenaries fighting the Welsh, but that his fondness for the Welsh and their bards made him change sides. He

lived for a time in an island called "Ely" (the name given to Lundy by the Normans, where Madoc lived and from whence he sailed on his second voyage), had traveled extensively in the Low Countries and in France, and was especially interested in stories of early discoveries of land in the west from "Seneca to Madoc."

Willem elaborates on Madoc's fame as a sailor, which he derived, writes Willem, from his grandfather being "half a Viking." He tells how Madoc went to the Court of Louis VII of France, disguised as a monk, as an envoy of his race. It is known that Owain Gwynedd sent two Welsh monks with letters to the French king, offering his support against Henry II.

Willem introduces a romantic element into his story, giving Madoc a love-interest whom Willem calls the "River Nymph," who was likened to a mermaid because she encased her legs in fish-nets! Later we were to discover, significantly, that Madoc was termed a "mer-man" (Man of the Sea). Willem claims that the "River Nymph" and the bards urged Madoc to seek out the Fountain of Youth, which at first he sought on the Isle of Ely, but later decided must lie much farther out to sea.

The remainder of the narrative by Willem was notably esoteric in nature, relating how Madoc found *"paradis ravi par le soleil, resplendissant com fruits de mer,"* how he returned to "Wair for two new ships" for a second voyage to found a new kingdom of "eternal youth, love and music, where all should share in the abundance of good things." The expedition was said to be armed with "ten painted pearls to probe the rivers" of the New World, or *paradis*.

According to Willem, in "Ely" Madoc sought the "seaman's magic stone," which would ensure a safe return to his new-found paradise—that *pierre laide*, used by the Icelanders. This is wholly reminiscent of the "magical" luminous stones used by the brother of Jared, in the Book of Mormon, to guide the voyagers safely across the sea to the Promised Land, and the Liahona, that "marvelous director" of the same book.

Willem's narrative hints that the *paradis ravi par le soleil* might not have been Madoc's final goal, but that this might be "six days distant from a treacherous garden in the sea," which Willem called *La Mer Dégringolade*. This mysterious "garden" in the ocean, "which no storm could ever dissipate, and which swallowed up ships," was quite obviously the Sargasso Sea, which stretches from the Gulf of Mexico north and east past Florida nearly as far as the Azores.

According to Willem, Madoc discovered an island, surrounded by enormous, strange fishes. He calls this island "one of the Isles of Llion." We were reminded that John Dee had based his claims about Madoc on the *Fortunata* map, which purportedly showed the route of both Nicholas of Lynne and Madoc and indicated an island, far out in the Atlantic, called *Gwerdonnau Llion*, discovered by Madoc. Dee believed that the island was somewhere "close to the sea of weed," and that it must therefore have been either "Bermoothes or an islande in the Bahamas." Dee believed it was possible that this was one of the islands in the Atlantic Ocean known to disappear beneath the sea from time to time. This would equate them with the Isle of Lyon, the fabled kingdom of Lyonesse from the legend of King Arthur which one day disappeared beneath the sea. This would place Arthur's explorers in the region of the Sargasso Sea. This was confirmed by Cnoyen's statement that "...a certain priest who came of that race famed in legend by King Arthur and who knew of his countrymen's voyage to a strange sea filled with weed."

There is reason to believe that Madoc may have sought refuge from a storm in the Bahamas, on his way back from America after his first voyage, probably on the island of Bimini. The Spaniards learned of the existence of Bimini from the mainland Indians who gave it this name; and it was from these Indians that the Spaniards learned that the "Fountain of Youth" which Ponce de Leon sought was none other than the Isle of Bimini. Moreover, according to Peter Martyr, they had learned of its existence from "Matec."

———

The overwhelming evidence indicated that Madoc ap Owain Gwynedd was a Templar. Disguised as a monk, he attended the Court of Louis VII in France just as the Knights Templar of Hugues de Payens were returning from the Holy Land with whatever they recovered from the caverns beneath the Temple Mount. Not long after his return to Wales, Madoc constructed his "magical ship," the *Gwennan Gorn* and sailed away under a square sail with splayed Templar cross.

Madoc possessed a "marvelous director," a magnetic compass perfected and used by the Templars, and he had a map which guided him to the "Promised Land," a map ostensibly drawn by his Scandinavian ancestors. The Welsh manuscripts in the Cottonian Collection relate that Gruffydd ap Conan (died 1137) was, on the maternal side, descended from the Scandinavian Kings of Dublin, Ireland. Mr. Gisle Brynjulfsson, of the Royal Society of Northern Antiquities in Copenhagen, an authority on the Gwynedd ancestry, has written: "It also deserves mention that Madoc, supposed to have visited America at the close of the twelfth century, was a grandson of this same King Griffin (Gruffydd) and that he is likely to be acquainted with the Scandinavian accounts of Vinland and the other western countries, this being well known to the Scandinavians in Ireland." [as cited in *Who Discovered America?* Zella Armstrong, Lookout Pub., Chattanooga, Tenn., 1950]

Thus we discover that Madoc was a descendant of King Olaf the White of Dublin, and in direct descent from the Kings of Norway, the Earls of Orkney, and the Möre clan, ancestors of the Sinclairs. More importantly, at least to our interests, he was a descendant of the Clan Gunn, the most likely source of his map and knowledge of the New World.

Chapter Fourteen

Carre-Shinob

In 1590, Montezuma reigned as Emperor of the magnificent Aztec Empire in Mexico. In the same year that empire was destined to fall with the arrival of the Spanish Conquistador Hernán Cortes (Cortez). This ruthless conqueror had been sent by the governor of Hispaniola to explore the coast of Mexico and Central America.

Disembarking from their ships at Vera Cruz, Cortes marched inland with 400 soldiers in full metal armor, fifteen men riding horses (which the Aztecs had never seen before), and seven cannons drawn by these same beasts. In addition, the Spaniards had impressed into service 1,300 Indian warriors and another 1,000 porters.

Because Cortes had exceeding white skin and wore shining silver armor, the Aztecs equated him with Quetzalcoatl, a white-skinned and bearded god who had arrived long ago from "across the eastern sea." Quetzalcoatl had taught the Aztecs great things, then departed, promising that at some future time he would return. This strange bearded invader riding an even stranger beast fit the description of this god, and so they offered little or no resistance.

Even before Cortes reached Tenochtitlan, the great Aztec capital encompassing some five square miles and comprising more than 140,000 inhabitants, Montezuma sent several Aztec noblemen and more than a hundred porters bearing gifts to the "god." The gifts were fabulous beyond description: boxes of precious gems, jewel-encrusted gold vases, silver vessels, richly adorned capes made from the colorful plumes of the sacred Quetzal bird, and two huge disks the size of cart wheels, one of gold and the other of pure silver, engraved with glyphs and sacred writing.

The wealthy gifts merely whetted the conquistador's appetite for riches. He marched into Tenochtitlan, placed Montezuma under "house arrest," and ordered all gold and other treasure to be collected and delivered to the Spaniards.

One of the chroniclers of the expedition, Bernal Diaz del Castillo, described Montezuma's treasury in the "Sunken Gardens" (vaults) beneath the palace as being a massive room piled to the ceiling with gold and silver, much of it in ingots and much of it worked into fine jewelry, statuettes, masks and other items, while boxes of precious gems lined the walls." Cortes, upon seeing it for himself, wrote: "It seems incredible that any worldly ruler should possess such riches."

In the midst of seeking out the treasure, Cortes was called away to meet a force of Cuban troops, commanded by Panfilo de Narvaez, marching to wrest the treasure from him. He left one of his lieutenants, Pedro de Alvarado, in charge of Tenochtitlan in his absence. But Alvarado was not a seasoned leader. During the annual May celebration called the "Incensing of Huitzilopotchli," 600 Aztec performers assembled in the streets, adorned in costumes of Quetzal feathers, and wearing gold jewelry embedded with precious jewels. Enraged that the Aztecs had withheld some of their treasure, Alvarado ordered his soldiers to attack the performers. Hundreds of unarmed Aztecs were murdered in the streets. Bernardino de Sahagun, in his *Historia de Nuevo España*, wrote: "The pavement ran with streams of blood, like water in a heavy shower."

Incensed by the merciless slaughter, the Aztecs retaliated against the invaders, whom they now knew could not be gods as they had supposed. While the Spaniards were busily engaged in battle, Montezuma summoned his nobleman and priests and issued instructions for the secret removal of the vast treasure. More than 1500 royal bearers were assembled and loaded down with as much treasure as they could carry and led quietly out of the city and towards the north. For weeks they trekked along the route which the northern tribes called the "Trail of the Old Ones." At last they arrived at their destination, seven sacred caves, and there deposited the treasure out of reach of the avaricious Spaniards.

Meanwhile, the Spaniards found themselves surrounded. Cortes induced Montezuma to intercede with his people, saying "We will willingly depart if the way is opened." Montezuma reluctantly agreed and pleaded with his people, calling upon them to lay down their weapons and allow the Spaniards to pass unmolested. But the Aztecs remembered the massacre of the dancers who had put aside their arms, and became enraged at Montezuma. They summarily stoned him, striking him several times in the head. On 30 June 1520 the great Aztec emperor succumbed to his wounds and died.

The Spaniards attempted to flee with as much remaining treasure as they could carry, but the angry Aztecs pursued them and recovered most if it. More than a third of Cortes' army perished during the flight from Tenochtitlan.

Cortes rallied a new army and returned in 1521, conquering the Aztec nation completely. He became absolute ruler of the land from the Caribbean to the Pacific, but his vast coveted treasure was gone and remained his one most nagging defeat. He managed only to learn that Montezuma's treasure had been removed from the "Sunken Gardens" beneath the great palace and carried to the far north and concealed within seven large caves. This became the foundation of the legend of the famous "Seven Cities of Cibola," and would constitute the basis of a frenetic search by the Spaniards for the next three centuries.

The Aztecs claimed to have once lived far north of Mexico, near an inland sea with many marshes, and on an island in that sea. The very name Aztec is derived from Aztlan, a word meaning both "Island of Herons" and "White Land." This description aptly fits the region of the Great Salt Lake, not only to its islands' population of herons and other birds, but the "White Land" would seem to indicate the surrounding Salt Flats. The name Aztlan, as we have witnessed previously, also derives from "Land of Atlas."

The Aztecs referred to their place of origin as *Chicomoztoc*, which means "Seven Caves." The Aztecs, Toltecs, Incas and Mayans, as well as numerous sub-tribes living in the Central America land-neck, have traditions of sacred caves in the land of the north, from which caves their cultures originated. The Mayans, for example, describe their ancestors as seven tribes which emerged from seven sacred caves. Aztec traditions are similar, describing a sacred cave with seven mouths through which seven tribes, one of which being the Aztecs, emerged from the underworld.

The Aztecs began leaving their northern home in about 1168, and migrated into what is now northern Mexico during the thirteenth century. Vanquishing other tribes in their path, they moved into the Valley of Mexico near the beginning of the fourteenth century where they founded the cities of Tenochtitlan and Tlateloco on islands of Lake Texcoco in 1325.

The Aztec dialect was Nahuatl, a language belonging to the Ute-Aztecan linguistic stock which exists in the Western United States, and from which was derived the Shoshonean languages, which includes the Ute dialect.

The Ute Indians revered their ancestors, the Aztecs, as the "Old Ones," and have preserved many of the legends concerning them. One of these legends pertains to the "Trail of the Old Ones" which ran from Mexico northward through Utah to the Uintah Mountains. According to the Utes, the Old Ones appointed them guardians of the sacred treasure, and Aztec priests made frequent trips to obtain some of the sacred gold and to pay respects to their gods. The Utes believed that these priests could turn themselves into pumas at will. And the Utes maintain to the present day that the sacred caves are situated high in the Uintah Mountains.

Based upon all available evidence, and upon the oral traditions of the Utes, it seems certain that Madoc visited the Uintah Mountain region. It may well have been Madoc who induced the Aztecs to migrate south to Mexico where he had already established a colony. Madoc's arrival in America in 1170 A.D. corresponds almost exactly with the Aztec calendar-tradition that their southern migration began circa 1168 A.D.

In addition to becoming their king, Madoc became a great teacher and bene-factor of the Aztecs, teaching them the arts of building, writing, planting and many other things in the European fashion. The Aztecs came to revere him as a god—the god "Matec"—and they equated him with their greatest god, Quetzalcoatl. John P. Brown, in his book *Old Frontiers*, has concluded: "The god really existed and he may have been Madoc, who arrived in Mexico on the second of his voyages, earned the affection of the Indians, taught them, and eventually left them, but promising to return. ...The Indians thought that the Fair God, Quetzalcoatl, had returned to them when Cortez came."

The Utes maintain that there is a temple of the Old Ones somewhere on Rock Creek in the high Uintahs. There are ostensibly two carved bears guarding the entrance to the temple, and according to one old Ute Indian, Waubin Q. Wanzitz, nearby was a marvelous white horse, carved from stone. This statue stood for many years on a sage-brush flat facing towards the mountain, supposedly a direction indicator to the temple site.

Tab-Wash (Tabuache), son of Nauhnan, and grandson of Chief Tabiona (Tabby), was a particular friend of mine. Wash (as he was called) had seen the white horse statue and recounted the Indian tradition for the origin of the temple and the statue:

Many years ago, when the Utes were a free people, and roamed the mountains which they loved, they had much gold and fine things made by their ancestors—the Ancient Ones. The Utes had never seen a white man. Then, in the year of the great trembling of the earth [earthquake], there came a white man on a white horse. He was a great teacher. He told the Utes that many white people would be coming, more numerous than the trees on the mountains, and he said they should hide up the temples of the Ancient Ones, for these men would be greedy, and would not honor the sacred things. In the year of the trembling earth, Towats [the Great Spirit] spoke to the medicine men and told them to cover up the temples of the Ancient Ones. All the sacred places were covered. In that year the white horses made of stone were carved by the great white medicine man on the white horse, so that the Utes would never forget. [*The Gold of Carre-Shinob*, Kerry Ross Boren & Lisa Lee Boren, Bonneville Books, Springville, Utah, 1998, pp.141-42.]

I asked Wash how long ago the great trembling of the earth had taken place. "Oh, maybe ten Wash," he replied, meaning ten of his lifetimes. Wash was then over ninety, so it must have been between 800 or 1,000 years ago, about the same time as the arrival of Madoc in America. It seems probable that it was Madoc who carved the white horse statue.

The Utes are among the few tribes which have bearded men among their number, indicating intermarriage anciently with the white race; true Indians, or course, have no facial hair. Brigham Young informed Captain Dan Jones, a Welsh convert, "of a Welsh settlement on the Rio Colorado and that he believed that the Moquis were descendants of Madoc" [*Madoc*, Deacon, op.cit., pp.151-52]. Moreover, Madoc is said to have recorded his own history and the history of the Native Americans on brass and gold plates, with strange hieroglyphic writing that was a combination of the Welsh language and symbols familiar to the Aztecs. Even if Madoc himself did not visit the Uintah Mountain region, this would still explain the stacks of brass and gold plates said to be part of Montezuma's treasure.

All of this goes a long way to indicate that Madoc, or at least the Templars, had visited America and left behind remnants of their influence. Major Amos Stoddard, writing about the Mandans, postulated:

"Travelers describe certain private societies among the Indians, *which apparently resemble our lodges of Freemasons*. Their rules of government and the admission of members are said to be nearly the same. No one can be received as a member of the fraternity, except by ballot, and the concurrence of the whole is necessary to a choice. They have different degrees in the order. The ceremonies of initiation and the mode of passing from one degree to another would create astonishment in the mind of an enlightened spectator. Is not this practice of European origin? In the early periods of English history the knowledge of Freemasonry was mostly confined to the druids; and Wales was more fruitful of this description of men than any other part of Europe. They were almost the only men of learning in those days." [*Sketches of Louisiana*, Major Amos Stoddard, Philadelphia, 1812.]

The Spaniards wasted no time in mounting expeditions to the north in search of Montezuma's treasure and the legendary "Seven Cities of Cibola." On Monday, 23 February 1540, the northern quest began, with Francisco Coronado as Captain General. They crossed into what is now Arizona and on June 23rd marched onto the Colorado Plateau. Having reached the Indian village of Zuni, the Spaniards believed they were now in the country of Cibola. The chronicler Baltazar de Obregon, circa 1584:

The principal reason why the discovery of, and expedition to, the provinces of Cibola and the original home of the Mexicans was desired was that the marquis [Cortes] had found, among the tribute, possessions, and treasures of the powerful King Montezuma, some chronicles, drawings, and paintings which revealed the origin, spread, and arrival from those regions of the Culguas and the ancient Mexicans. [*Handbook of American Indians North of Mexico*, F.W. Hodge, Bureau of American Ethnology, Smithsonian Institution, 1910, vol.2.]

We noted with considerable interest the similarity between the names of "Culguas" and the "Colchis," ostensible ancestors of the Aztecs, and their origins in the region of the north of Mexico.

At the Gila River in Arizona in July 1540 the Zuni Indians told Coronado of a place far to the north where the natives lived on the shores of a great body of water they called Laguna del Norte—the Lake of the North. These Indians were reported to wear trinkets of gold and to know the location of gold sources in the mountains called, in Spanish, the *Sierra Madre de Oro*—the "Mother of Gold" mountains (Uintah Mountains). Coronado determined to send some of his men to the north in search of it.

Coronado dispatched his friend Don Garcia Lopez de Cardenas and twelve men towards the north from Zuni in search of a route to the Laguna del Norte. Near the

111

Grand Canyon, Cardenas dispatched a small party of seven men to seek a northern route. This second party was captained by one "Tomás Blaque."

This expedition arrived in the vicinity of present-day Vernal, Utah, and coincides with Ute Indian oral tradition which relates the story of the first white men ever seen by them. The Spaniards tortured and killed several young braves, including a son of the chief, in an attempt to learn the source of the gold. The Utes overcame them, and sent the Spaniards away minus their horses, and warned them never to return. But they would return. [For additional information, see *The Gold of Carre-Shinob*, op.cit.]

"Tomás Blaque" was not a Spaniard. He was none other than Thomas Blake, a Scottish soldier of fortune, son of William and Agnes Mowat Blake, and a former member of the Scottish army commanded by Oliver Sinclair! In a petition made some years later he stated that he had served in the pacification of New Granada in 1532 before coming to Mexico in 1534 or 1535, and that he had enlisted with Coronado and served with the army until its return three years later. For twenty years he was the only man of British blood who was allowed to reside in Mexico, and he was the only Englishman, so far as is known, to take part in any of the Spanish explorations in what is now the United States.

Shrewd and experienced as the Scotsman Thomas Blake undoubtedly was, he was fated to gain little gold through his service with Coronado. Shortly after his return he married Francisca de Ribera, widow of a prominent "old conqueror" who had been a nuncio and fiscal of the Holy Inquisition in Mexico. About 1550, like many another veteran of Coronado's expedition, Blake applied for aid from the crown because he "suffered great need." Blake was alive and residing in Mexico in 1556, when he was found there by Robert Tomson, an Englishman whose remarkable accounts of travel in Mexico and the West Indies appear in the writings of the English chron-

icler Richard Hakluyt (a chronicler of the Madoc voyages and close personal friend of Dr. John Dee.)

Not only did Thomas Blake serve under Oliver Sinclair in Scotland before arriving in Utah in 1540, but Blake's mother, Agnes Mowat, was kin to the Sinclairs as well as to the Earls of Moray. Oliver Sinclair disappeared in 1545 with an immense amount of Catholic treasure, never to be heard of again. There was no doubt among his contemporaries that he had sailed for the New World. Was it coincidence, we wondered, that Oliver Sinclair and Thomas Blake, both involved with treasure having a common source, should arrive in the New World in the same time frame?

Though the Spaniards continued to make incursions into the Uintah Mountain region in search of the treasure of Montezuma and the source of the sacred gold of the Aztecs, the Ute Indians managed to keep the secret from them. To the Utes, this place was "Carre-Shinob"—"Where the Great Spirit Dwells."

Chapter Fifteen

Keeper of the Yellow Metal

When the priests and nobles of Montezuma deposited the vast treasure of the Aztecs in the sacred caves of Carre-Shinob in the year 1520, they delegated the Utes Indians to be the guardians and over-seers of the sacred hoard. In the beginning, only the tribal medicine man was permitted to know the great secret, but in time all of that would change.

Pan-a-Carre Quinker ("Iron Twister"), son of Moonch by his Piute wife Tishum Igh, was born about 1808. In his youth, Pan-a-Carre Quinker felt a yearning in his soul for an unfulfilled destiny. He decided to make a solitary journey to the Land of the Sun to seek a vision from Towats.

Towats is the Great Spirit. His symbol is the Sun and he is the father. Earth is the Mother and she produces all life through the love of Towats, through the Sun upon her bosom. In the Ute dialect the sun is called "Tanna." The Land of the Sun was a sacred place high in the Uintah Mountains where the Sky Reader, the Prayer Maker, the Vision Dreamer (i.e. Medicine Man or Shaman) went to smoke peyote, chant, and speak to the Great Spirit. It was a holy place, high on the mountain above Spirit Lake, on a large flat stone known as the Medicine Rock.

A legend persists that just before dawn, when the moon is full, and the morning mist wafts across Spirit Lake, the face of an Indian maiden is reflected from the surface of the water; and often at night a white elk can be seen walking across the surface of the lake, accompanied by the gentle sound of tinkling bells. The tale sounds like a myriad of other folk myths, except that this particular account has a genesis based upon

an actual event associated with the arcane legend of sacred Indian treasure. And the story also revolves around the Medicine Rock.

The Medicine Rock was first shown to me when I was a young boy by an old-timer named James Rogers Lamb who, as it happened, was my uncle's father. Old Jim knew whereof he spoke. He had lived among the Indians as a young man and had taken an Indian wife, Yellow Bird, who was one of the numerous daughters of Chief Washakie of the Shoshones.

Jim Lamb was a veritable fount of history of the Uintah Mountain region, having experienced much of it personally. He was especially knowledgeable about the history and customs of the Ute and Shoshone tribes, both of which he had lived among and he spoke both dialects fluently. Lamb Lakes, which are situated in an alpine basin adjoining Spirit Lake on the east, were named for him. Jim Lamb is the source of much of the history behind the legend of Spirit Lake, together with Chief Walker's own account related to his friend Isaac Morley.

The Utes and Shoshones were ancient enemies, even though they were cousins, and for many years they had fought bloody territorial battles. The dispute culminated in one final great battle between the tribes at Hickerson Park, where many warriors perished on both sides. Because there were so many empty teepees and wailing squaws, a council of peace was held and they at last came to an agreement: everything north of the crest of the high Uintahs was to belong to the Shoshones, and everything to the south would belong to the Utes. Spirit Lake and the surrounding region, known as the Land of the Sun (Tavaputs), was sacred to both tribes, and was therefore considered neutral ground.

The Land of the Sun was avoided with superstitious fear by everyone except tribal chieftains and medicine men, for it was ostensibly the place where Towats dwelt. The Medicine Rock, high on the mountainside above the lake, was the place where the shamans practiced their magic. Here they would fast and pray, chant holy songs, and burn holy smoke to inspire medicine dreams. It was a holy and sacred place. It was an important place to Walker.

Following the peace negotiations between the tribes, Walker's father Moonch had married the sister of Chief Fuchawana of the Southern Shoshones; she became the mother of Walker's half-brother Tabby. When Pan-a-Carre Quinker was still an infant, his father Moonch made a pilgrimage to Spirit Lake. Holding his squirming son by one foot, Moonch dipped the boy three times in the icy waters of the lake. This was not a baptism in the conventional sense; it was both a "toughening" and to imbue the child with the spirit of Towats to make him great as a man grown.

For all his wealth and power as a man, Pan-a-Carre Quinker was not content, for though he was a great warrior, his heart had not found love among the women of his own tribe. He rode down from Spirit Lake to Hickerson Park where the Shoshones had made their annual summer encampment. He hid himself in the trees and began to watch his old enemies, for even though they were on neutral ground, there was still animosity between the tribes because of stolen horses.

One day he saw a young maiden picking bullberries on a hillside with some of the older squaws, and he became enthralled with her beauty. He continued to watch her for several days, hoping to find an opportunity to catch her alone. He would not have

hesitated to take her captive and carry her away to his Sanpete Valley homeland, though he preferred her willing interest. But he was an enemy of her people and it was unlikely that she would welcome his advances. Fate conspired to bring him good fortune.

The young girl at last drifted off by herself. Finding a particularly abundant berry patch, she lingered, and did not notice that the other women had moved on. Seeing his opportunity, young Pan-a-Carre Quinker started to approach her, but before he could do so, he saw a young Shoshone brave stalking the girl. The Iron Twister vied for position where he could watch.

The Shoshone brave had been spurned by the girl and sought his revenge by attacking her. He sneaked stealthily up behind her, threw her to the ground, and began to beat her severely. Pan-a-Carre Quinker sprang up and ran across the clearing to her defense. Pulling the Shoshone brave off the struggling girl, the two warriors were soon locked in vicious combat. But the Iron Twister was a better warrior and killed the Shoshone brave.

The girl was equally frightened of her rescuer, for he was an enemy of her people, but he soon calmed her fears. He spoke her language, and in quiet tones told her about himself, and when she had quieted, she told him about herself.

Her name was Sasquina, which in the Shoshone dialect means "White Elk," and she was fourteen snows in age. More importantly, she was the daughter of Chief Fuchawana; her brother, also called Fuchawana, was the tribal medicine man. Pan-a-Carre Quinker was a handsome man and according to legend the two young people fell instantly in love. She brought him to her village and when her father learned that the Iron Twister had saved Sasquina from harm, Pan-a-Carre-Quinker was welcomed as an honored warrior.

Pan-a-Carre Quinker and Sasquina were married in Hickerson Park, with the blessing of her tribe, and they spent their honeymoon at Spirit Lake. They romped and played together and at last the Iron Twister's heart was full. Sasquina was soon pregnant with their first child, and to mark the happy event, he made her a necklace from the backbone of an elk, an animal that was sacred to Towats. Then he went on a hunt with her people, and when he returned she was nowhere to be found.

Pan-a-Carre Quinker hunted frantically for his bride. At last the signs made it clear what had happened. Sasquina had gone down to the lake to fetch water and had somehow fallen in and drowned. He never found her body, but he did find one of her tiny moccasins in the water, bobbing on the ripples, the tiny trader bells she had sewn onto it gently tinkling. The strongest warrior in the West was brought to his knees in grief.

Pan-a-Carre Quinker could not understand why this terrible tragedy had happened to him just as love and happiness had found him. He climbed the steep trail to the Medicine Rock and fasted and prayed for many days, calling upon Towats to tell him why it should be so. Towats heard him. Towats told him more than he ever expected.

Towats appeared to him in all his radiance and spoke with him face to face. He showed him a glorious vision of the sacred caves of Carre-Shinob and the golden treasures of his ancestors, the Old Ones. He told Pan-a-Carre Quinker that he was to be the guardian of this place, and also of the Sacred Mines from whence the gold derived. Towats said to him: "No more will your name be Pan-a-Carre Quinker, but you shall have a new name: you shall be called Yah-keerah, Keeper of the Yellow Metal."

As for his grief, Towats promised him a sign that Sasquina had not died in vain. When Yah-keerah (white men, unable to pronounce his new name, called him "Walker") came down from the Medicine

Rock, it was near the dawn of day, and the morning sun gave birth to a mist on the surface of the lake. He was startled to hear the gentle tinkling of bells, exactly like the tiny trader bells which Sasquina had sewn to her moccasins. He stopped and looked across the water and saw a herd of elk swimming towards him out of the mist. Their leader, a large white elk, suddenly rose to the top of the water and walked on the surface of the lake!

The white elk walked across the water and came to stand before him on the shore. It was then that Yah-keerah saw the bone necklace around the animal's neck—the bone necklace he had given to Sasquina, whose very name meant "White Elk."

To the present day the legend persists that at certain times one can hear the tinkling of the bells (I have heard them—or was it my imagination?), and some have even claimed to have seen a white elk in the mist on the surface of the lake; and who are we to doubt it?

It is difficult to sort the truth from legend after so many years, and quite often we find that legends are the basis of truth. The truth is that Yah-keerah claimed to have seen a vision wherein Towats spoke to him in a medicine dream, and showed him the hidden place called Carre-Shinob with its great sacred treasure. That great cavern of riches, which has never been found by the greedy, and seen by only a few, lies somewhere near Spirit Lake.

Shoshone legend also decrees that near Spirit Lake is an ancient burial ground, and that old Chief Fuchawana is buried there. His son, Fuchawana the younger, a Shoshone medicine man, eventually left his own people and went with Yah-keerah to Sanpete. He became a great shaman of the Sanpete and Uintah Utes, and was revered by them as one of the few men privileged to be called a guardian of Carre-Shinob.

Chief Walker, Keeper of the Yellow Metal, was a very spiritual man. He conversed with Towats on many occasions.

In 1843, not long after the death of his father, Walker was at Fort Uintah in the Uintah Basin on a trading expedition. While there he fell quite suddenly ill and was taken in by the post trader, Antoine Robidoux, but he fell into a deep coma and apparently died. Robidoux turned him over to his people for burial.

Then, even as the squaws were mourning and beating their breasts, Walker suddenly recovered and awoke to tell a strange tale. He said that his spirit had left his body, to soar like an eagle above the mountains. He found himself northward in Shoshone country, above the plains of Wyoming. There he met Towats, high in the clouds, who spoke to him, saying, "Look down." He looked and saw a wagon train—"rolling wickiups"—being driven by white men wearing "high hats" (silk and beaver top-hats). Towats told him that it was to these men that he was to reveal the secret of Carre-Shinob; but not to just any of them, but to one man among them, one of their leaders, a man of great good whom Towats showed him.

"When will this man come?" Walker asked.

"Soon," Towats replied.

On 14 June 1849, Chief Walker appeared suddenly in Salt Lake City at the head of a large contingent of Utes, to speak with Brigham Young about the intentions of the Mormons towards his people. Brigham replied diplomatically, "No Indian will be turned from a Mormon's door as long as I remain their chief." Walker was pleased with the response and suggested that they smoke the pipe of peace. According to Brigham Young, "When Walker had filled his pipe, he offered the Lord the first smoke, pointing the pipe and stepping toward the sun." After recognizing his sun god, Walker passed the peace pipe around the circle of Mormon leaders. As the pipe was passed among them, Walker's eyes fixed upon Isaac Morley.

"I have seen you before," Walker told the surprised Mormon patriarch. "I have seen you in a vision. You will come and live among my people. We will be brothers." On 28 October 1849, Isaac Morley set out for the Sanpete Valley with 244 colonists to settle in the midst of the Ute Indians.

———

The settlement of Sanpete Valley was the beginning of a most unusual friendship between Isaac Morley, president of the Mormon colony, and Walker, chief of the Sanpete Utes. The Mormon colonists pitched their tents for the first time in Sanpete Valley on 21 November 1849. [For a more complete account of the settlement of Sanpete Valley, see *The Gold of Carre-Shinob*, Boren & Boren, op.cit.] Morley pointed prophetically at an eminence rising in the distance and said: "There is the termination of our journey in close proximity to that hill. God be willing, we will build our city [there]." Some of the colonists were dissatisfied with the choice. Seth Taft gave vent to his feeling by exclaiming, "This is only a long, narrow canyon, and not even a jack-rabbit could exist on its desert soil!" But Father Morley was adamant, saying, "This is our God-appointed abiding place; and stay I will, though but ten men remain with me."

There was a compelling reason why Isaac Morley chose "Temple Hill" as the site of the new city. Chief Walker had pointed out the hill as being sacred to the Utes. His ancestors, the "Old Ones," he explained, once had an altar on the hill's crest where human sacrifices were performed. Morley inquired whether there were any remains of the stone altar still visible, but the chief said there was not. There were ancient caverns beneath the hill, however, Walker said. Morley's curiosity was instantly piqued. He asked Walker to show him the caverns, but the chief balked. "Heap bad place," he said fearfully. "You no go there—never come out!"

"Why is it dangerous?" Morley asked. "Are there evil spirits there?"

"Worse," said Walker. "You will see when the warm weather comes." He refused to elaborate further. Shortly thereafter he and his people departed while the colonists settled in for the winter.

Morley pondered the words of Chief Walker for some time. Something about the story of stone altars and sacrifice struck a familiar chord. A learned scholar of the Book of Mormon, he searched its pages for a clue. He found what he was looking for in Alma 1:15:

And it came to pass that they took him; and his name was Nehor; and they carried him upon the top of the hill Manti, and there he was caused, or rather did acknowledge, between the heavens and the earth, that what he had taught to the people was contrary to the word of God; and there he suffered an ignominious death.

Being devoutly religious and a strong adherent to the teachings of the Book of Mormon, Isaac Morley recorded the following in his journal:

...No sooner had I read this passage than I recognized the place as the very hill where the Nephites had sacrificed Nehor on the sacrificial altar for the sake of the preservation of the ancient Church. Here once an ancient temple stood, and here one day again would stand another in these Last Days... This was, even as Chief Joseph Walker said, a sacred hill, and so I called the place Manti, even as it was called in days gone by...

During the first winter at Sanpete Valley, a very few of the settlers had time to erect log cabins before the snow became too deep for gathering logs. A few families turned their wagon boxes on end with canvas covers stretched across them for wind breaks, and they suffered greatly from the penetrating cold. The majority of the colonists, including Isaac Morley, made dugouts in the south side of Temple Hill.

By 23 March 1850 the snow had nearly disappeared and the colonists discovered that water had soaked three feet into the ground. They began digging irrigation ditches, ploughing and planting. Then, on an evening of a certain warm day, the settlers were disagreeably confronted from every direction by a loud hissing and rattling from snakes. Upon awakening from hibernation, hundreds of rattlesnakes had made their way unnoticed from caves within Temple Hill, and were suddenly in the colony.

Rattlesnakes are most dangerous when awakening from a comatose hibernation because they are temporarily blind and will strike at anything that moves. The spotted serpents were seen twisting and coiling over practically every rock on the hillside, and many were already under foot. The men immediately armed themselves with pine knot torches and began the battle of extermination. One settler killed thirty in a matter of a few minutes, and the total of the first night's slaughter was over five hundred!

The extermination continued for several evenings before the crisis ended. Since rattlesnakes travel during the early evening, it was not uncommon for the colonists to awaken in the morning to find a rattlesnake curled on the foot of the bed or in a cupboard. "They invaded our homes with as little compunction as the plagues of Egypt did the palace of Pharaoh," wrote one settler. While horses and cattle were bitten, not one settler was poisoned by the invading horde.

The friendship between Morley and Walker grew rapidly. Morley permitted the starving Indians to retrieve the frozen carcasses of cattle that were dying daily; of the 250 cattle brought into Sanpete Valley in November, only 100 remained alive when the snow melted. He also invited Walker's people to come and eat the Mormon "tiegup"—a Ute term for food acquired by persistent begging. Walker was willing to trade valuable furs, oxen or ponies for "tiegup," but Morley refused to accept them, giving the supplies as a token of friendship. Morley wrote to Brigham

Young: "It seems to be a trying time all around, and those who have the most wisdom can make a display of it for the most good."

Walker had another surprise for his friend Morley: he announced that he was ready to be baptized for the remission of his sins, and had convinced his brother Arapeen and others to do likewise. He would have it no other way than have it done that very day. On 13 March 1850, Chief Walker waded into the ice-choked waters of City Creek and submitted to immersion under the trusted hands of Isaac Morley, becoming the first of his people to be confirmed a member of the Mormon Church. Several other distinguished "Lamanites" entered the baptismal waters on March 20, after which President Morley wrote to Brigham Young:

The door is opened and they are coming in, with expression of good feelings, and kindness as could probably be expected from uncultivated minds. A stone from the quarry needs polishing to become useful, and we believe there are some here that may be made, (with watchful care) to shine as bright gems in the Temple of the Lord, yes, stars that may spread their twinkling light to distant tribes....We feel to say that there never was a mission opened with brighter prospects to the scattered children of Ephraim than the one in which we are engaged, and shouldn't be willing to leave unless called away by as good authority as that by which we were sent here. Did we come here to enrich ourselves in the things of this world? No. We were sent to enrich the Natives, and comfort the hearts of the long, long, oppressed. Let us try the experiment and if we fail to accomplish the object, then say, boys come away. Amen.

On March 23, Charles Shumway and a few brethren arrived in Salt Lake City where Shumway complained to Brigham Young that Morley paid more attention to the needs of the Indians than he did the colonists under his charge. But for the present, Young did nothing. In fact, though

Brigham Young agreed with Shumway in principle, on April 12 the First Presidency wrote its Third General Epistle in which reference was made to the Sanpete settlement by saying. "The citizens have laid the foundation of a great and glorious work." The Presidency dwelt on the accomplishments under Morley's direction and prophesied that those who persevere to the end in following the counsels of heaven will be a thousand fold richer than those who leave to search for gold, as many Mormons were then planning.

Even while Brigham Young was discouraging Mormons from searching after gold, he had gold on his own mind. His tolerance of Morley's favoritism towards the Indians stemmed from the discovery of an immense source of gold known by the Utes, and revealed to Father Morley. Brigham was already planning a visit to Sanpete Valley to applaud the good works of Isaac Morley.

Chief Walker

Chapter Sixteen

The Sacred Mine

Shortly after Chief Walker's baptism, the wily chieftain came alone to Morley's newly-built log cabin and asked to talk to him in private. Morley sent his family away to a neighbor's house while he spoke in secret with the solemn chief. Morley recorded the event in his journal:

...Walker appeared to be very nervous and uncertain. He never seemed comfortable indoors, and at first I attributed it to this, but there was something different in his demeanor that I could not discern the meaning of. "I will show you something," he said, removing a small buckskin pouch tied on a long leather thong about his neck. He dumped the contents onto the table-top. Even in the dim light I could see that the pile of thumb-sized rocks were gleaming with yellow color, and I recognized it immediately as being as pure gold as I have ever seen. Walker called it "money-rock," and I was quite surprised at his casual attitude towards the great fortune before him. [*The Journal of Isaac Morley*, transcript in possession of the Author]

Morley asked the chief why he allowed his people to suffer want if he had so much wealth at his disposal, to which Walker replied that the gold belonged to Towats, and was therefore sacred. The place where the gold was hidden was protected by Towats, he said, and Indians were forbidden to go there.

Walker recited the long history of the gold of Carre-Shinob, then informed Father Morley that Towats had once appeared to him in a vision and told him the secret of the sacred gold should be given to the "high hats" when they came. He also said that Towats had shown him that Morley was the

man to whom the secret should be revealed. "I will show you where is money-rock," he told the Mormon leader.

Morley refused to accept any of the gold for his own use. He convinced Walker that the secret should be given to the Mormon Chief, Brigham Young, for the benefit of all Mormons. Inasmuch as the Mormon Chief was a prophet and shaman of the great Towats, he said, he should be the one to rightfully possess the gold.

Walker agreed to provide the gold to Brigham Young, under certain conditions, but first he must take Morley to Carre-Shinob, because Towats had commanded it. They would go in May, said Walker, when the snow had gone from the high mountains. In the meantime, Isaac Morley wrote promptly to Brigham Young. Though undated, the letter was probably written sometime before March 20, and was one of the sealed letters which Charles Shumway had delivered into Brigham Young's hands on March 23:

"...Thinking this to be a matter of the utmost urgency, and for your eyes only, I remit this letter among those sealed as matters of intelligence concerning the Natives of this place. Walker has this day come to see me, bringing with him a pouch of what appears to be the purest gold, in the form of nuggets uniformly the size of the nail of the thumb or larger. He reports these to have come from an ancient mine somewhere high in the mountains to the east of this place, and has offered to take me there, and to give me the gold on the basis of our friendship. He tells a marvelous story of a vision, in which the spirit of Towats appeared to him, making him the keeper of the "money-rock," as he calls it, until the Mormons came, at which time he was told to give it to them. He perceives, somehow, that I am the man that Towats chose to have the gold, but I have managed to convince him that you as the great Mormon Chief, should have it, and he is willing that it should be so....

"I firmly believe in the truth of Walker's statement that such a mine does exist somewhere in the mountains, and I am willing to go with him there to verify it, if you see it in your wisdom for me to do so. Walker says the trip will take two or three weeks, as soon as the snow melts in the mountain passes. The snow goes daily here in the valleys, and should be gone in the high country before a month or two has passed....

"The door is opened for a marvelous work in these last days, and an expression of good feelings from Walker has given us the prospect of filling the bellies of the Saints with food and our temples with decorations befitting the Lord of Solomon. If the mine is as rich as Walker purports it to be, then might our temple rival even that of Solomon's in its richness....

"I would never permit others to enrich themselves, nor would I enrich myself, at the expense of the Natives who daily perish from cold and hunger and disease. It is my fervent hope that the Lord of Hosts has chosen me as a means to bring forth this wealth for His purposes, that His people, red and white alike, may be relieved of their suffering....

"Walker will do nothing until hearing from you, which I pray will be by return messenger, for it is the nature of the uncivilized mind to forever change...."

Brigham Young's response to Morley's letter has not been found, but we get a sense of it from an excerpt of Morley's journal under date of 14 April, 1850:

"Today received a letter in hand from Pres. Young and the First Presidency, commending me for the progress of the Sanpete settlement and requesting shingles for the Council House of Great Salt Lake City... Pres. Young has written to Walker, and I have sent word for him to come in that I may read it to him. Having full authority from Pres. Young to proceed to the mine, I will make the necessary preparations with Walker when he arrives. He is anxious to leave for the mountains soon, as Sowlett and other members of his tribe daily threaten his life."

Brigham Young put the gold to good use. During the summer of 1849, one dollar bills had been issued and signed by Brigham Young, Heber C. Kimball and Thomas Bullock, clerk. The paper currency was based upon a promissary note, the Church having nothing in its treasury with which to support it.

Late in the fall of 1849, at about the time Isaac Morley led the colonizers to Sanpete Valley, Thomas Rhoades, a member of the Mormon Battalion, arrived from California and paid a tithing of $17,000 in gold dust gleaned from Sutter's Mill. With this gold dust, Brigham Young began the coinage of gold coins, best known as "Mormon Money." John M. Kay and Willard Richards, under the supervision of Thomas Bullock, established the "Deseret Mint" in the home of Dr. William Sharp, dentist. The gold coins were cast in the values of $2.50 to $20.00, and were engraved on one side with an emblem of "clasped hands," surrounded by the official engraving title and value amount, while the obverse was engraved with the "all-seeing eye," surrounded by the logo, "Holiness To The Lord." These are all Masonic (Templar) symbols.

By late in the year 1850, and continuing for several years thereafter, an abundance of these gold coins began to circulate, and there was great speculation about the source of the metal used. The Church remained silent, and has continued to be silent on the subject ever since.

On 7 July, 1850, Isaac Morley officiated

at the dedication of a new bowery in Manti, at which Chief Walker attended with over 200 members of his tribe. During the course of his speech, Father Morley gave instructions to the settlers regarding future dealings with the Indians, and challenged Walker's people to accept baptism. So great was their esteem for Morley by this time, 120 Utes were baptized under his hands on this occasion, "causing all the Saints to rejoice."

Brigham Young arrived in Sanpete Valley on Sunday, 4 August 1850, on a personal visit. The settlement's only cannon was fired in salute from Temple Hill. On the following day, Young was escorted by Morley and others to sample the trout fishing, and in the afternoon Brigham officially christened the settlement, giving it the name "Manti" as suggested by Isaac Morley. He also dedicated the hill above the settlement as a future temple site, based upon Morley's opinion that it was once the site of an ancient Nephite temple.

According to Morley's journal, the fishing expedition was a cover to afford Brigham Young an opportunity to meet secretly with Chief Walker. William Potter served as interpreter, for though Walker spoke English, he generally preferred to negotiate in his own language for the benefit of his sub-chiefs. Walker agreed to allow gold to be taken from the sacred mines, but he imposed specific conditions. The location would be revealed to only one man, mutually trusted—not even Brigham Young was to know the location of the gold. The penalty of death would be inflicted on the man chosen to retrieve the gold should he reveal the location to any other person without permission from the Utes, and any white man who attempted to follow the chosen man would also suffer death. Finally, the Indians would at no time assist in the removal of the gold, and the man chosen must take only as much gold as was needed in one trip at a time—no mining operation would be allowed.

While they awaited the choice of the right man, Isaac Morley made another trip to the sacred mines in the early summer of 1851. On the return trip he encountered the camp of a group of Mexicans, led by one Antonio de Reinaldo. The Spaniards were also in the mountains after gold. Morley managed to elude them, but their presence was reported promptly to Brigham Young. By the end of the year, Brigham would have the Spaniards on trial for violating his newly enacted anti-slavery statute, rushed through the Territorial Legislature by Representative Morley [see *The Gold of Carre-Shinob*, chap. two].

In May of 1852, Brigham Young again visited at Manti. He brought with him the man chosen to bring gold from the sacred mines—Thomas Rhoades, who was Church Treasurer, and who had brought the gold from Sutter's Mill in 1849. They met with Isaac Morley and Chief Walker and it was agreed that Rhoades was a man mutually trusted. Rhoades made his first trip to the mines shortly thereafter, taking 14 days, and retrieving 62 pounds of pure gold.[*Footprints In The Wilderness, A History of the Lost Rhoades Mines*, Kerry Ross Boren & Gale R. Rhoades, Publishers Press, Salt Lake City, 1971]

At the Reinaldo trial, Isaac Morley testified against the Mexicans, and they were found guilty of violating the anti-slavery act, for which Morley had been the sponsor. Arapeen testified at the trial in behalf of the Mexicans, stating that the selling of Piede and Paiute slaves to the Mexicans had long been practiced, and he saw no wrong in it. The Mexicans were released on the condition that they would never return to Utah.

Arapeen was volatile over the prohibition to sell slaves. One day he appeared with several Piede children to a group of Mormons on the Provo River and demanded of their leader, Daniel Jones (the same man to whom Brigham Young revealed his belief that the Hopis were descendants of Madoc), that the Mormons buy the slaves, since he could no longer sell them to the Mexicans. When Jones refused to buy the children, Arapeen grabbed a young Piede boy by the feet and dashed his brains out on a rock.

Chief Walker was equally irate. He rode up to Morley's house in Manti and demanded to know why his friend Morley had made a law prohibiting him from selling Piede slaves to the Q'uatz.

"Because slavery is not the Mormon way," Morley said.

"And Walker will not stop selling slaves to the Mexicans," Walker spouted. "That is not our way." He whirled and rode away and remained cool towards the Mormons for some months thereafter.

Then, on 17 July 1853, Walker's smouldering anger was incited to war when James Ivie, who lived in Spring Creek in Utah Valley, struck a belligerent brave over the head with a broken gun barrel, killing him. [note: James R. Ivie was married to a daughter of Alfred D. Young, whose mother, Mary Boren Young, was sister of Coleman Boren, author Kerry Ross Boren's great-grandfather]. Angered because the Mormons refused to turn Ivie over to him for justice, Walker declared war on the settlers. Outbreaks occurred all over the Territory. At Manti, Father Morley ordered the settlers into a newly constructed fort.

Though the Walker War raged for several months throughout much of the Territory, with many killed on both sides, it is a tribute to the respect Walker held for Morley that no attacks were made upon Manti, in the very center of Walker's realm. Then, on 8 April 1853, Walker asked Morley to deliver a message to Brigham Young: "Tell Brother Brigham we have smoked the tobacco he sent to us in the pipe of peace: I want to be at peace, and be a brother to him."

Brigham Young's response to Father Morley reveals his true personal philosophy, unmasked by diplomacy: "That is all right, but it is truly characteristic of the cunning Indian. When he finds he cannot get advantage over his enemy (he will) curie down at once, and say 'I love you.'"

Within days of making the statement, Brigham Young was in Manti to confer with Morley about using his influence with Chief Walker to effect a peace. No sooner had he done so, however, than Brigham Young levied a political attack upon Morley for having too much influence with the Indians.

The tension arose between the two Church leaders during the fall of 1853, but had its roots even earlier. The original political structure at Manti consisted of a tripartite division into a militia, a city council, and the ecclesiastical authority, which at Manti was Isaac Morley. Samuel K. Gifford recorded in his diary the conflict that arose over the construction of a fort during the Walker War:

The Military, whose right it was to take charge of building forts, proposed to make a good stone wall all around nine blocks, taking in the outside streets. The City Council thought they ought to have the say of where and how the fort should be constructed. Then came the Church Authorities and said the Priesthood must rule. And soon the debate became quite warm. But as none wished to go against the Priesthood, Father Morley succeeded in getting in a row of houses built on the east side of the nine blocks, leaving the street outside the doors opening to the west.

The Azariah Smith journal, under date of 27 February 1854, recorded a visit by Apostle Erastus Snow whereat he preached, "reproving the People for their backwardness in building a fort and also for their disunion and contention." The Manti City Council minutes show that even though Isaac Morley was not a member of the Council, he attended regularly, and the Council made its decisions according to his wishes.

The problems began from the first day of settlement when there was a disagreement over the exact place of settlement.

Among the leaders of this contention were Seth Taft and Jake Butterfield. After losing all of his cattle to the severe winter, the carcasses being given to the starving Indians, Taft bundled up his wife and two daughters in the spring of 1850 and returned to the Salt Lake Valley where in time he became bishop of the 9th Ward. Butterfield, a Mormon Battalion veteran, was a bitter critic of Morley throughout 1849-1850, and at last he was excommunicated and banished by a Bishops' Court in February 1850 at the instigation of Isaac Morley.

Even more significant was a venal feud between Isaac Morley and Bishop John Lowry, Sr., who was supported by Titus Billings and Elijah Averett. The greatest issue between them was Lowry's "distaste" for Indians and Morley's favoritism of them. Lowry's problems with the Indians began when Chief Walker asked Brigham Young if it was possible for him to marry a Mormon woman. Young gave his consent on condition that the woman agreed.

Walker had his eye on Bishop Lowry's daughter, Mary. Dressed in his finest Spanish-style clothing, Walker entered the Lowry home without knocking. He expressed his intentions to the frightened girl, describing his great wealth, and even promised to forsake his Indian ways and adopt those of the white man if she would marry him. Afraid of the consequences should she refuse him, Mary Lowry blurted out that she was already married to a white man. Walker demanded to know who it was, and Mary told him it was her sister's husband, Judge Peacock. Walker angrily plunged his knife into the kitchen table and left.

Bishop Lowry, when he learned of the incident, went directly to Father Morley and demanded that Chief Walker be reprimanded. Morley insisted that Walker had been entirely within his rights to propose and had done nothing wrong; moreover, Morley pointed out that Mary Lowry's lie, when found out, could incite another Indian war. Lowry left in a huff, accusing Morley of caring more about the Indians than he did his own people.

Bishop Lowry found himself in a quandary. He confronted his daughter and demanded that her lie be made truth. That same night Mary married Peacock, then fled to Salt Lake City. John Lowry never ceased blaming Morley for the entire affair. It was not long before the tension exploded into another confrontation.

In 1853, Morley pulled out of a commitment to finish construction of a council house in Manti, and used the funds to aid Walker's ailing people, thereby arousing the ire of Lowry's faction. Averett and Billings, stonemasons, found themselves out of a job, and went directly to Salt Lake City to confer with Brigham Young and Heber C. Kimball in an attempt to effect Morley's replacement. They complained that Morley had summarily changed a decision made by all the Church leaders in order to help the Indians. Upon their return, a special ward meeting was convened on Wednesday, 23 November 1853, and the resultant confrontation between the two factions resulted in Isaac Morley's resignation.

Morley was a very powerful man; probably no other man in the Territory held more influence besides Young himself, and Morley was the only man who could handle the Sanpete Utes. His knowledge of the sacred gold made him an ever present threat in Young's mind, no matter how faithful Morley had proved himself to be. But Young could not be so forward as to come out publicly against Morley, so he made arrangements for Morley's removal behind the scenes. Averett reported that upon being told of the situation at Manti, "President Young turned away, saying that he knew all about it and did not wish to hear any more."

Heber C. Kimball was even more outspoken. In a speech given at Manti, and recorded in the Manti Ward minutes for 23

November 1853, he said that:

"President Morley was as good a man as there was on earth but he was getting old and childish and he was a man of poor temporal economy and that was the cause of things not going better here; that his mind did not run into temporal affairs but was taken up in spiritual affairs therefore was not calculated to be President of a Branch."

Isaac Morley's reputation was at stake. It was strange the Church authorities, of all people, should have accused him of being too spiritual, but as we shall see, there were deeper motives to the statement than meets the eye. Moreover, to accuse him of "poor temporal economy" was ludicrous, for Manti was the second largest and best developed community in Mormondom, and one of dozens he had personally founded.

On the day of his forced resignation, Isaac Morley began by protesting that he had tried to support Bishop Lowry, but confessed that he knew he had "crossed him" at times, and added, "If this has offended him I do think it ought not to of had that effect on him." The Manti Ward minutes for 23 November 1853 records the consequences of his situation.

"President Morley said brethren I wish to choose you a new President, yet I wish a place among you. I would say further for your benefit; had the brethren who has recently visited Great Salt Lake City - I say had they of laid the case before the Presidency in its true light I think it would be appeared in a different light from what it now does.—Pres. Morley appeared very humble and burst into tears and sat down."

Prior to his resignation, Morley wrote to Brigham Young on 5 November 1853, asking, "In what duties have I failed?" Young responded on November 15 by writing: "Permit me to say that I was some what surprised that one of your years, judgement, and experience should allow himself to be affected and weighed down by mere reports."

Morley had heard rumors that he was also going to be forced to resign from the legislature, but Young told him that had he felt any need to replace him, he would have notified him in person, as he had always done in matters of consequence. "I do not wish you to even dream of resigning," Young wrote. "Bring your certificate of election and take your seat in the assembly." But Young's suspicions that Morley held too much influence with Walker and his Utes, and had become a liability, expresses itself clearly in the concluding paragraph of his letter to Morley:

"I have reflected upon your age, circumstances, and probable feelings and feel today that it would please me much if you would arrange your affairs with the view of returning and living with us here in this city at the earliest reasonable date."

Following his resignation on November 23, Father Morley went to Salt Lake City to confer with Brigham Young on his options. Their discussion took place on December 12 and Young demanded that Morley remain and send for his family immediately. They also discussed Morley's friendship with the Indians, but what was said is not recorded. However, on the following Sunday morning Morley took the pulpit in the Bowery to address the Saints on the subject of "Indian Activities in Sanpete."

Following the April 1854 general conference of the Church, Isaac Morley returned to Manti to put his business affairs in order. He visited for the last time with his old friend, Chief Walker, who was camped on Meadow Creek, to tell him that Brigham Young had called him away. Morley wrote in his journal:

"There were tears in Walker's eyes. He was ill, and thought we might never see one another again. I told him that Towats would never allow brothers to be parted, and that should either of us die, or us both, we would meet again in the Lord's Heaven. He seemed pleased and comforted at that. 'When Walker die,' he said, 'my brother

Morley will speak to Towats when I am buried?' I told him I would. We parted with an embrace, which thing is not customary with Walker. He is the most unforgettable man I have ever known."

On 29 January 1855, after a protracted bout with pneumonia, Chief Walker died at his camp on Meadow Creek in Millard County. A day or two later, several Ute Indians rode into Salt Lake City looking for Isaac Morley. They informed him of Walker's death and urged him to come. Heber C. Kimball and others cautioned Morley that Walker had often expressed the desire to have several Mormons killed and buried with him, to accompany him on his journey to the land of medicine dreams. Morley, however, had given his promise to Walker to consecrate his grave and commend his soul to Towats, and left immediately with the Indians.

The body of Walker had already been buried, entombed in a deep crevice near the top of the mountain above Meadow Creek. It was early February when Morley arrived there, led by Arapeen and a few sub-chiefs. As they neared the burial place, the sound of crying could be heard emanating form the tomb. Two Piede children, a boy and girl, had been entombed alive, condemned to slowly starve to death, their crying calculated to scare away evil spirits which might try to steal Walker's soul on its three-day journey to the great beyond. [For additional information on the burial, and Morley's comments on the plight of the children, see *The Gold of Carre-Shinob*, chap. 5, pp.46-49.]

As Morley opened his Book of Mormon to prepare for the service to consecrate the grave of Walker, Arapeen stopped him. This was only a temporary burial place, he said; Walker had requested to be buried at Carre-Shinob! Morley protested that he was nearly seventy years of age, too old to make such a rigorous journey, but Arapeen reminded him of the promise he had made to his dead brother, and further threatened that his refusal might precipitate another

war. Besides, Arapeen was willing to let nineteen year-old Caleb Baldwin Rhoades, son of Thomas Rhoades, accompany them on the journey to assist the elder Morley. Thomas Rhoades, the only other white man then permitted near the sacred mines, was indisposed by illness during 1855, and unable to make trips into the mountains after gold.

At Meadow Creek the two white men joined Chief Arapeen, his brother Tabby, and five other Utes—Un-gas-ton-igats, Cessapoonch, Un-gaco-choop, Rabbit, and Fuchawana (the brother of Sasquina)—and removed the body of Chief Walker from the crevice tomb at Meadow Creek, and entombed him in the sacred caverns of Carre-Shinob among his ancestors.

Walker was interred in a sitting position within a chamber of Carre-Shinob, where also reposed the bones of his grandfather, Sanpete, and other Keepers of the Yellow Metal. Like Sanpete, Walker was adorned with golden Aztecan artifacts—mask, breastplate, anklets, bracelets, necklaces and rings. Because of the superstition prevalent among the Utes, only Fuchawana, a shaman, entered the burial chamber with the two white men.

After Father Morley had consecrated the grave, they emerged into the bright sunlight, where only Arapeen and Tabby were to be seen. To Morley, Arapeen said, "You no come here anymore." "Don't worry," Morley replied, "I am too old."

———

Isaac Morley remained an active legislator in Utah Territory for another two years, until 1857, at which time he declined the nomination for another term. His decision was partly based on Brigham Young's continued pressure for him to resign and become full-time Church Patriarch. He spent the rest of his life traveling throughout Utah Territory administering patriarchal blessings to the Saints.

Morley never ceased his colonizing enterprises. A firm believer in the "United

Order," he helped to establish the Muddy Mission in Nevada, and the communal town of Orderville in Kane County, and North Bend (later called Fairview) in Sanpete County. During his lifetime he founded more than ten communities in at least six states or territories.

In March 1864, while living with his daughter Lucy Diantha Allen and her family in North Bend, Isaac Morley developed severe rheumatism. As he lay in his sick bed for some months, another Indian war—the Black Hawk War—broke out in Utah Territory. Once more the Utes rose up against the Mormon settlers, and Father Morley's mood plunged into a despair from which he never recovered. While the Black Hawk War raged around him, Isaac Morley died at his daughter's home on 24 June 1865. He was seventy-nine. At his own request prior to his death, his remains were laid to rest at the foot of Temple Hill in his beloved Manti.

Chapter Seventeen

The Secret of Temple Hill

In retrospect, we have seen that Isaac Morley founded the town of Manti, Sanpete County, Utah, naming it for a hill of the same name mentioned in the Book of Mormon (Alma 1:15), whereon stood a sacrificial altar, according to that source. But Morley wrote in his journal that this was a sacred hill, that "Here once an ancient temple stood, and here one day again would stand another in these Last Days." The Book of Mormon does not mention a temple at this place and so Morley must have had another source for his information. In his journal he says only that Chief Walker claimed it was "a sacred hill," but Walker knew nothing of temples. Morley must have had an arcane source, and that is exactly what we discover when we review his origins.

———

Isaac Morley was born 11 March 1786 at Montague, Massachusetts, son of Thomas E. Morley (1758-1836) and Editha Marsh (1762-1836). He had been well educated in the finest schools of Salem, Massachusetts (as his journals and letters attest), but was endowed with a pioneer spirit that urged him, in 1810, at the age of 24, to venture 600 miles to the wilderness of the Western Reserve, a tract of land in what is now the northeast section of the state of Ohio. He constructed a cabin and cleared the land where the town of Kirtland was soon after built, then returned to Montague to marry his childhood sweetheart, Lucy Gunn. They were married on 20 June 1812, just two days after Congress declared war against Great Britain. Of their nine children, all born at Kirtland, seven grew to maturity—six girls and one boy.

Isaac Morley served as a Fifer in the Ohio Militia under Capt. Clark Parker and Generals Wadsworth and Perkins in the War of 1812, serving from 22 August until 2 October 1812, and again from 1 December until 27 February 1813, marching to Huron after the surrender of British General Hull.

A cooper by trade, Isaac was initially a Presbyterian, but in 1828 he was baptized into the Campbellite church by Pastor Sidney Rigdon. Shortly thereafter, Morley, Rigdon and Lyman Wight established their own church, a socialistic order called "The Family," on Morley's farm near Kirtland. A number of families settled there in a communistic society called a "common stock family," sharing all things in common.

In September 1830, four Mormon missionaries—Oliver Cowdery, Parley P. Pratt, Peter Whitmer, Jr., and Ziba Peterson—visited Kirtland, converting many to the new faith. On 15 November 1830, Isaac Morley was baptized and confirmed a member of the Mormon Church by Parley P. Pratt.

In February 1831 the Prophet Joseph Smith came to Kirtland and lived, with his family, in the Morley household until a log house could be constructed for their use. Eventually, Isaac donated his entire farm to the up-building of the Church. He remained one of Joseph Smith's closest and most trusted friends until the Prophet's martyrdom at the hands of a mob at Carthage, Illinois, on 27 June 1844.

Isaac Morley followed the Saints throughout the years of their persecutions in Ohio, Missouri and Illinois, and was a prominent Church leader during this period. He founded the towns of Kirtland, Far West, and Lima, in Ohio, Missouri and Illinois respectively. Lima, Illinois, was first named Yelrome, which is Morley spelled backwards. He was a participant in many of the significant events of that period, and was imprisoned on several occasions as a Mormon leader hated by the Missourians. In November 1833, Isaac Morley, Sidney Gilbert, and John Corrill were jailed at Independence, Missouri, on false charges, and offered up their lives as a sacrifice for the Saints, but managed to effect their release one day prior to their scheduled execution. Morley's courage and integrity were never questioned.

As a colonel in the Nauvoo Legion, Isaac Morley played a pertinent role in suppressing the mob rule which culminated in the murder of Joseph Smith and his brother Hyrum. On 10 September 1845, Morley's house, cooper shop and granary at Lima were burned to the ground by the mobs and he fled with his family to Nauvoo. He was instrumental in the completion of construction of the Nauvoo Temple and there, in January 1846, with Brigham Young and Heber C. Kimball officiating, Isaac took seven additional (polygamous) wives, in keeping with the doctrine of plural marriage. One of these, Lenora Snow, was sister of future Church President Lorenzo Snow, and poetess Eliza R. Snow.

Two of Isaac Morley's daughters, Cordelia Calista and Lucy Diantha, had been "sealed" to the Prophet Joseph Smith as plural wives. Smith had asked for the hand of Cordelia before his death, but as she was in love with Frederick W. Cox, she declined. However, she was sealed to the Prophet posthumously on 27 January 1846 by Heber C. Kimball, the latter having married another of Morley's daughters, Theresa. Lucy Diantha Morley had also declined Smith's first proposal of marriage, being in love with Smith's personal body-guard, Joseph Stewart Allen. Nevertheless, at the urging of her father, Lucy finally consented to be sealed to Joseph Smith in

1837. On 15 September 1838, she bore the Prophet a child in Clay County, Missouri, whom she named Caroline Delight (Allen). Caroline Delight was my great-grand-mother.

On 4 February 1846, Isaac Morley bundled his eight wives and other family members into wagons, crossed the frozen Mississippi River, and started westward with the migrating Saints. He became a founder of Winter Quarters (now Florence), Nebraska, where his first wife, Lucy Gunn, died on 3 January 1847, after suffering for two months with typhoid fever. He buried her in the "Mormon graveyard" at Florence, next to three of their grandchildren who died from lack of food and medical atten-tion during their privations after leaving Nauvoo.

On 23 January 1848, Isaac Morley was appointed president of the second migra-tion to "Zion," the first having been led by Brigham Young the previous year. Morley's company, consisting of 1,229 souls, 397 wagons, and numerous chattels, left Winter Quarters on 1 May 1848, and after many hardships arrived in the Valley of the Great Salt Lake on 23 September.

He settled first in Session's Settlement, a few miles north of Salt Lake City, but soon established his own community, "Morley's Settlement," which he later named Boun-tiful, a name derived from the Book of Mormon. On 16 February 1849, President Brigham Young sustained Isaac Morley as President of the High Council of the newly organized Great Salt Lake City.

On Thursday, 26 April 1849, a regular fast-day service was conducted in the "Bowery" at Salt Lake City. Even though a strong southerly wind prevailed, many Saints gathered to fast and pray and hear President Morley, Apostle John Taylor, and Patriarch John Smith (uncle of Joseph Smith) speak. During the meeting the Nauvoo Legion was reorganized and was composed of two cohorts, four regiments in a cohort, two battalions in a regiment, and five companies in a battalion, with Major Daniel H. Wells in command of the entire legion. Isaac Morley, who had been a full colonel at Nauvoo under Lt. Gen. Joseph Smith, was made lieutenant of a company composed exclusively of men over fifty years of age, called the "Silver Greys."

Prior to 1 February 1849, the federal government refused to provide any form of government for the Mormons in Utah, being uncertain of their allegiance. Following the Treaty of Guadalupe-Hidalgo, on 2 February 1848, the United States claimed ownership of the northern section of Mexican Territory, which included Utah. The Mormons therefore accepted the responsibility of instituting a provisional government, and beginning on March 4th a constitution for the new "State of Deseret" was drawn up by a committee of ten men, with Albert Carrington as chairman. Isaac Morley proposed the name "Deseret" to Brigham Young, from a Book of Mormon term meaning "honey bee," signifying Mormon industry.

The organization of the new state called for a governor, a legislature consisting of two houses (the senate and house of representatives) and a judiciary with other state officials. William W. Potter was appointed the first territorial marshal of the new provisional state. The first election was held 12 March 1849 at the Bowery, the constitution was adopted, and Brigham Young became Governor, Heber C. Kimball became Chief Justice, and Isaac Morley became Senator.

Then, following the October 1849 general conference of the Church, Isaac Morley was appointed by Brigham Young to head the colonization effort of Sanpete Valley.

———

No sooner had Isaac Morley arrived in Sanpete Valley on 21 November 1849, than he turned his attention towards the promontory which came to be known as Temple Hill. He was so adamant that settle-ment be made in proximity to that hill that he alienated a number of the colonists who favored more convenient locations in the valley. He strongly averred, "This is our God-appointed abiding place, and stay I will, though but ten men remain with me."

Why was the hill so important to him? Chief Walker of the Sanpete Utes had informed him that the "Old Ones" had once erected a sacrificial altar on the hill's crest, and thus the hill was considered sacred to the Indians, but this seems insufficient cause for Morley's intense interest in the site. In fact, the answer is gleaned from several passages in Morley's journal, even though parts of it are cryptic and coded. The first extract comes from a conversation Morley had with Chief Walker.

"...For the third time in as many days, Chief Joseph Walker has stopped by my tent to visit. He seems to have a great deal on his mind, and is of a spiritual frame of mind, anxious to speak at length about his visions and the history of his people. ...He says there is a hill in the valley where we are destined to settle, and he has urged me to establish our residency in proximity to that hill, because it is a sacred place to his people. When I asked him why it was sacred, he told me that there once was a stone altar at the very highest point on the hill where his ancestors, whom he calls the Old Ones, used to make human sacrifices to their gods. He also says that the altar is no longer at that place, but it stood there in the time of his grandfather, who was once a chief of this people, and for whom the valley is named [i.e. Sanpete]. The stone altar, which had strange carvings on its base, was disassembled by the Spaniards who came to this region in search of gold and riches...."

This entry explains, in part, why Father Morley chose the location near the hill for the establishment of the city of Manti. He obviously made the connection between the stone altar and the passage in the Book of Mormon (Alma 1:15) concerning the sacrifice of Nehor on the hill Manti by the

Nephites in ancient America. But Morley also adds that "Here once an ancient temple stood,..." even though there is no such allusion in the Book of Mormon. Walker mentioned only a stone altar, but nothing of a temple. Did Morley have another source? There are several strong allusions to this in his journals.

"...From our camp I climbed the south slope of the hill, finding the snow nearly gone on that side, with the intent to examine the stone inscriptions which I now believe to have been part of the ancient temple that once stood on top of this sacred mound. ...I found several large stones that protrude from orifices in the ground, it seeming from a cursory examination that more than two-thirds of the stones lay beneath the surface. The exposed portions of these stones give every appearance of having been worked or crafted by some means human, and I suspect them to be the remains of the stone foundation of the ancient temple that by every indication dominated this hill in times of old. ...Having made copies of the several stone inscriptions, I compared them to the books and found seventeen likenesses, with fourteen others unidentified and seven others unintelligible. ...After [Sunday] services in the Bowery, I climbed to the top of Temple Hill with Bro. Gifford [probably Samuel K. Gifford] to examine the cannon [the Nauvoo Legion had provided the colonists with a cannon for protection]. Because several adventurous youths had within the week attempted to roll the cannon off the hill, Bro. Gifford was commissioned to secure the buttress of the cannon by a strong iron ring to a large stone at the hill's crest. In so doing, Bro. Gifford split the stone and found it to be hollow. It appears upon our examination of the stone that it was an ancient repository of records....and belonged, as I suppose, to the second temple...."

Father Morley speaks familiarly of the "ancient temple," but nowhere identifies it, unless it is mentioned among the coded sections of his journals. He even refers to a "second temple," inferring that he knew of at least two such structures that once existed on the hill. Moreover, he compared copies of the inscriptions found on the hill with other copies in "the books"—what books does he refer to? It seems apparent that he possessed some sort of translation guide to the hieroglyphics.

From the time of his arrival in the Sanpete Valley in 1849 until his recall in 1854, Isaac Morley searched continuously for something in or around Temple Hill. It was nearly an obsession with him, though he remained very secretive about it. Did he find something? Shortly after April conference in 1854, as he sadly prepared to leave his beloved valley after being forced to resign as President of the Sanpete Branch, he made a strange notation in his journal:

"...I have been stripped of my rank and pride. They know not what they do. That which would have enriched the church in wealth and wisdom is now hid from them evermore. The Lord in His wisdom keep His own. I have this day hid up the entrance, even as it was found, and will in all probability never more return. I have seen. I have beheld with mine own eyes. It is enough..."

Prior to his death in 1865, Isaac Morley gave specific instructions to his son, Isaac Morley, Jr., that his remains be brought back to Manti and interred at the foot of Temple Hill, on the west end, at a place chosen by Father Morley himself. He told his son that it was a sacred place, "in proximity to the secret of the Lord." No other explanation was ever forthcoming.

There is independent confirmation of a secret or mystery connected with Temple Hill. In later years, when the Manti Temple was erected atop the hill, two of the stonemasons who worked on its construction were the twin brothers, Elisha and Elijah Averett. The latter was the same who complained against Morley over the construction of the Manti Council House.

Elijah Averett, Jr. was a close personal friend of my maternal great-grandfather, Gardner G. Potter. Elijah Jr. was killed by Indians in Southern Utah during the Black-hawk War, and buried in the desert by Gardner Potter (son of William W. Potter, who was also killed by Indians—and Danites—in the Gunnison Massacre of 1853, and buried near Isaac Morley at Manti).

Elijah Averett, Sr. (whose journals can be found at the Utah Historical Society and at the University of Utah) directed the construction of the Manti Temple. The granite blocks were quarried from a site several miles up Manti Canyon and carried to the construction site on sleds and wagons. According to Averett, the quarry had apparently been used anciently, and displayed all of the signs of having been used for extensive building projects.

Moreover, Averett recounts the story of excavating for the western foundation of the Manti Temple when the ground caved in. There was discovered what appeared to be an extensive cavern or tunnel system beneath the hill, but "reminded in times past of how these caves were filled with rattlesnakes, we filled in the depression with rubble, then built a stone floor, and above that a stone wall, to buttress the foundation."

Pete Neilson, who once rode with Butch Cassidy's Wild Bunch, in later years reformed his ways and wrote a history of his adventuresome life (unpub. Ms.). He became a Temple worker during the last years of his life, performing ordinances in the Manti Temple. Neilson claimed that the foundation stone which lay beneath the altar of the Temple had been excavated from a cavern which lay directly beneath, and contained ancient inscriptions which, to him, appeared to be Greek letters. He claimed that these inscriptions could still be seen by accessing the underside of the altar through the Temple basement.

Sophus E. Jensen, who claimed to have seen ancient inscriptions on Temple Hill before the Temple was constructed, saw identical inscriptions at the stone quarry in Manti Canyon. Adelia Cox Sidwell, a relative of Father Morley, recalled in her reminiscences that "as kids we used to play on the south side of Temple hill, up near the top where the big rock protruded with the strange old writing on it."

My second great-grandfather, William Washington Potter (1809-1853), was an Indian interpreter, guide and scout, explorer extraordinaire, and one of the first settlers of Manti; in fact, he had accompanied Parley P. Pratt and others to the Sanpete Valley on a scouting expedition even prior to settlement, and was guide and scout of the Morley company in November 1849. He operated the first sawmill in Sanpete Valley, located originally in upper Manti Canyon, and produced most of the lumber and shingles for the construction in Manti, as well as other communities throughout the region.

Potter hauled flat stones up the canyon from the old stone quarry (many years before it was used for construction of the Manti Temple) to make a solid floor for his sawmill. On one particular trip to the old quarry, Potter turned over a large stone that had been half-buried in the earth to discover that the underside had been sculpted with several figures. Later descriptions of these carvings indicate that they were of heads resembling those found on ancient Greek temples.

Potter brought the carved stone to the attention of his friend, Albert Carrington, who had some scientific background. After studying them and making sketches of them, Carrington gave the carved stone to Apostle Jedediah M. Grant, who was then Mayor of Salt Lake City (and a brother-a-law of William W. Potter), who in turn gave them to Brigham Young. Eventually the carved stone was turned over by Young to the University of Deseret (together with a "seer stone") and what became of the stone thereafter is not known. One story claims that the sculpted stone was ultimately used in the architecture of either the Manti or Salt Lake Temple.

Orson Pratt, a scientist of some renown, examined the sculpted stone and made an official report of his findings, probably at the instigation of Brigham Young. He concluded that the two main sculptures (there were several smaller ones on the same block) were "in every way identical to those found, as I discover from prints, on the cornices and columns of ancient Greek temples such as the great temple to Athena at the Acropolis...." Pratt believed that one of the figures was a representation of Zeus.

Whatever these sculptures were, they do not seem to have been of Aztec origin, and later tribes did not sculpt, certainly not for architectural purposes. The bulk of the evidence seems to indicate a Greek origin of the sculptures and at least some of the inscriptions found on or near Temple Hill. We will discuss and compare these inscriptions in a later chapter.

We were reminded of earlier allusions to the land of Colchis, visited by Jason and the Argonauts circa 1194 B.C., in search of the Golden Fleece. And we were reminded, too, that Jason was alleged to have erected a temple on a mount in that faraway land, where they made offerings to the gods and performed the secret ceremonies of Orpheus.

Isaac Morley

Chapter Eighteen

The Secret of Sanpete

We have laid the groundwork and established a basis for something significant being associated with—and possibly hidden—in Sanpete Valley, Utah. It now becomes necessary for us to postulate what comprises the secret of Sanpete, and to present the available evidence to support it.

We believe the Sanpete Valley and surrounding region comprises the land known anciently as the Land of Colchis, and that Carre-Shinob in the Uintah Mountains was the source of the legend of the Golden Fleece. We believe that Jason and the Argonauts constructed a temple on the very hill where now stands the Manti Temple, and therein introduced the Orphic Mysteries. We believe that the "Garden of the Hesperides," belonging to the daughters of Atlas, which bore golden fruit, was identical with the source of the "Golden Fleece." We believe that Madoc ap Owain Gwynedd, Prince of Wales, became King of the Aztecs circa 1170 A.D., and that he constructed, or had constructed, another temple on the hill at Manti. We believe that Madoc, who was Grand Master of the Cambrian Order of the Knights Templar, brought with him to the New World a sacred relic known as the Ark of the Covenant, and that this sacred relic once reposed within Madoc's temple and was afterwards hidden up in caverns beneath the temple mount (in semblance of Solomon's Temple), or nearby. We believe that Madoc engraved a history of ancient inhabitants of America on gold, brass and copper plates, and hid them up for future generations. We believe that some of these records came into possession of Madoc's descendant, Dr. John Dee, who translated them into a book he called "*The Secret Book of Madog.*" We believe that John Dee was connected to the Templar treasure of the Sinclair family, and that some or all of that treasure eventually found its way to the Sanpete region. We believe that Isaac Morley was connected to the same arcane society as John Dee, and was further connected to the Templar treasure of the Sinclairs. We believe that the Templars visited the Sanpete region during the 14th century and left evidence of their presence there. We believe that John Brewer discovered evidence of both the Templar visit and the remnants of Madoc's civilization. We believe that the Sanpete Valley yet contains holy relics and is considered by certain factions to be a sacred place, instrumental in fulfilling prophetic designs for projected world history.

On the surface these claims may seem extravagant and incredible, but a review of the sequential facts will give the readers an opportunity to derive their own conclusions.

From very ancient times there existed the legend of a fabulous source of gold in a remote corner of the world, the source of immense wealth among monarchs of the ancient world. This vastly rich source became associated with such figures as King Midas (of the "Golden Touch"), Hercules and the legendary "Garden of the Hesperides," and the legendary "Golden Bough" of the Greeks. But above all it has remained best known as the "Golden Fleece" of Jason and the Argonauts. In earlier chapters we presented Jason's story and reviewed the connections between the Golden Fleece and the Ark of the Covenant, as well as the construction of Solomon's Temple.

From the earliest times there existed a belief in an unknown "promised land" across the vast Atlantic Ocean. In ancient times it was known as "Ultima Thule," the "end of the earth." It had been colonized in remote times by adventuresome sailors, most of whom are long since forgotten.

As a result of the confounding of the language at the time of the Tower of Babel, the "...Lord scattered them from thence upon the face of all the earth." (Gen. 11:8) The Jewish historian Josephus states: "After this they were dispersed abroad, on account of their languages, and went out by colonies everywhere. ...There were some also who passed over the sea in ships and inhabited the islands." (*Antiquities of the Jews*, Bk. 1, Chap. 5)

In the Book of Mormon, Moroni abridged the record of "...the ancient inhabitants...of this (America) north country. ...Jared came forth with his brother and their families...from the great tower, at the time the Lord confounded the language of the people, and swore...that they should be scattered upon all the face of the earth." (Ether 1:1,33)

The greatest sailors, as we have noted, were the "Sea Peoples," the Greeks and Phoenicians. The Greeks, like the Irish, were descendants of Calcol or Cecrops, who was grandson of Judah (1 Chr. 1:3-6) His brother Darda married Bahia Asia, daughter of Teucer, King of Troy in 1480 B.C. and became Dardanus, King of Troy, in 1449 B.C.

In her article *"Echoes of the Heroic Age"* (*National Geographic*, Dec. 1999), Caroline Alexander has written that "The Mycenaens themselves were descendants of Greek speakers who appeared on the Greek mainland around 1900 B.C. They eventually consolidated their petty chiefdoms into societies that revolved around a central palace. Heinrich Schliemann's discovery of elaborate gold burial goods showed that as early as the 16th century B.C. the Mycenaean ruling class had amassed a treasure trove of disposable wealth. Guarding both sea and hinterland, Mycenae was strategically placed to control trade in this rich region." The Mycenaeans were they who, among other Greeks, attacked Troy in 1194 B.C., simultaneously with the voyage of the Argonauts. Thus we have shown that early Greeks sailed to remote climes and brought back great gold treasure.

Pre-Columbian voyages to the New World are frequently met with skepticism. Nevertheless, as far back as 800 B.C. Hanno was reputed to have sailed around the west coast of Africa and "thirty days westwards of the Pillars of Hercules," and Periplus, writing later, suggested that Hanno might have discovered a new land.

Pharaoh Necho II sent out Phoenician sailing expeditions circa 600 B.C., one of which was reputed to have reached the coast of South America, where they left inscriptions.

In 400 B.C. Plato recounted Hanno's story and added the account of "the lost world of Atlantis," referring to "an island in the mouth of the sea in the passage of those straits, called the Pillars of Hercules...larger than Libya and Asia, from which there was an easy passage over to other islands and from those islands to that continent which is out of that region. Poseidon settled in this island, from whose son Atlas its name was derived, and divided it among his ten sons."

Atlantis has been identified with sites including the vicinity of Bermuda and the Gulf of Mexico. Atlantis supposedly disappeared in the midst of massive cataclysmic events, including "floods and earthquakes" and possibly volcanic eruptions. John Dee believed that America was Atlantis and that Atlas was its ancient king. He believed that only a portion of the land sank beneath the sea—the coastline of Florida that once extended past the Bermuda Islands, which Dee called the "Bermoothes."

Aristotle mentioned the Carthaginians as having colonized a land "many days' journey from the Pillars of Hercules," and

Seneca wrote prophetically that "The time will come when the ocean will loosen the chains of nature and we shall behold a vast country; a new Typhis shall discover a New World: Thule shall no longer be considered the last country of the known world." Didorus Siculus in 100 B.C. recorded that the Phoenicians had discovered a "large, sweet, fertile island opposite to Africa."

In the sixth century A.D., Saint Brendan, an Irish monk, is said to have set sail on the Western Sea in "an osier boat covered with tanned hides and carefully greased, provisioned for seven years." The island (even continents were termed islands anciently) which Brendan discovered is identified only as "Saint Brendan's Isle," but it is generally conceded to have been the American continent.

It is ironic that Joseph Smith was born on a farm, between Sharon and Royalton townships in Vermont, which adjoined the McIntosh farm, which latter place has been identified with an ancient temple site believed to have been established between 300-600 A.D. by Irish priests—perhaps Saint Brendan himself.

It has also been shown that on an least five occasions between 983 A.D. and 1030 A.D. the Norsemen visited the New World, establishing several temporary colonies. The Vikings further frankly admitted that the Irish had been there before them.

The Chinese historian Li Yen recorded in 800 A.D. that the Chinese had made early voyages to "Kamchatka" and an area now identified as the northwest coast of America. In 1962 a Peking University professor named Chu Shien-chi claimed that he had discovered old records in Chinese archives that showed that five Chinese, led by a Buddhist monk, sailed from China to Mexico in 459 A.D. via the Kuriles and Aleutians.

Also in 1962 a Soviet geographer, Samuel Varshavsky, made the claim that America was discovered 130 years before Columbus by an English Carmelite friar, Nicholas of Lynne, who was known to be living in 1386.

Among the nations which have claimed the honor of being the first to discover America are Arabs, Basques, Catalans, Dutch, Phoenicians, Polynesians, French, Germans, Hindus, Chinese, Japanese, Portuguese, Romans, Turks, and Welsh. And the latter make their claim through Madoc ap Owain Gwynedd, who sailed to America in 1170 A.D., 322 years before Columbus.

We have also mentioned the Greek sailor-explorer Milesius, a descendant of Jason, and brother-in-law of King Solomon, who sailed to America with the Phoenicians and returned with enough gold to decorate Solomon's Temple and fill the vaults beneath with the greatest treasure ever known. It becomes clear that "King Solomon's Mines" were in America, and were connected with the "Golden Fleece." And through Madoc we can also make a connection to Carre-Shinob, in the Sanpete region, a gold source of immense proportions sufficient to rank as this legendary ancient trove.

In our book *The Gold of Carre-Shinob* we presented a complete account of this amazing source of gold and sacred treasure, and in our book *The Widow's Son* we gave a lengthy account of Madoc ap Owain Gwynedd and his "discovery" of America and kingship of the Aztecs. We also covered in detail the connections between Madoc and the Book of Mormon, and we refer the reader to these sources for much additional information.

The catalyst in all of these things was that mystical, enigmatic figure Dr. John Dee. We have mentioned previously that he was the reputed author of *The Chemical Wedding of Christian Rosencreutz* which brought Rosicrucianism to the forefront. As we have seen, he became Grand Master of the Order of the Rosy Cross (Rosicrucians). He was a descendant of Madoc and author of *The Secret Book of Madog*.

John Dee was born on Saturday 13 July 1527 to Rowland and Johanna Dee. His father was a gentleman sewer at the court of King Henry VIII. In addition to Madoc, Dee also claimed to be descended from Roderick the Great, Prince of Wales, as well as from King Arthur. At the age of fifteen he attended St. John's College, Cambridge, where according to his own account he studied eighteen hours a day. He became a Fellow of the newly founded Trinity College where he gained his lifelong reputation as a sorcerer after devising some special effects for a production of Aristophanes. In 1548, on his second trip to the Continent, he became a student at Louvain in the Low Countries. In Paris in 1550 he delivered a series of lectures on Euclid, before so many listeners "that the mathematical schools could not hold them; for many were fain, without the schools at the windows, to be auditors and spectators, as they best could help themselves thereto" (*Compendious Rehearsal*).

On returning to England he found favor with King Edward VI and was given an annual pension of a hundred crowns, which he exchanged for the living of Upton upon Severn in Worcestershire. He became rector of Long Leadenham, Lincolnshire, later the same year. On the accession of Queen Mary he was imprisoned on suspicion of trying to kill her "by enchantments." One of his cellmates, the Protestant Barthlet Green, was burnt at the stake in 1556, but Dee was pardoned and on Mary's death he found himself in favor with the new queen, Elizabeth.

His huge library, amounting to more than 2000 books and 200 manuscripts, many of them saved from the dissolution of the monasteries during the Reformation, made him one of the most learned men in the country and much revered for his knowledge. He wrote his most important books over the next two decades, including the *Propaedeumata Aphoristica* (observations on astrology and astronomy, 1558), the mystical *Monas Hieroglyphica* (1564),

his "Mathematical Preface" to Euclid's *Elements of Geometry* (1570), and his expert treatment of exploration for the benefit of Elizabeth's imperial ambitions, *General and Rare Memorials Pertaining to the Perfect Art of Navigation* (1577). He also became so involved in writing a tract on the reform of the calendar in 1582 that he neglected to renew the licences for his parsonages.

This sudden loss of income led him to seek the patronage of a succession of foreign princes from 1583 to 1589: Prince Albert Laski and King Stephen Bathory in Poland, and the Emperor Rudolph II and William of Rosenberg in Bohemia. On returning to England he found that his library had been looted by former friends who had helped themselves to many of his most treasured books and possessions. He spent the next few years trying to restore them while seeking paid employment.

His appointment as warden of Manchester College in 1595 ended his influence at court. He seldom returned thereafter. When he did return, in June 1604, it was to present a petition to King James I in an attempt to dispel his reputation as a sorcerer. He asked to be put on trial and executed if found guilty, but James dismissed the petition. The image of John Dee as a reclusive crystal-gazing magician endured ever after.

In point of fact, however, what was then considered magic was actually the search for a crucial link between science and religion. Dee was convinced of such a link and tested it to the limits, staking his entire reputation on it. He remained convinced of it, but his career marks the final break between science and religion in western thought.

Jane Dee (1555-1605), born Jane Fromonds at Cheam on 22 April 1555, was a lady-in-waiting to Queen Elizabeth and became John Dee's second or third wife in 1578. Dee described her as "testy and fretting." She was the mother of his children

Arthur (1579-1651), Katharin (b. 1581), Rowland (b.1582), Michael (1585-1594), Theodore (b.1588), Madimia (b.1590), Francys (b.1592), and Margaret (b.1595). Jane Dee died of the plague, which may also have killed Rowland, Madimia and Margaret, and was buried in the Collegiate Church of Manchester on 23 March 1605.

John Dee died in London on 26 February 1609, and was buried in the chancel of Mortlake Church. According to the chronicler Elias Ashmole, "When Doctor Dee lay sick of the sickness whereof he died, his maiden daughter Katherine conveyed away his books unknown to him [to sell them to buy food] about a fortnight before he died which when he came to understand it broke his heart."

In 1577, at the pinnacle of his extraordinary career, John Dee began his diaries. On the eve of his fiftieth birthday, he was one of the most renowned men in Europe in the fields of science, astrology and mathematics. He had managed to withstand his reputation as a sorcerer which had dogged him since his Cambridge days. He kept his diaries as part of his work as a scientist, entering details of his life in the margins of almanacs, next to the printed data on the planetary configurations for each day. He later explained to Queen Elizabeth that his aim was to discover "the heavenly influences and operations actual in this elemental portion of the world."

Dee kept personal diaries, chemical diaries, and spiritual (or spirit) diaries. The earliest surviving volume of John Dee's spirit diaries begins with this prayer:

"O Lord Jesus Christ, I most humbly beg your Divine Majesty to send me the timely help of some pious wise man and expert philosopher. And if no such mortal man is now living on earth, then I beg your Divine Majesty to consider it fitting to send me from heaven your good spiritual ministers and angels, namely Michael, Gabriel, Raphael and Uriel, and any other true and faithful angels of yours who may instruct me."

He explained that he had spent many years seeking wisdom in more conventional ways—in books and discussions with learned men—but "after all my foresaid endeavor I could find no other way to such true wisdom attaining, but by thy extraordinary gift." Dee wrote that he had started invoking the archangels Raphael and Michael in 1569, and praying for wisdom ten years later (*Dee's Mysteriorum Libri V*, Sloane MS 3188, British Library). He knew from the Old Testament that the patriarch Enoch had conversed with God, and Dee's greatest desire in life was to know all things and solve all mysteries, which he could only do if he could, like Enoch, converse directly with God. He had also read about "the Show-Stone [i.e. a Seer Stone], which the high priests did use, by thine own ordering: wherein they had lights and judgements in their great doubts." He longed for "a good seer, and skryer of spiritual apparitions, in crystalline receptacles," who could act as his medium and describe visions that he was unable to see for himself. Dee himself recorded only two instances in his spirit diaries when he saw anything in the crystal Show-Stone.

Dee went through a number of "seers" between 1569 to 1581 and quickly exposed them as charlatans. Then, in March 1582, Edward Kelly came to Dee's home at Mortlake. He introduced himself as Edward Talbot. For the next seven years, Kelly would be Dee's "skryer" and have a most profound influence on his life.

Although Edward Kelly (1555-1597?) dominates John Dee's diaries, almost nothing is known for certain about his life. He was Irish, born in Worcester, England, and may have trained as an apothecary. The antiquary Anthony Wood professed that Kelly had studied at Oxford and was assistant to the mystic and mathematician Thomas Allen, though there is no record of it. Legend persists that he had his ears cropped in 1580 for forging documents or money, and was involved in necromancy in a Lancashire churchyard.

Kelly possessed great magnetism, and while he made enemies easily, he also impressed some of the wealthiest, wisest and most powerful men of his day. Though Dee was distrustful of him at first, their partnership only ended in 1589 when Kelly found more lucrative employment as court alchemist to Count William of Rosenberg and the Emperor Rudolph II. Kelly helped to develop the abandoned gold mines of Jilové, south of Prague. According to the Czech writer Ivan Sviták he used magical transmutations with mercury to extract microscopic amounts of gold from waste material. He amassed a huge fortune and bought about twenty houses in Prague, including the so-called House of Dr. Faustus at the cattle market (Charles Square).

From 1591 to 1593 Edward Kelly was imprisoned at Krivoklát, west of Prague, not for any disfavor, but to prevent him from being kidnapped by Lord Burghley's agents. In 1594 he was in Peter of Rosenberg's army, fighting against the Turks, but shortly thereafter fell into debt. In 1596 he was imprisoned in the castle at Brüx, western Bohemia, after wounding an assistant of the alchemist Sebald Schwertzer. It is said that in an escape attempt in November 1597 he broke a leg and died of his wounds, but according to Ivan Sviták the master-illusionist in fact survived to join a group of foreign alchemists practicing in Russia. ["*John Dee and Edward Kelly*," I. Sviták, Kosmas—the *Journal of Czechoslovak and Central European Studies*, 5, 125-38, 1986.]

Through Edward Kelley and the "Show-Stone," Dee communicated with angels, among them (according to his diaries) Michael, Raphael, Gabriel, Uriel and others. They revealed to him many ancient signs and symbols and their meanings and significance. On 26 March 1583, Dee recorded in his diary the following vision:

26 Mar. Tuesday, hor. 10 ante meri-diem. First appeared a cloud, and that vanished away. Three [angels] came in, they made curtsy to the chair, and two went away. Then the third which remained lay down on the ground as before. There came like a lamb's head, and licked him....He showeth a book, as he did before, all gold. The leaves of the book are all lined, full of square places, and those square places have characters in them, some more than other, and they all written with colour, like blood, not yet dry. He pointed orderly to them with his finger, and looked toward the skryer [Kelly] at every pointing...He took from under the table a thing like a great globe, and set that in the chair, and upon that globe laid the book. He pointeth to the characters, and counteth them with his finger, being 21: and beginning from the right hand, toward the left. [*The Diaries of John Dee*, Edward Fenton, ed., Day Books, Oxfordshire, 1998, pp.55-56].

The 21 characters were these:

Dee's diaries contain a marvelous entry immediately following the appearance of the angel—Dee calls him "*Medicina Dei*"—with the golden book and the 21 characters; the entry had direct implications upon the subject of hidden treasure in the New World:

"△: [Dee's symbol for himself] Our desire is to know what we are to think of the man which came out of my oratory and laid the fiery ball at Mr Adrain Gilbert his feet yesterday, as he sat in my study with Mr Kelly and me. Whether it were any illusion, or the act of any seducer?

MEDICINA DEI: No wicked power shall enter into this place.

E.K.: The Stone has become very dark.

MEDICINA DEI: As the building is grounded and ended upon three, so must the mysteries hereof be practiced with three.

△: Must Adrian Gilbert be made privy of these mysteries?

MEDICINA DEI: Thou hast said. Behold, these things shall God bring to pass by his hands whose mind he hath now newly set on fire. The corners and straights of the earth shall be measured to the depth: and strange shall be the wonders that are creeping in to new worlds. Time shall be altered, with the difference of day and night. All things have grown almost to their fullness.

△: Then this Adrian Gilbert shall carry the name of Jesus among the Infidels to the great glory of God, and the recovery of those miserable people from the mouth of hell into which, for many hundred years past, and yet continually, they do fall. May he require description of the countries, for his better instruction?

MEDICINA DEI: I instructed thee beforehand, and told thee, that both of you must jointly learn those holy letters: to the intent that the finger may point to the head, and the head to the understanding of his charge, for discoveries making of the sea and their bounds.

△: You perceive that I have divers affairs which at this present do withdraw me from peculiar diligence using to these characters and their names learning by heart: and therefore, I trust, I shall not offend if I bestow all the convenient leisure that I shall get about the learning hereof.

MEDICINA DEI: Peace. Thou talkest as though thou understoodest not. We know thee, we see thee in thy heart. Nor one thing shall not let another. For short is the time that shall bring these things to proof: wherein he that liveth shall approve himself alive. Beautiful are the footsteps of his coming.

E.K. He holdeth his hands abroad. He draweth the curtain."

[*The Diaries of John Dee*, op.cit., pp.56-57.]

The message is quite clear. The "corners and straights" of the earth are latitudes and longitudes, and "measured to the depth" is a reference to the ocean. The "new worlds" are foreign lands, where time is "altered" by the "difference of day and night," i.e. different time zones. The "Infidels" to whom Adrian Gilbert will carry "the name of Jesus" (i.e. Christianity) are the American Indians, who live in countries where Gilbert must be informed as to the directions. Finally, Dee and Kelly are both instructed to learn the "holy letters"—i.e., the characters are the key to discoveries across the seas, in America. How can we know this? Adrian Gilbert is the key.

Adrian Gilbert (1545-1628) was a navigator and brother of Sir Humfrey and Sir John Gilbert. He gave his half-brother Sir Walter Raleigh £10 when Raleigh first went to court, and served as his agent for about thirty years. In the summer of 1583 he was given a grant "to discover and settle the northerly parts of Atlantis, called Novus Orbis, not inhabited or discovered by any Christians hitherto but by him. The said Adrian Gilbert, John Dee, and John Davis to be exempt from all customs, forever." (*Calendar of State Papers*, vol. 161, no.24.) Towards the end of his life he became alchemical assistant to Mary, Countess of Pembroke.

Adrian Gilbert's brother, Sir Humfrey Gilbert (1537-1583), was a renowned navigator and advocate of direct trade with Asia and the native Americans. He was among the first Englishmen to suggest that North America should be colonized, to "settle there such needy people of our country, which now trouble the common wealth, and through want here at home are enforced to commit outrageous offences, whereby they are daily consumed with the gallows." [see *The Voyages and Colonising Enterprises of Sir Humphrey Gilbert*, D.B. Quinn, London, 1940.] On his second voyage to the New World—which Dee helped to plan—he sailed near Nova Scotia. His flagship, the

Delight, was wrecked off Newfoundland, and on the return journey he was drowned when his own ship, the Squirrel, sank at sea.

The third brother, Sir John Gilbert (b.1536), was a naval administrator who subscribed to his brother Humfrey's expeditions, despite his constant concern that his brother's death might leave the whole family without an heir.

Sir Thomas Gerard (d.1601) was one of the leaders, with Sir George Peckham, of the English Catholic group of expansionists. In the early 1570s he had been involved in an attempt to free Mary Queen of Scots from captivity, was imprisoned for treason, and was released after paying a heavy fine. On 19 April 1582, an informer known only as "PH" wrote to Lord Burghley: "There is a muttering among the papists that Sir Humfray Gilbert goeth to seek a new found land, Sir George Peckham, and Sir Thomas Gerard goeth with him. I have heard it said among the papists, that they hope it will prove the best journey for England that was made these 40 years."

Also present on Sir Humfrey Gilbert's second and final voyage in 1583 was my ancestor, Francis Bryan II (1549-16—), son of Sir Francis Bryan I (1490-1550) and Lady Joan Fitzgerald. This is significant because Francis Bryan II also sailed with Sir Francis Drake, and his father, Sir Francis Bryan I, who was a courtier at the court of Henry VIII, had preceded John Dee as Grand Master of the Rosicrucians.

The Gilberts were also nearly related to this writer on another line. Their mother, my direct ancestor by virtue of her marriage to Sir Philip Champernoun, who was also a courtier to Henry VIII, had been married three times; one of these marriages produced her son, Sir Walter Raleigh, who later married a granddaughter of Elizabeth Bryan Carew, sister of Sir Francis Bryan I, Grand Master of the Rosicrucians.

Sir Walter Raleigh (1552-1618) was a courtier, navigator and writer. When Dee met him in 1583, the year his half-brother Sir Humfrey Gilbert died at sea, he was at the height of his favor with the Queen. In October 1595—after his first term of imprisonment in the Tower of London—he was back in favor, and had just returned from his voyage of exploration around Trinidad and up the Orinoco River (the route of Jason and the Argonauts) in search of El Dorado—supposedly the world's greatest source of gold, with which he hoped to ransom his life. Durham House in the Strand, London, where he entertained Dee, had belonged to Queen Elizabeth; she gifted Raleigh with it in about 1583. Raleigh was a member of Dee's Rosicrucian society, but he also operated a group of his own, which came to be known among his detractors as the "School of Atheism," and consisted of some of the greatest figures of the era: Christopher Marlowe, Sir Philip Sidney, Francis Bryan II, Richard Hakluyt, Sir Christopher Hatton, Sir Francis Bacon, William Shakespeare, Sir John Scudamore, and Edward de Vere the Earl of Oxford, and many others.

The influential acquaintances of John Dee seems endless. Some of them, as we shall see, are instrumental to our story.

—from a True and Faithful Revelation, etc. (London, 1659) Dr. John Dee

Chapter Nineteen

The Morley Connection

John Dee—seer, mystic, magician, astrologer, astronomer, scientist, mathematician, and promoter of the advancement of the English empire, was actively involved in the opening, exploration, and settlement of the New World. In this enterprise he had many accomplices.

John Davis (ca. 1552-1605) was a navigator, one of many who were to ally themselves to the charismatic Dee. His exact date of birth is not known, but in 1568 Dee and an assistant ("W.EM"—probably Wm. Emery, Sr.) "Elicited by magic" the date of 3 May 1552. Davis was himself a mystic, and a skryer of none other than Humfrey Gilbert.

Davis made three voyages to discover a northwest passage to the Orient, and established that Greenland is separate from America. A voyage to the South Seas in 1591-3 ended in failure when his colleague Thomas Candish claimed that Davis had fatally deserted him. Davis provisioned his ship with 14,000 dried penguins and returned to England to find that his wife Faith had taken a lover, a forger named Milburne (whom Sir Walter Raleigh described as "a fugitive and dissolute person"), who tried to discredit Davis to protect himself from his revenge. Although historians such as Geoffrey Elton and Christopher Morris have stated that his reputation remained untainted, he appears to have been one of the principal despoilers of John Dee's vast library; almost every page of Dee's meticulous library catalogue contains the notation: "Jo. Davis spoyle" against one or more books. On his final voyage, to the East Indies, he was hacked to death by Japanese pirates.

Thomas Heriot [Harriot] (1560-1621) was mathematician, astronomer, and tutor to Sir Walter Raleigh. He was a member of Raleigh's "School of Atheism," which was connected to Dee's Rosicrucian order. Heriot traveled to Virginia as surveyor on Sir Richard Grenville's expedition of 1585-6. He impressed the native Americans with various instruments, including a "perspective glass whereby was showed many strange sights." He returned with some of the first potatoes to be brought to England. John Davis, whom we have mentioned, said that "for theoretical speculations and most cunning calculation," Heriot was matched only by Dee. Heriot, like Dee, was also renowned as a magus, and served as an alchemist for Raleigh and the "Wizard Earl" of Northumberland in the Tower of London in the early years of the reign of James I.

Sir John Hawkins was an early Elizabethan explorer, whose subscription for his voyage to Mexico was raised by John Dee and Sir Lionel Duckett, both of whom also backed the expedition of Martin Frobisher. Both Hawkins and Frobisher returned with so much gold they were investigated by David Lewis, Judge of the Admiralty court, on suspicion of being pirates. The gold was finally determined (by Dee) to be iron pyrites—"fool's gold"—but the whole affair seems highly suspicious. Especially since Dee had supplied Davis with copies of the Zeno-Sinclair maps! According to Steven Sora, "Dr. Dee's collection also included the charts and maps of the Zeno-Sinclair expedition; the explorer Sir Martin Frobisher had obtained these from Dee." [*The Lost Treasure of the Knights Templar*, Sora, op.cit., p.231.]

Frobisher carried the Zeno-Sinclair

maps in his 1576 expedition in search for a route to Cathay; he mistook the eastern coast of Greenland for "Friseland"—the ancient name of America. He returned home with iron pyrites for gold and a kidnapped Inuit native who later died from pneumonia; unless the story of his "mistake" was a cover for his true discoveries.

Friseland has also been described as "an imaginary island in the North Atlantic." As late as the nineteenth century its identity was still being debated by serious geographers like Alexander von Humboldt [*Mapmakers of the Sixteenth Century and Their Maps*, R.W. Karrow, Chicago, 1993]. Dee's theory that Friseland had been conquered by King Arthur formed the basis for his claims for Queen Elizabeth's titles to lands across the Atlantic Ocean [see *John Dee's Natural Philosophy*, N.H. Clulee, p.182].

Estotiland was the name most frequently associated with America. Mercator's world map of 1569 (and Mercator was Dee's close friend) shows Estotiland as a part of the North American mainland, while in Ortelius' Theatrum Orbis Terrarum it appears as an island between Greenland and Canada. The Italian geographer Niccolo Zeno claimed that his forbears had discovered it in the late fourteenth century, and found it a place of woods, grain crops and primitive inhabitants. In John Dee's diaries we find the following entries:

[1577]

"Nov. I declared to the Q. [Queen] her title to Greenland &.c., Estotiland, Friseland."

"6 Nov. Sir Humfrey Gilbert came to me at Mortlake.

[1578]

"30 June. I told Mr. Daniel Rogers (Mr. Hackluyt of the Middle Temple being by) that King Arthur, and King Malgo both of them, did conquer Gelandium, lately called

Friseland. Which he so noted presently in his written copy of Monumethensis: for he had no printed book thereof..." [*The Diaries of John Dee*, Fenton. Ed., op.cit., pp.2-3]

Sir John Hawkins, on his expedition to Mexico, sought evidences of Madoc, and reported to Dee and others on his return that he had been informed by Mexican chieftains with whom he traded that they believed they were descended from "ancient Brytons." Incidentally, Sir John Hawkins' nephew, William Hawkins (d. 1613), served with Sir Francis Drake in his voyage of circumnavigation of 1577-80, and is believed to have furnished Dee with an account of the voyage on his return (*Lansdowne MS*, British Buseum, No. 122, ff.22-28).

David Tobias, the current owner of most of Oak Island and the moving force behind its excavation, believes that Sir Francis Drake had the pit constructed to hide part of his privateering treasure.

Drake began capturing small ships in American waters while quite young. In 1572 he joined forces with William LeTestu, a French pirate who was later captured and hung for his participation with Drake. In 1576 Drake had a private meeting with Queen Elizabeth to present his plans to sail into the Pacific to discover lands to claim in her name. Drake was inspired by John Dee's book *General and Rare Memorials Pertaining to the Perfect Art of Navigation* (1577), and Dee became a patron of the voyage, together with Francis Walsingham, the Earl of Leicester, Christopher Hatton and Edward Dyer, all mentioned in Dee's diaries that year.

The Madoc cult was also heavily interwoven into the circle of Dee's acquaintances. We noted previously that among the early exponents of the Madoc legend were Dr. David Powel and Humphrey Llwyd, both Welsh writers of great renown. Dr. Powel's version of the *Historie of Cambria* was mainly based on the chronicles of *Caradoc of Llancarfan*, which covered a period of Welsh history up to the end of the first half of the twelfth century, to the death of Caradoc in 1156. Powel frankly admitted that his revised version of the *Historie* was "augmented and continued out of records and best approved authors." One of these authors was Humphrey Llwyd, of Denbigh, who assisted his friend Powel with his *Historie*, in addition to providing his translation of Caradoc. Inasmuch as Llywd did not continue his translation of Caradoc after 1559, so far as is known, Powel had to turn to other sources for the latter part of his book and, as Richard Deacon adds, "supplementing and presumably checking his information with his friend, Sir Philip Sydney, Sir Humphrey Gilbert and other Elizabethan explorers."

The mention of Sydney and Gilbert in association with Powel and Llwyd gave us an immediate connection to the esoteric and arcane society, the "atheistic school" headed by Sir Walter Raleigh. Sir Humphrey Gilbert, who was Raleigh's half-brother, had established an English colony in the New World at Newfoundland, and died at sea, and we had already seen that Raleigh championed the Madoc theory in his own writings. Sir Philip Sydney was a known esotericist, the author of the masterful *Arcadia*, and a close friend of John Dee. Moreover, both Sydney and Dr. Dee had hosted the appearance of Giordano Bruno and Louis de Nevers (Grand Master of the Prieuré de Sion) at Oxford. And when Dr. David Powel, D.D. at Oxford, published his *Historie of Cambria* in 1584, he dedicated it to his friend, Sir Philip Sydney.

Suddenly the door to discovery of significant connections was opened to our inspection. The first published work in Tudor times to affirm the discovery of America by Madoc was a pamphlet entitled *A True Reporte*, written by Sir George Peckham (d. 1608: "The chief adventurer and furtherer of Sir Humfrey Gilbert's voyage to Newfound Land," according to

Hakluyt) and dedicated to Sir Francis Walsingham, and published in 1583, a year prior to Powel's *Historie*. Sir George Peckham and Sir Thomas Gerard, who had accompanied Sir Humphrey Gilbert, were keen to establish their own titles in the New World. In return for maps and propaganda, Dee was offered a total of 10,000 acres of the newly discovered territories, including huge areas of what is now New England and New York, and included Westford, Massachusetts, where was buried Sir James Gunn. [*John Dee's Natural Philosophy*, Clulee, op.cit., pp.187-8.]

Sir Francis Walsingham (ca.1530-1590) was a keen advocate of colonial expansion and naval exploration, and frequently consulted Dee about navigation matters. From 1573 he was chief secretary of state and Queen Elizabeth's head of a secret service for which Sir Walter Raleigh and Christopher Marlowe, among others, had been engaged as spies. Dee, too, was one of Walsingham's spies, and incredibly his code name was "007"!

The pamphlet by Peckham set out "to prove Queen Elizabeth's lawful title to the New Worlde, based on not onlie upon Sir Humfrey Gilbert's discoveries, but also those of Madoc." It referred to David Ingram, of Barking, who had sailed with Sir John Hawkins, as one source of its information, and more importantly, to "an ancient Welsh chronicle" as the other. It soon became apparent that the latter source was Dee's manuscript called *The Secret Book of Madog*. Incidentally, Ingram confirmed the account, claiming to be the first of many travelers to hear Welsh words spoken by Indians in America.

Humphrey Llwyd (1527-68) was, in addition to being a widely read writer, something of an authority on cartography, his *Cambriac Typus* being one of the earliest known maps of Wales.

He was a Member of Parliament, first for East Grinstead and then for Denbigh Boroughs, and he carried on a lengthy correspondence with Ortelius who, in his *Theatrum Orbis Terrarum*, described Llwyd as "a noble and erudite man." And we were not surprised to discover that, according to Richard Deacon, "Humphrey Llwyd was also a friend of that strange, learned alchemist-scientist, John Dee, who made a hobby of collecting evidence of ancient voyages of exploration...."

Richard Hakluyt was familiar to us from his connections with Raleigh, Marlowe and, of course, John Dee. Hakluyt gave by far the most substantial arguments and evidence in support of the Madoc story to emerge from Tudor and Elizabethan times. He was at Christ Church, Oxford, when Louis de Nevers, Grand Master of the Prieuré de Sion, met with John Dee and Sir Philip Sydney and others, and from that time forward his interest in Madoc and American explorations blossomed.

Hakluyt himself, as far as is known, never ventured farther than Paris. After leaving Oxford he spent much of his time in country vicarages before becoming Archdeacon of Westminister. He described himself as "a dedicated person" in becoming the historian of "great traffiques and discoveries" of his countrymen over a period of 1,500 years. A man of great integrity, a geographer as well as an historian, he was indisputably the greatest expounder of overseas explorations. His great efforts produced his great work *Principall Navigations*. An astute researcher, Hakluyt took on the "burden and huge toil" of bringing up to date the discoveries by consulting every work available, as well as old and long forgotten manuscripts. He examined ancient Welsh bardic odes, quoting some stanzas from Meredudd ap Rhys. He found supporting evidence from foreign sources, from the Spanish Chronicles and Cortes to Dutch records. Hakluyt became a firm advocate of Madoc's voyage, writing that "I am of the opinion that the land whereabouts he came was some part of the West Indies." Again, it was of no great surprise to discover that Richard Hakluyt

was a close friend and associate of Dr. John Dee, and mentioned frequently in his diaries.

Dee was undoubtedly the strongest Tudor-Elizabethan protagonist of the Madoc claim to the discovery of America, and claimed to possess manuscripts written by Madoc himself, and some of his descendants, which proved the claim, which Dee vowed was being compiled from ancient sources into a book.

"But Dee had a passion for secrecy," Deacon tells us, "and kept a great deal of his knowledge to himself, committed only to his '*Secret Book*,' which he is said to have showed to Queen Elizabeth when she visited his library at Mortlake. But, alas, a mob, inflamed by stories of his black magic and incited by his enemies, broke into his house and looted many of his books and manuscripts."

But Dee's book, which he titled *The Secret Book of Madog*, survived the purge. Because of his extreme secrecy, few ever actually saw the book. Hakluyt, who consulted him frequently and cited him as a source of information on more than one occasion, claimed that Dee had shown him "onlie that fyrst parte which pertaineth to [Madoc's] navigations and not else that he [Dee] had wryteen."

We had, therefore, established Dr. John Dee's interest and involvement in the Madoc story, and we had been able to confirm that he compiled a record which he called *The Secret Book of Madog*, translated from gold plates ostensibly kept by Madoc himself. We had discovered that Dee was one of the "invisible superiors" of the Rosicrucian establishment, and was the reputed author of the Rosicrucian Manifestos which began to circulate shortly after his death. He was the probable author of *The Chemical Wedding of Christian Rosenkreutz*, which contained elements of the Grail romances and the Knights Templar, and which was promulgated, after his death, by Johann Valentin Andrea

(1586-1654); and Andrea, as we had seen, established the Christian Unions, each headed by an anonymous prince and assisted by a "council of twelve." And, through Andrea, Dee had ties to the "Invisible College" which became the Royal Society. Andrea had also been Grand Master of the Prieuré de Sion, succeeding Robert Fludd, and Fludd (a translator of the King James Bible) became John Dee's successor as England's "leading exponent of esoteric thought." Fludd's father was treasurer of Queen Elizabeth I and served in her court along with Sir Francis Bacon. At that time England was sending aid to France, whose finance minister was Louis de Nevers. Fludd, de Nevers, and Andrea were all Grand Masters of the Prieuré de Sion.

In England, Bacon and his circle were pressing Elizabeth for their own "New Atlantis" agenda. Dr. John Dee, another in the circle of the Invisible College, had the ear of Queen Elizabeth. It came as no surprise to discover that all of the men associated with Dee in the enterprise of establishing the Madoc legacy—Christopher Llwyd, Dr. David Powel, Richard Hakluyt, Sir Walter Raleigh, et.al.—were also associated in a mutual arcane society dedicated to the establishment of a government or monarchy in the New World. They called themselves the Dragons.

In 1823, three years before his death, John Adams, the second president of the United States, had a flat stone inscribed and put on the grave of his great-great-grandfather who had immigrated to America in 1639. The inscription reads: "In memory of Henry Adams who took his flight from the Dragon persecution in Devonshire in England and alighted with eight sons near Mount Wollaston." ["*Bend Me a Maze*," Patricia Villiers-Stuart, quoted in Anthony Roberts (ed.): Glastonbury, Ancient Avalon, New Jerusalem, Rider, London, 1978 & 1992, p.166.] It should be noted that Charles Adams, son of President John Adams, was a close personal friend of

Joseph Smith, founder of Mormonism. Henrietta Bernstein, in her book *Ark of the Covenant, Holy Grail: Message For The New Millennium* (DeVorss & Co., Marina del Ray, 1998, pp.147-48), capsulizes the Dragon story as follows:

...the Dragons were a group of people who looked forward to a more harmonious way of life which they wanted to establish in America. They derived their name from the Druids, who were also called "Dragons"—those who knew how to control the key lines, often called the "Dragon lines" of the geodetic earth currents.

At the beginning of the seventeenth century, many famous names were associated with the Dragons, including Thomas Hariot, the mathematician; his pupil Sir Walter Raleigh, who wrote *History of the World*; Dr. John Dee; Christopher Marlowe; and others. These men belonged to Francis Bacon's group of Rosicrucians. While some Dragons lingered on in Devonshire and remained a persecuted minority, others emigrated to the new colonies which would eventually become the United States.

There are, however, even more outstanding connections which strongly supports our hypothesis that this arcane society established itself in the United States under the auspices of Joseph Smith, and that the key figure in that society was Isaac Morley. If this were indeed the case, one would expect a connection to John Dee, and that is precisely what we find, with both Isaac Morley and Joseph Smith.

But the connections go far beyond that: ancestors of both Joseph Smith and Isaac Morley were personal acquaintances of John Dee, and were members of the so-called Dragon society of the Rosicrucian order!

Joseph Smith's third great-grandfather, Robert Smith, was born in Lincolnshire, England, and emigrated to Boston, in America, in 1638. He was closely related, by marriage, to Sir Isaac Newton, who succeeded Robert Boyle as Grand Master of the Prieuré de Sion; Boyle, a member of the Invisible College, had succeeded Andrea.

Newton had written of the significance of the dimensions of Solomon's Temple. He believed that a select few had possessed the Philosophers' Stone throughout history, and this group included Solomon, Moses, Plato, Hermes, and Jesus. Newton believed in God but followed the Arian doctrine that Jesus was not equal to God the Creator. When Newton died, most of his writings were scattered and lost. The English economist John Maynard Keynes came across Newton's papers in 1936 at an auction. After studying them in great detail, he concluded that Newton was the "last of the magicians."

Newton and Boyle associated closely with the mystical philosopher John Locke. Locke was connected to the Guise family, a Templar stronghold, and became a student of the mysterious history of Rennes-le-Château, long before Saunière's nineteenth century discovery. Locke was also involved in forming a constitution for the Carolinas in America, a hundred years before the version by Jefferson (and Jefferson was a successive Grand Master of Dee's Rosicrucian order). Moreover, Joseph Smith's direct ancestor, Thomas Locke (Lok), was of the same family, and all were closely associated with Dee.

Benjamin Lok was an alchemist who studied at Dee's house at Mortlake between 1580 and 1582. His alchemical treatise *A Picklock to Riply his Castle* was copied by Dee's son Arthur at some time after 1602. Benjamin, Zacharie, and Thomas (Joseph Smith's ancestor) were among the fifteen children of Michael Lok (1532?-1615?), who was one of the principal investors in the ill-fated voyages of Martin Frobisher in the mid-1570s, and became governor of the newly formed Cathay Company in March 1577.

Robert Smith, the Prophet's immigrant ancestor, married Mary French, daughter of Thomas French, Jr., and Mary Scud-amore. Thomas French, Sr., was an alchemist and mystic, one of the circle comprising the Dragons, and an intimate associate of Dr. Dee. Originally from Scotland, he had been associated with the Sinclairs of Rosslyn, and Thomas French, Jr., had been associated with Isaac Newton; Newton claimed direct descent from the Sinclairs. Thomas French, Jr., was a member of the mystical Boston Philosophical Society, and instrumental in establishing the Masonic roots of government in America.

Mary Scudamore was the daughter of William Scudamore and Frances Lechmere. Her grandfather, John Scudamore (ca. 1542-1623), was Gentleman Usher to Queen Elizabeth, patron of the noted mathematician Thomas Allen, and benefactor of the Bodleian Library. In his will he expressed the hope that he would be received "into the company of the heavenly angels and blessed saints." His second wife Mary was one of Dee's most loyal friends at court, and with Blanche Pary had tried to obtain for him the mastership of the Hospital of St. Cross at Winchester. Dee noted in his diary for 7 June 1580: "Mr Skydmor and his wife lay at my house and Mr Skydmor's daughter, and the Queen's dwarf Mrs Tomasin. 8 June, My wife went with Mistress Skydmor to the Court, &c." Queen Elizabeth described her dwarf, Mrs. Tomasin, as "our dearly beloved woman," who was allowed to appear at court wearing the Queen's old clothes.

Rosicrucians during the latter part of the nineteenth century maintain that Joseph Smith's ancestor, Robert Smith, was near relation—probably a nephew—of Hugh Smith, Arctic explorer who sailed with Arthur Pitt and Charles Jackman in 1580; his accounts of his travels are included in Hakluyt's *Principle Voyages of the English Nation*. Dee mentions him in his diary under 23 March 1581: "At Mortlake came to me Hugh Smyth, who had returned from Magellan Straits, and Vaygatz, after that &c." John Dee's copy of a rudimentary map and instructions of Vaygatz and a northwest passage for Pitt, Jackman and Smith still survives (British Library, Cotton Otho MS E VIII, ff.77-9).

There is also an indication that Dee, like Joseph Smith, practiced a form of polygamy. Dee called it "cross-matching," or more correctly the "new and strange doctrine" of marital cross-matching.

It began on 4 April 1587 when a voice spoke out of the Show-Stone to Edward Kelly, saying to him: "As unto thee, barrenness dwelleth with thee, because thou didst neglect me, and take a wife unto thyself contrary unto my commandment. Therefore thou shalt have the womb which thou hast barren and fruitless unto thee, because thou hast transgressed that which I commanded thee."

On April 18th the spirit called "Madimi" appeared to them and commanded that they should share their wives; Dee questioned whether this was not an unlawful thing, and there came a writing within a half-moon in the Stone which read: "Nothing is unlawful which is lawful unto God." Kelly, however, was reticent. Dee wrote: "...Upon Mr Kelly his great doubt bred unto me of Madimi her words yesterday spoken to him, that we two had our two wives in such sort as we might use them in common, it was agreed by us to move the question whether the sense were of carnal use (contrary to the law of the commandment) or of spiritual love and charitable care and unity of minds, for the service of God advancing." When told that it was both, Dee lamented: "The one is expressly against the commandment of God; neither can I by any means consent to like of that doctrine. And for my help in that verity, I do call down the power of the Almighty God, the creator of heaven and earth, and all the good angels. Assist me, O Christ. Assist me, O Jesu. Assist me, O Holy Spirit."

Eventually, Dee accepted the doctrine, though he declared it to be "strange to the women." It is mentioned here only briefly in context with Isaac Morley's later acceptance of the practice of plural marriage.

———

If Joseph Smith's ancestry was integrally connected to John Dee, then Isaac Morley's ancestors were even more so. Most notable was Christopher Marlowe, the poet, whose line "come live with me and be my love" became a standard for generations of poets to follow. Marlowe chose the more archaic spelling of the name Morley, though his father used the latter name. Marlowe was a member of Dee's Rosicrucian order, as well as the Dragon society.

The Morley family was very ancient and very prominent in England. In fact, the ancient name was Möre, and the family originated in Norway of nobility, and were cousins of both the Gunns and Sinclairs. In England, the family became "Keepers of the King's Forest," and at that time were given the title "Möre-leigh," or "Möre of the King's Forest." Inasmuch as the keeper of the forest included the duties of keeping the King's parks, the Morleys also took the surname "Parker." It was their duty to keep the forests and parks stocked with deer and other wild game for the pleasure of the King's hunting.

Though the Morleys and Parkers were the same family, the name was used interchangeably. In time, Morley also became a title, and the Parkers became the Lords of Morley. They became prominent and powerful, holding several lordships through careful marriages, and in addition became hereditary Archbishops of Canterbury.

Among the acquaintances of John Dee was Edward Parker, tenth Baron Morley (1555-1618), a former recusant who spent some time abroad before succeeding to the barony in 1577. He renounced his hereditary right to the office of Lord Marshal of Ireland, in return for the right to print a book about how to instruct children in the oath of allegiance. His son William (1575-

1622) became fourth baron Mountegle (or Monteagle) through his mother Elizabeth Stanley (the Stanleys, hereditary Earls of Derby and Monteagle, are ancestors of Lisa Lee Boren) as well as eleventh Lord Morley. In 1605, Lord William was the recipient of the mysterious letter betraying the Gunpowder Plot (a plot to assassinate Queen Elizabeth). Of this same family was Matthew Parker, Archbishop of Canterbury, a patron of Richard Lyne, one of the leading English painters and engravers of his day, who painted the mystical characters on Dee's "magic table." [see *The Diaries of John Dee*, op.cit., p.75 (28 April 1583); p.335.]

Dee mentions the Morleys frequently in his writings. For example, in his diary under date of 1582, Dee recorded: "9 June. I writ to the Archbishop of Canterbury: a letter in Latin. Mr Dr Awbrey [Dr. John Aubrey] did carry it. ...13 July. Mr Talbot came about 3 of the clock after noon, with whom I had some words of book dealing: who parted in friendly terms. He said that the L. Morley had the L. Monteagle his books...."

Three days later, Dee made the following notation: "16 July. ...came Sir George Peckham to me, to know the title for Norombega: in respect of Spain and Portugal parting the whole world's discoveries. He promised me of his gift out of his patent 5000 acres of the new conquest, and thought to get so much of Mr Gerard's gift, to be sent me with seal, within a few days."

The name "Norombega" comes from an Abnaki Indian word meaning quiet waters between two rapids, and refers roughly to the New York-New England area, from which Dee was promised 10,000 acres (in the vicinity of Westford, Massachusetts) in return for providing maps and other information. Did the "Morley books" have something to do with this?

Isaac Morley married his cousin, Lucy Gunn, a direct descendant of Sir James Gunn, the Westford Knight. But she was also a direct descendant of Sir Francis Russell, second Earl of Bedford (1527-1585) [see Appendix - Genealogy], one of John Dee's closest friends and associates.

Sir Francis Russell was born at Chenies, Buckinghamshire, the same year as Dee, and was a son of Sir John Russell and Anne Sapcote; he died 28 July 1585 at Bedford House, Strand, Middlesex. He married Margaret Saint John (1533-1562), who died at Woburn Abbey, Bedfordshire, an estate inherited by Sir John Russell, the first Earl, from Sir Francis Bryan, who was succeeded as Grand Master of the Rosicrucians by John Dee, upon Bryan's death in 1550.

Sir Francis Russell was a politician and diplomat. He was also Sir Francis Drake's godfather, and visited Dee in 1577 in connection with Drake's voyage of circumnavigation that began later the same year. Dee wrote in his diary for the year 1583:

"15 June. The Lord Albert Laski [1536-1605; Count Palatine of Siradia, Polish landowner and patron of the alchemical, occult and Paracelsian sciences] came to Mortlake to me. About 5 of the clock came the Polonian Prince Lord Albert Laski down from Bisham [in Berkshire, home of Lord and Lady Russell], where he had lodged the night before, being returned from Oxford whither he had gone of purpose to see the universities [and to meet with cosmologist Giordano Bruno who was lecturing there on the immortality of souls "and on the quintuple sphere"], where he was very honourably used and entertained. He had in his company the Lord Russell, Sir Philip Sydney and other gentlemen: he was rowed by the Queen's men, he had the barge covered with the Queen's cloth, the Queen's trumpeters, &c. He came of purpose to do me honour, for which God be praised."

Sir Francis Russell and Margaret Saint John were the parents of ten children. Lucy Gunn Morley descended through Francis Russell, Jr. (1555-ca. 1603) who married Anne Forrester.

Elizabeth Russell (1555-1604) married

in 1582 to William Bourchier, of the family of Sir Francis Bryan.

Margaret Russell (1560-1616) married in 1577 to George Clifford, the Earl of Cumberland. Dee notes her in his diaries in 1593: "25 Oct. Mr Gray, the Lady Cumberland's preacher, his wrangling and denying and despising alchemical philosophers. ...26 Nov. John, sometimes Mr Colman's servant, came to me from the Lady Countess of Cumberland, &c. 3 Dec. The Lord Willoughby, his bountiful promise to me. The Countess of Kent, his sister, and the Countess of Cumberland visited me in the afternoon...." On 27 August 1595, Dee mentions the baptism of his daughter Margaret Dee, and notes that her godmothers were the Countess of Cumberland and the Countess of Essex. She designed the memorial in Hornsey church to Richard Candish (Cavendish), politician, diplomat and translator of Euclid into English; he was a close associate of Dee and died about 1601. Margaret Russell, Countess of Cumberland, spent much of her later life fighting for her daughter Anne's right to succeed to the family estates. The poet Edmund Spenser (a member, with his friend Raleigh, of the Dragons) dedicated his "Four Hymns" (in praise of love and beauty) to her and her sister, the Countess of Warwick.

Anne Russell (1548-1604) remained one of Dee's most loyal friends at court. Queen Elizabeth was present at her wedding in 1565 to Amrose Dudley, Earl of Warwick. She was an investor in Frobisher's second voyage. According to her niece, Lady Anne Clifford, "she was more beloved and in greater favor with the said Queen than any other lady or woman in the kingdom." She is mentioned frequently in Dee's diaries, especially in behalf of her intercessions with the Queen in his behalf. Examples in 1594 and 1595, respectively: "3 May. Between 6 and 7 after noon the Queen sent for me to her in the privy garden at Greenwich, when I delivered in writing the heavenly admonition;

and her Matie took it thankfully. Only the Lady Warwick and Sir Robert Cecil his Lady were in the garden with her Matie. ...31 July. The Countess of Warwick did this evening thank her Matie in my name, and for me for her gift of the Wardenship of Manchester...."

John Russell (1553-1584) was a member of parliament, serving on a committee concerned with ports, and when he died in July 1584 he was buried with honors in Westminister Abbey. He married, on 23 December 1574, Elizabeth Cook (1523-1609), relict of Sir Thomas Hoby, who was twenty-five years her senior. Lady Russell became renowned as one of the most learned women in England, together with her sisters Ann (mother of Sir Francis Bacon) and Mildred (who married Lord Burghley). She devoted her gifts primarily to organizing grandiose funerals and writing memorial inscriptions in Latin, Greek and English. Her nephew, Roger Cook (b. 1552), was Dee's alchemical assistant from 1567 to 1581. He returned to Dee's service briefly in 1600, but by 1606 was working for the "Wizard Earl" of Northumberland, and was later employed as an alchemical assistant at the court of Rudolph II until the Emperor's death in 1612. (Rudolph II was invested with the Order of the Golden Fleece, one of the most illustrious chivalric orders in Europe. Dee mentions it in his diary under date of 8 October 1584.)

Perhaps this is an appropriate place to mention John Dee's bid for the mastership of the Hospital of St Cross at Winchester. He utilized the influence of both the Countess of Warwick and Lady Scudamore to secure it. Dee's diaries recount these as follows:

"9 Nov. [1592] Her Matie's grant of my supplication for Commissioners to come to me. The Lady Warwick obtained it."

"28 Oct. The letter to the Lady Skydmar. Hora 6 _ a meridie. I writ and sent a letter to the Lady Skydmor in my wife's name, to move her Majesty that either I might declare my case to the body of the council, or else under the Great Seal to have licence to go freely any whither &c."

Dee envisioned setting up a private research institute, from where he could "enjoy the commodious sending over into divers places beyond the seas for things and men very necessary: and for to have the more commodious place for the secret arrival of special men to come unto me there." [Compendious Rehearsal, Dee.] It is clear that the Gunn and Morley families, not to mention those of Joseph Smith, were an integral part of Dee's secret plans "beyond the seas."

Francis Bacon, Baron Verulam, Viscount of St. Albans

Chapter Twenty

Arca Testamenta

Manly P. Hall, a renowned authority on philosophy, comparative religion, and the esoteric doctrines of antiquity, in his book, *America's Assignment with Destiny* [Philosophical Research Society, Los Angeles, 1931, pp.49-50], makes the following profound statement: "The explorers who opened the New World operated from a master plan and were agents of rediscovery rather than discoveries." He proclaims Columbus to have been an Initiate and part of the Great Plan.

"Prevailing historical accounts which deal with the discovery and colonization of the Western Hemisphere must some day be completely revised. ...Time will reveal that the continent now known as America was actually discovered and, to a considerable degree, explored more than a thousand years before the Christian Era. The true story is in the keeping of the Mystery Schools, and passed from them to the Secret Societies of the medieval world. The Esoteric Orders of Europe, Asia and the New East were in at least irregular communication with the priesthoods of the more advanced Amerindian nations."

Grace A. Fendler, in her well-researched book, *New Truths about Columbus* [Los Angeles, 1934], also shows Columbus as an agent of rediscovery: "There is strong evidence that Columbus' own authentic discovery of America took place at some time previous to his voyage under the Spanish flag. In the famous Capitulations, or the Contracts between Columbus and the Spanish Sovereigns, Columbus undertakes to annex to the Crown certain Islands and Lands declaring he has already discovered them. The second Papal Bull of 1493 takes official cognizance of Islands and conti-nental lands found and to be found."

In *Ark of the Covenant, Holy Grail* [De Vorss & Co., Marina del Rey, CA, 1998], Henrietta Bernstein states: "The 'Invisible Society' is a secret fraternity, an Invisible Government of the world whose members are dedicated to the service of a mysterious inner plan, to bring society to a higher consciousness. ...In each generation only a few are accepted into the inner sanctuary as invisible Adepts of the work. There is little doubt that their sainted names will be remembered in the future, together with the prophets of the ancient world. They are represented by great individuals such as Cervantes, Cagliostro, St. Germain, Andreae, Bacon, More, Raleigh, Washington and Franklin."

Having established this much, we now enter the realm of revealing a secret; a secret kept for centuries by the Templars, and before them the Cabalists of the ancient Mystery Schools. The Templars revered the Ark of the Covenant as the most sacred relic in world history, and to them it was Arca Testamenta—the Ark of the Testament. They made a distinction between the Ark of the Covenant and the Ark of the Testament. In fact, the Templars believed there were several Arks—as many as six. They also believed that the Ark of Noah was in fact the Ark of the Covenant. Henrietta Bernstein explains Masonic belief:

The ancient Mysteries are often hidden in an allegorical manner or demonstrated with symbols. It is necessary to study the symbols of Masonry to begin to understand that Noah's Ark is actually the Ark of the Covenant delivered to our civilization from Atlantis. There is evidence that when

Atlantis was about to sink in the Deluge, some of the high priests who were fore-warned took their most treasured possession, in the Ark of the Covenant, and journeyed to other parts of the world, which included Egypt. Noah, a priest of Atlantis, was the courier for the Ark of the Covenant to be taken to Egypt. There the Atlanteans established a great philosophic and literary center, which would later profoundly influence the religions and sciences of countless races and peoples. [Bernstein, op.cit., p.10]

It should be remembered that John Dee believed that Atlantis and America were synonymous. Moreover, Joseph Smith taught that the Garden of Eden was in America, and that patriarchal history down to the time of Noah occurred there, and further that Noah constructed his boat in America and ended up on Mount Ararat, in the Old World.

The Ark of the Covenant, to the Templars, transcended the common religious view of the Christian world. "This may disturb a lot of people," writes Bernstein, "but the true nature of the Ark is not religious." The Templars maintained that the Ark was not the container, but the contents of the chest, which constituted the "Ancient of Days."

In the Zohar, a Cabalistic holy book of the Hebrews, recorded in 1290 A.D., but dating from very ancient tradition, there are fifty pages devoted to the Ark of the Covenant. In the Zohar we read that Yahweh, the God of Israel, ordered Moses to build a chest for the "Ancient of Days," giving precise details for its construction (the same as those in Exodus 25:10), and commanding that the "Ancient of Days" be carried in the chest on the journey of the Hebrews from Egypt to the Land of Israel.

The chest itself, because of the sacred geometry of its construction, together with other holy relics contained within, possesses great power. According to Cabalistic teachings, when the chest is opened a vortex of energy is activated, enabling one to penetrate the dimensions of space and time. This was the source of the experience of past, present and future visions of the high priests, prophets and seers of ancient days. They further maintained that the scrolls and scripts contained within the chest possessed great energy because of sacred words inscribed thereon.

Space does not permit a full study of the Ark of the Covenant in this narrative, except where it pertains to our hypothesis. Suffice it that the Templars believed that as many as six Arks were built (and perhaps even more later) for the specific purpose of forming a powerful communication device.

At the time of King David there existed the "True Ark" and four replicas; these were symbolized by the five-pointed "Star of David." During the reign of King Solomon, who built the Temple to house the "Ancient of Days," he revised that symbol to represent a six-pointed star (the Star of Solomon). The reason for the addition stems from a fascinating tradition. Solomon married the Queen of Sheba (Arabic Ethiopia), by whom he sired a son named Menelik, who inherited the throne of Ethiopia (and who became direct ancestor of the last King of Ethiopia, Haile Selassie). Menelik, envious of the power of the Ark, designed to steal the Ark from Solomon's Temple and remove it to Ethiopia. Learning of the plot, Solomon removed the True Ark from the Holy of Holies to the sacred caverns beneath the Temple, and replaced it with a replica. By certain wiles, Menelik succeeded in stealing the replica Ark (an ancient legend says he flew the Ark to Ethiopia on a magical flying carpet), never realizing he had been duped.

Modern Ethiopians still claim to possess the Ark, which they call the "tabot." Many of their round, Templar-like churches contain tabot replicas, but they claim that the original Ark reposes in St. Mary's Church in Ethiopia, carefully guarded, and known as the Tabota Zion. [see *The Sign and The Seal*, Graham Hancock, Crown Pub., New York, 1992.]

Henrietta Bernstein has also recognized the plurality of Arks, and speculates on the reason and purpose for there being more than one:

It is believed that copies of the Ark serve a positive function by their placement. People who really understand the grid can send messages with the Ark. ...The Ark of the Covenant can also be used for interstellar communications. The grid systems encapsulating the earth can be employed laterally between human beings and other species, but it is also an effective grid system vertically, through other dimensions, for interstellar communications. It is conceivable that we were once a sacred planet and were conscious of inter-dimensional connection to the rest of the universe. [Bernstein, op.cit., p.13.]

The Templar secret—or at least one of them—was that the Ark contained a holy relic known as the Emerald Tablet which, according to Bernstein, "contains the records of the entire cosmology, past, present and future of this galaxy or solar system. This includes physics, sacred geometry, alchemy, geomancy, astrology, astronomy—the formula for time and space. It also contains the blueprint for the entire scheme of the universe—the microcosm and the macrocosm, the upper universe and the lower universe. This system carefully explains the deepest depths of the Divine Nature and shows the true tie that binds all things together. When we organize our view of reality according to those laws, we become one and forever united with God." (P.15)

The Templars believed that Moses was initiated as a High Priest in Egypt, and obtained a copy of the Ark of the Covenant in the Sanctuary of the Great Pyramid which he carried away with him to the Holy Land. After talking to God on Mount Sinai, where he received the "Law" of the Ark, Moses wrote and concealed these great secrets in the first five books of the present Bible, also known as the Pentateuch and the Torah.

Moses is said to have instituted the mysteries of the Ark into teachings which were given to a chosen few. These teachings were never to be written, but transmitted by word of mouth from one generation to the next. They took the form of philosophical and allegorical keys which revealed their hidden significance; they were called by the Jews the Cabalah (Kabbalah, Qabbalah).

Albert Pike, in his great Masonic book *Morals and Dogma*, states:

The primary tradition of the single revelation has been preserved under the name of the "Kabbalah," by the priesthood of Israel. The Kabbalistic doctrine, which was the dogma of the Magi and the Hermes, is contained in the Sepher Yetzirah and the Zohar and the Talmud. ...The Zohar, which is the Key to the Holy Books, opens also all the depths and light, all the obscurities of the Ancient Mythologies and of the sciences. Originally the center of the Atlantean wisdom-religion was said to be a great pyramidal temple standing on an acropolis. From here the Initiate-Priests of the Sacred Feather went forth, taking their wisdom concealed in the Sanctuaries. ...It was the dogmas of this Science that were engraven on the table of stone [the Emerald Tablet] by Hanock [Enoch] and Trismegistus. Moses purified and re-veiled them, for that is the meaning of the word reveal. He covered them with a new veil, when he made of the Holy Kabbalah the exclusive heritage of the people of Israel and the inviolable Secret of the priests."

The source of the Ark has been stated as Atlantis, and a careful study shows that this mysterious continent was the source of much else. The history of Atlantis is the key to Greek mythology, says Ignatius Donnelly, in his book *Atlantis and the Antediluvian World* [New York and London, 1882]. He states that there can be no question that the gods of Greece were human beings, and that the Garden of Eden from which humanity was driven was a possible allusion to the earthly paradise located west of the Pillars of Hercules and destroyed by volcanic cataclysms—i.e. Atlantis.

Dr. Augustus Le Plongeon, one of the most important writers on the ancient Mayan civilization, published his alphabetical key to Mayan hieroglyphics in 1886. When comparing this to the ancient Egyptian hieratic alphabet, he found that signs on the Pyramid of Zochicalo were both Mayan and Egyptian. He concluded that these inscriptions indicated that the Mayan pyramid was a monumental structure erected to commemorate the submergence and destruction of a great land he equated with Mu (Plato's Atlantis).

This should not be summarily dismissed as speculation. There are considerable parallels. The Atlanteans were sun worshipers which has been perpetuated in the ritualism of both Christianity and paganism. The cross and the serpent were Atlantean emblems of divine wisdom, and Atlanteans wore the green and azure radiance of the plumed serpent, and the "winged" or "plumed" serpent was also applied to Quetzalcoatl, the Central American god. Bernstein goes so far as to state, "They [Atlanteans] were the progenitors of the Mayans and Quiches of Central America." The center of the Atlantean wisdom-religion was said to be a great pyramidal temple standing on an acropolis. From here the Initiate-Priests of the Sacred Feather went forth, taking their wisdom to every corner of the world. The capital of Atlantis was called the City of the Golden Gates, and Atlanteans wore rich gold ornaments and adorned their temples with gold long before Solomon's time.

In summary, esoteric tradition maintains that the Ark of the Covenant originated in Atlantis, and Atlantis was ancient America, or part thereof. The Ark found its way to Egypt, and from thence Moses brought it to the Holy Land, where Solomon erected a temple to house it circa 950 B.C. By this time, five replicas of the True Ark had been made, and distributed to various parts of the world. A secret society arose around each of the Arks, to preserve and protect them for future generations. One of these, ostensibly the True Ark, was brought from Jerusalem to Ireland circa 586 B.C., and hidden up in the great "mergech" inside the sacred hill of Tara.

Joseph of Arimathea, the uncle of Mary, mother of Jesus (according to the biblical version), was a tin merchant, in charge of tin mines in the Mendip Hills of Cornwall, England. Anna, the grandmother of Jesus, was a native of Cornwall. It is said that in these early years, Jesus accompanied Joseph to England and studied with the Druids on the Isle of Avalon (Glastonbury), where he was initiated into the Druidic Mysteries, at which he became an Adept.

After the Crucifixion, Joseph of Arimathea fled with members of his family and others, including Mary Magdalene, ostensibly the wife of Jesus according to Templar doctrine, to France. The Magdalene remained in France and thus began a royal bloodline through the offspring of Jesus, who became the ancestors of the Templar or Grail families. Joseph of Arimathea went on to England, settling at Glastonbury, and brought with him the mysterious "Holy Grail," which some—such as Henrietta Bernstein—equate with the Ark of the Covenant. Joseph of Arimathea and Mary, mother of Jesus, both died and are interred at Glastonbury. From earliest times, Glastonbury was known as "The Secret of the Lord."

Without entering into continuing debate, we might mention that the "Secret of the Lord" might have been Jesus himself! Gildas, the wise Albanicus (425-512 A.D.), who some claim was the uncle of King Arthur, took refuge in Glastonbury Abbey after being driven by Saxon pirates from the island of Steepholme. He became a monk there, where he wrote his monumental early history of Britain, De excidio Britanniae, wherein he states: "Christ the True Sun afforded His light, and knowledge of His precepts, to our island in the last years, as we know, of Tiberius Caesar." This was in 37 A.D., four years after the Crucifixion. Some authorities believe that Jesus survived the Crucifixion, and accompanied Joseph of Arimathea to Glastonbury, in England, or perhaps appeared there after his Resurrection, a more acceptable theory for Christians.

One of the earliest manuscripts found to date relating to Joseph of Arimathea coming to Glastonbury is an anonymous tract called Grand-Saint-Graal. This ancient text recounts how Joseph and his companions left Sarras in the region of Marseilles, France, and crossed the English Channel to Glastonbury. The ancient manuscript is most revealing:

Joseph of Arimathea and his companions wandered away from Sarras until they came, after much journeying, to the seashore. That night the brave Galaaz was by the grace of God conceived. The next day Joseph and his company prayed before their sacred Hebrew Ark of the Covenant, kneeling before their Hebrew or Holy Grail, weeping and requesting that they be made strong to cross the sea into that promised land where they would multiply and become the best people. ...The first to go were the Grail Bearers. They departed on foot, bearing the Holy Vessel, without dread of the sea, and walked across water dry shod. ...They made a safe crossing. Next morning they were in Britain. ...Britain was full of wicked folk, all Saracens. Joseph predicted the reign of King Arthur, whose adventures would last for twelve years. ...Then great, terrifying wonders caused by the Grail would occur in Britain....that Joseph of Arimathea brought the Hebrew wonder, which was his Holy Grail, to Glastonbury where he was interred, that the Abbey where he was buried stood under the "Cross of England," that "Corbenie" was the name of the castle built to house the Holy Grail, that "Corbenie" was located in a foreign land where during services at this Grail Castle the Grail was placed on a silver plate. The priest there stood under the sound of a thousand voices and the beating of hundreds of birds' wings overhead ...[Grand-Saint-Graal, "Henry Lonelich," Incident 31 ff., History of the Holy Grail, a translation of Grand Seint Graal, 1450 A.D.; written originally in French prose at Glastonbury between 1191-1212.]

Glastonbury lies on the main road from London to Exeter, in Somerset, near Bath. The river Brue winds serpentine through Somerset, forming an island in the stream in early times, separating Glastonbury from the mainland by marshes and streamlets. On this island were many apple trees, and the isolated strip of land became known to the early Romans as Insula Avallonia, or the Isle of Apples, shortened by the Britons to Avalon. Out of the marshy meadows rises a hill with an elevation of about 500 feet, called the Tor, or Tower Hill, and on its summit are the remains of St. Michael's oratory. The nearby town of Glastonbury lies in the midst of orchards surrounded by water-meadows.

While many have never even heard of this little town in England, it has been the site of Druidism, ancient Goddess worship, the genesis of European Christianity, as well as the birthplace of the Arthurian cycle. Subterranean chambers are found beneath the Tor and, in fact, all over Glastonbury. They were reputed to be ley lines, or Dragon lines, with magnetic energy emanating from deep in the earth.

We have mentioned that the mother of Jesus was buried at Glastonbury, as was Joseph of Arimathea; regarding the burial of Joseph, Lionel Smithett Lewis states that after moving the burial site several times, in 1928 he was placed in the ancient St. Katherine's Chapel, the north transept in St. John the Baptist Church in Glastonbury. To protect the remains, the initials of Joseph of Arimathea (J.A.) Carved with a caduceus between the letters, were explained as being those of "John Allen."

King Arthur was buried at Glastonbury. An authentic account of the discovery of

Arthur's grave is given by Giraldus Cambrensis, who was present on the occasion, and William of Malmesbury, a contemporary. Later, King Henry II had the remains exhumed. Arthur's bones were found buried in a hollowed oak tree (the oak was sacred to the Druids) at a depth of sixteen feet, marked on the surface by two small pyramids. The remains of Guinevere were found, as well as those of Modred, Arthur's son and slayer. Under a stone was found a leaden cross which Giraldus claimed Arthur actually held in his hands. The cross was inscribed with the words: "Here lies buried the renowned King Arthur in the Island of Avallon." The great Masonic writer Manly P. Hall connects Arthur and Merlin to the Masons as follows:

"Arthur was the Grand Master of a secret Christian Masonic brotherhood of philosophic mystics who termed themselves Knights. Arthur received the exalted position of Grand Master of these Knights because he had faithfully accomplished the withdrawl of the sword (spirit) from the anvil of the base metals (his lower nature). As invariably happens, the historical Arthur soon was confused with the allegories and myths of his order until now the two are inseparable....The medieval Rosicrucians were undoubtedly in possession of the true secret of the Arthurian cycle and the Grail legend, much of their symbolism having been incorporated into that order...."[*The Secret Teachings of All Ages*, Manly P. Hall, p.CLXXX]

Glastonbury contained many secrets, one of which was the burial place of the Ark of the Covenant, or Holy Grail. It is believed that the configuration of the architecture possessed the sacred geometry to reveal the hidden secrets of the Abbey, which had been built on the site of the old Wattle Church, said to have been erected with the aid of Jesus himself in honor of his mother Mary (there still exists a carved inscription on ancient stone which reads: "JESUS : MARIA."). A hint of this sacred message is found in the recorded manuscripts of the ancient monks of the Abbey which states: "That which the brethren of old handed down to us, we followed, ever building on their plan. As we have said, our Abbey was a message in ye stones. In ye foundations and ye distances be a mystery - the mystery of our Faith, which ye have forgotten and we also in ye latter days...." [*The Gate of Remembrance*, Frederick Bligh Bond, England, 1918, p.147.]

During the reign of King Henry VIII, there was a dissolution of all the abbeys during the Reformation. Sir Francis Bryan, Henry's favorite courtier and friend—who was also Grand Master of the Rosicrucians—was given mastership of Glastonbury Abbey, which was being kept by monks under the leadership of Abbot Whiting (into whose family the Bryans would marry).

In February 1520, Sir Francis Bryan had been the houseguest of the Duke of Buckingham at Thornbury and at his town house in London. On 8 February, they were entertained by the Earl of Oxford's minstrels and players, and then they set out in great state for a pilgrimage to Glastonbury Abbey, which was then under Buckingham's jurisdiction. They arrived about 29 April and remained until at least 22 May. On 29 April, they paid respects to the holy relics of Joseph of Arimathea, and attended high mass; Buckingham gave 20 d. to the support of "an idiot of the abbey of Glastonbury," and various other amounts for oblations. The remainder of their time there seems to have been divided between visits and oblations to the holy relics: the casket containing the bones of Joseph of Arimathea, the graves of Arthur and Guinevere, as well as those of the numerous saints and kings, the Holy Thorn Tree (which Joseph of Arimathea planted from the Crown of Thorns), etc., and enjoying minstrels, a French poet, archery, and trading horses, listening to a harpist, and much more.

The Duke of Buckingham, whose wife was the aunt of Sir Francis Bryan, was something of a mystic himself. Was their pilgrimage to Glastonbury also connected to the search for something known to be hidden there? It seems likely, for on October 26, 1520, Buckingham announced a proposed pilgrimage to Jerusalem, telling his assembled associates (which included the dean of his chapel, his almoner [financier], and a surveyor, among others), "Ye see I wear a beard, whereof peradventure ye do marvel; but marvel not of it, for I make a vow unto God that it shall never be shaven unto such time as I have been at Jerusalem...."

Buckingham's plans were halted when Henry VIII learned of it. Henry had the Duke arrested and eventually beheaded. Then, in 1539, Henry ordered the arrest of Abbot Richard Whiting, who was commanded to reveal the location of all of Glastonbury's hidden treasures. When Whiting refused to tell, he was hanged and quartered, and parts of his body displayed throughout England. Then, following the tearing down of Glastonbury Abbey, stone by stone—a thing unprecedented with Henry's treatment of other abbeys—the abbey and its surroundings were dissolved of all power and authority and virtually abandoned for several generations to follow.

Before elaborating on the significance of these events, another factor should be considered. On 29 September 1538, just one year before the destruction of Glastonbury Abbey, Sir Francis Bryan received a grant from John Scudamore of Herefordshire (Joseph Smith's direct ancestor), in charge of Augmentation accounts, which included "a relic said to be a piece of the Holy Cross adorned with silver gilt, which belonged to Stratford, Essex, delivered to the lord Cromwell on the King's warrant." [*Calendar of State Papers*, reign of Henry VIII.]

159

The Emerald Tablet of Hermes

Chapter Twenty-One

New Atlantis

Sir Francis Bacon was the Lord High Chancellor of England under King James I, the highest office in the land next to the King. He was a principle founder and mover of the Rosicrucian movement and became Grand Master of the Order after Dee. He produced a great body of literature, which some believe included the actual works of Shakespeare, and was responsible for the King James version of the Bible (over which translation was the great Robert Fludd, Grand Master of the Prieuré de Sion).

Dr. John Dee had been born in Wales in 1527, a physician, philosopher, scientist, astrologer, alchemist, cabalist, mathematician and astrologer and diplomatic emissary of Queen Elizabeth I. He was deeply steeped in the metaphysics of the Hermetic tradition, and successor of Sir Francis Bryan as Grand Master of the Rosicrucian Order. Henrietta Bernstein is one who recognizes the significance of the association between these two great men.

Sir Francis Bacon and Dr. John Dee were part of the adept group which were in process of forming the democracy of an enlightened Republic of America. This was part of the great plan: the Republic of the Americas would be the Utopia, the Zion, the physical structure demonstrating the principles of the Ark of the Covenant. It was necessary for the physical Ark to reach America and the logical persons to carry out this plan were Sir Francis Bacon and Dr. John Dee. [*Ark of the Covenant*, Holy Grail, Bernstein, op.cit. Pp.144-45.]

Bacon was connected to the "Invisible College," the collection of scientists and alchemists, physicians and writers, that served as the conduit for an underground stream of knowledge, knowledge that caused men such as Giordano Bruno to lose their heads. Much of what these learned men wrote was written under pseudonyms, or under total anonymity, but under his own name Bacon published a fascinating work titled *The New Atlantis*. It was a barely-concealed reference to the New World.

The so-called new Atlantis was by description nearly identical to the Arcadia of the Sinclairs and d'Anjous—a Utopia where the true Renaissance man could be free to publish and study science without fears of a censoring government or a church inquisition. Here in "New Salem," as Bacon referred to it (i.e. New Jerusalem), a secret society resided, to which few were admitted and even fewer were privy to the secrets. This secret society, said Bacon, had as its founder a wise king, and the order this wise king started was called Solomon's House. He made a strong point that Jews were allowed to reside on this secret island and practice their arts and sciences.

In about the year 1582, Dr. John Dee began making visits to Glastonbury, together with his companion Edward Kelly, and thereafter a number of such visits were reported. In his book *New Light on the Ancient Mystery of Glastonbury* [Somerset, 1990], John Michell makes an observation of Dr. John Dee during this period: "In the 16th century, soon after the Abbey's dissolution, the sage John Dee sought the stone among its ruins, and is said to have learnt its secrets with the aid of his spirit medium, Edward Kelley...." (pp.158-9) This statement is not wholly correct, inasmuch as Dee had not met Kelly at this early date. It is more likely that he was inspired in his search by Sir Francis Bryan, who was then Rosicrucian Grand Master.

Bernstein postulates that Dee and Bacon utilized the known underground tunnels beneath Glastonbury Tor to access the hiding place of the Ark of the Covenant. "It is conceivable," writes Bernstein, "that this is the manner in which John Dee and Francis Bacon were able to take the Ark of the Covenant, have it in their possession for awhile, and recreate it. Then, when finished, replace it. There is also the possibility that other copies could have been made by Francis Bacon at this time, to be placed in other locations in Britain, America and other countries. Both Bacon and Dee would have had the authority to carry out this covert operation because of their high positions in the Freemasonic and Rosicrucian order."

It is interesting to observe that in one of the earliest settled areas of the State of Vermont, not far from Joseph Smith's birthplace, is a town named Glastonbury. It has the reputation of being a very mysterious place, replete with unexplained disappearances, numerous UFO sightings, and one correspondent described Glastonbury, Vermont, as "a gateway to another dimension." Similar descriptions have been made of Glastonbury in England.

I became acquainted with the great writer John Steinbeck at a time when he was writing his final book, dealing with the subject of King Arthur and the Holy Grail. I spoke with him by telephone shortly after he had visited Glastonbury. He said he had a "transcendent" experience while standing atop Glastonbury Tor. He was euphoric. "I have discovered something phenomenal here at Glastonbury," he said, "something that could alter history as we know it." He promised to elaborate when he returned, but died before accomplishing it. His book was published posthumously by his wife and literary agent, with no mention of his discovery.

The "Invisible Empire," so often philosophically preached by the initiates, was about to take on a physical reality in the New World. The Philosophical Empire had been concerned primarily with the survival of knowledge; the New Salem could put that knowledge into physical government. The power of the Church in Europe to destroy all nonconformists could be eliminated in the New Atlantis by separation of Church and State, and the Esoteric Orders, which believed in a secret doctrine of pre-Christian origin, handed down from great antiquity, could begin a restoration of ancient philosophical systems.

The Rosicrucians spearheaded the formation of the American Republic. In 1660 the book *New Atlantis* was published in London, begun by Sir Francis Bacon, Lord Verulam, Viscount St. Alban's, and completed by R.H. Esquire. *The New Atlantis* described an existing secret society, of which Bacon was a founder. The book was replete with Masonic symbolism. Bacon's plan as outlined in the New Atlantis was to recreate and build a united brotherhood of the earth. The "New Atlantis" was to be formed on the American continent, set apart from ancient times for the great experiment of enlightened self-government. The explorers who opened the "New World" were aware that they did so according to a master plan, managed by enlightened adepts equipped with ancient knowledge and having a chosen and special bloodline. One of those adepts, having a secret bloodline, was certainly Sir Francis Bacon. Henrietta Bernstein has written:

"Research confirms Sir Francis Bacon was the rightful heir to the throne of England, although history tells us that he was never acknowledged as such by his mother, Queen Elizabeth I, or his father, the Earl of Leicester. The infant Francis was given over to Sir Nicholas Bacon, Lord Keeper of the Great Seal of England and his wife Lady Ann Bacon [Ann, sister of Elizabeth Cook, wife of John Russell, of the ancestry of Isaac Morley]. Elizabeth was known as the Virgin Queen. Even her marriage to Leicester was kept a secret. Elizabeth did, however, arrange for the young Francis Bacon to be given the highest education possible befitting an heir to the throne. Francis was a genius and he had a higher mission to fulfill. Bacon was the founder of democracy and the true genius behind the colonization of America." [Bernstein, op.cit., p.170.]

Robert Dudley, Earl of Leicester (1532?-1588), in addition to being Queen Elizabeth's favorite (and by some accounts her secret husband), was brother of Ambrose Dudley, Earl of Warwick, who married Anne, daughter of Francis Russell, Earl of Bedford (Isaac Morley's wife, Lucy Gunn, being Bedford's direct descendant). Leicester had been one of Dee's former pupils in mathematics, geometry and navigation and remained one of his most influential friends. It was Dudley who introduced Dee to Queen Elizabeth and suggested that he should choose the most astrologically propitious date for her coronation. He was an advocate of colonial expansion and was one of Sir Francis Drake's principal backers. The antiquary Anthony Wood later stated that no one knew the Earl better than Dee. Leicester is mentioned frequently in Dee's diaries. In fact, the first entries in his diaries, beginning in 1577, reads: "16 Jan. The Earl of Leiccster, Mr. Philip Sydney, Mr Dyer, &c. [This visit connected with Drake's circumnavigation] 22 Jan. The Earl of Bedford came to my house...."

Sir Francis Bacon's ascendancy to the Grand Mastership of the Rosicrucians, succeeding John Dee, who had in turn succeeded Sir Francis Bryan, was a natural progression, because via his secret birth he would have been a grandson of Sir Francis Bryan, for whom he was likely named.

Bacon became Lord Chancellor of England under King James I, and supervised the colonization of the states of Virginia and the Carolinas in America, and the goddess Pallas Athena, Bacon's personal emblem, can still be seen on the flag of the State of Virginia, her spear in hand. Athena also appears on the headings of Bacon's literature and on the headings of the Shakespeare plays and sonnets; Athena is known as the "Spear-Shaker." The Athena symbol was one of many codes and ciphers used by Bacon and his group to secretly record the history of the seventeenth century. Athena was considered the most significant goddess of the enlightened democracies, which included Atlantis, Athens, and eventually the Republic of America. Because Bacon and his associates chose Athena, Goddess of The Muse, who was also called the "Spear-Shaker," they were known as the "Shakespeare Group." The group consisted of such esteemed writers and poets as Lancelot Andrews, Toby Mathews, John Donne, Ben Jonson, Edmund Spenser, Sir Walter Raleigh, Francis Drake, George Withers, Christopher Marlowe, Francis Bryan II, and many others.

"Through Bacon and his group of writers," says Bernstein, "the Shakespeare writings were brought forth to explain the history of the period.....The man from Stratford, William Shakespeare, who could not even spell or write his name, was simply used as a guise." Much of the Shakespeare writings are coded Masonic rituals and messages. Masonic emblems adorn the title pages of Shakespeare's Great Folio of 1623. Ben Jonson, who introduced the Shakespeare works to print, said of Sir Francis Bacon: "Of greatness he could not want." Of the man William Shakespeare he wrote: "The most learned of works could not have been written by the least learned of men."

As Lord Chancellor to King James I, Sir Francis Bacon headed the group responsible for the editing and revising the King James version of the Bible. He chose learned men, such as Robert Fludd, Grand Master of the Prieuré de Sion, to translate the text wherein are cryptographically concealed messages. For example, in the 46th Psalm of the King James Version of the Bible, the 46th word down from the first verse is the word SHAKE, and the 46th word up from the end is the word SPEAR. William T. Smedley, author of the book *Mystery of Francis Bacon* [Health Research, U.S.A., 1967, p.138], writes that "It will eventually be proved that the whole scheme of the Authorized [King James] Version of the Bible was Francis Bacon's."

It is interesting to note that the original manuscript of the Bible given to Bacon by King James I to edit, as well as the originals of the Shakespeare writings, have never been found. It seems reasonable to suppose that such manuscripts of great importance would have been preserved. Baconians believe that Sir Francis Bacon did preserve them—in America.

The first permanent English settlement in North America was established in Virginia in honor of Queen Elizabeth, the Virgin Queen, and named for her by Sir Walter Raleigh. Among the charter holders of the Colony of Virginia was Dee's friend Richard Hakluyt. Sir George Sommers was appointed governor in 1609. When he sailed for the New World, Sommer's ship foundered on the Hog Islands, so named because of the wild swine found there. The Hog Islands were later named the Bermudas—Dee's "Bermoothes" and also of Shakespeare, whose play *The Tempest* is said to represent this colonization of America.

In 1609, King James I granted a charter to the Bermuda Company, and in 1612 Richard More (of the Sinclair-Gunn-Morley "Möre" clan) and sixty colonists from Virginia settled on one of these islands. In the same year, coins were struck for use in the Bermudas which were called "Hog Money"; the obverse bears the image of a boar, while the reverse shows a ship in full sail. This is significant because the image of the boar is identical to the crest of Lord Bacon in minute detail.

Why such emphasis on a hog? Outside the obvious, that a hog represents "bacon,"

there is a deeper aspect. Francis Bacon's Boar Crest from the binding of a presentation copy of Novum Organum, 1620, is a startling representation of a map of America! On the left front shoulder of the boar is what appears to be a depiction of the Ark of the Covenant, nestled in the cradle of a crescent moon. Its placement on the "boar map" shows it to be in the vicinity of present-day Utah, or a little south thereof, depending upon the determination of the ostensible boundaries. (Sir Francis Bacon was known as Hom Lunar—the Moon Man.)

Francis Bacon's history is ever shrouded in mystery. Sir Walter Raleigh said of Bacon: "And thy great genius in being concealed, is revealed." Many students of Bacon's life believe that he faked his death in 1626, disappeared from England, traveled for a time in Europe, and later became deeply involved in the formation of the Republic of America.

Between the years 1610 and 1660 a great deal of the material concerned with the plan of development for America was transferred from Europe to the New World, and the most likely place for its deposit was Virginia, America's first English colony. The secret societies such as the Rosicrucians, Freemasons, and the Fellows of the Royal Society had representatives in the colonies. Once again, Bernstein enlightens us:

Once the Jamestown settlement had gained some order and permanence, descendants of the men who formed the original Baconian Society left England and settled in Jamestown. It was through this connection that the Great Plan began to revolve in America. There were marriages between the families of the original custodians of the philosophical heritage. The mingling of the blood of these settlers like the Bacons, produced many of America's prominent citizens. [Bernstein, op.cit., p.182.]

These intermarriages seem indeed to

have been a reality. My own ancestor, Francis Bryan II, married Ann, a cousin of John Smith, founder of Jamestown, and Bryan himself was a member of the original Jamestown Colony. Bacon's family was also well represented in Virginia, and are traced from Robert Bacon of Drinkstone, Suffolk (who was father of Sir Nicholas Bacon, Lord Keeper of the Great Seal for Queen Elizabeth), to Nathaniel Bacon, who was a leader of Bacon's Rebellion in Virginia in 1676, and who died 1 October 1676 after setting fire to Jamestown.

It is believed, in Masonic circles, that Henry Blount, a true descendant of Sir Francis Bacon, who adopted the name Nathaniel Bacon after arriving in America, brought the sacred records and a copy of the Ark to Jamestown, and buried them under the Jamestown Church Tower in 1635.

In 1676 the Ark of the Covenant and its treasure were secretly moved from the Jamestown Church and placed in a ten-foot-square vault, buried twenty feet below the central tower of the original brick church in Bruton Parish. This was the first church in the first Virginia capital, Middletown Plantation, later to become Williamsburg. The treasure was transferred under cover of Bacon's Rebellion, exactly a century before the birth of the American Republic.

In 1938, Marie Hall, wife of Manly P. Hall, was able to locate the Bacon vault and began to seek permission from local authorities to excavate. From a Masonic record found at Williamsburg, she found confirmation in a written instruction which said: "Under the first brick church in Bruton Parish, Williamsburg, Virginia, lies Francis Bacon's Vault." Interestingly, the annals of the Williamsburg Masonic Lodge, as well as the Vestry records of Bruton Parish for this time period are missing. An early book on colonial architecture mentions that the size of the original church was 60 feet by 24 feet internally, approximately the same dimensions as the old Wattle Church at Glastonbury.

Marie Hall's research is recorded with the United States Government at Washington, D.C. The information shows that while she was digging around Williamsburg, she was approached by two prominent Masons, whom she called "Masons of the Inner Group"; one was owner of the London Times and the other a descendant of Sir Walter Raleigh. Says Bernstein: "Mr. and Mrs. Hall often talked with me about what was in the vault in Virginia. I believe Mr. Hall knew that the Ark had been taken out because he said to me on two different occasions that he thought the Williamsburg vault was empty."

In his book America's Assignment with Destiny, Manly P. Hall states that "Thomas Jefferson examined the 'repositories' of the Bacon group in colonial America, checked their contents and caused them to be resealed for future ages."

Bernstein believes that the vault beneath Bruton church may yet contain Bacon's books, and manuscripts such as the Shakespeare writings and the King James Version of the Bible, as well as the autobiography of Sir Francis Bacon. However, she believes that the Ark was removed from Williamsburg when the nation's capital, Washington, D.C., was erected, and makes a good argument that it was placed in the Washington National Cathedral.

The Washington National Cathedral was dedicated in 1990 after 83 years of construction. In its garden the cathedral possesses a cutting of the thorn tree from Glastonbury, and a chair from Glastonbury Abbey is located in the cathedral proper. The cathedral itself, based on original plans by Washington and Jefferson, was the last great Gothic Church built in the style of the early Templar Churches of Europe. There is an underground crypt at a place where the two arms of the cathedral cross, which is dedicated to Joseph of Arimathea. Next to the crypt area of Joseph of Arimathea is a small chapel called Glastonbury Cathedral. Here stands a throne chair carved of stone taken from Glastonbury Abbey. The Washington National Cathedral is built on fifty-three acres on Mount St. Albans, and in England Sir Francis Bacon was Lord Verulam and Viscount St. Albans. On the south portal of the cathedral, between two massive sets of doors, is a statue of St. Alban. The thorn tree from Glastonbury grows in front of St. Albans School for Boys. The cathedral is administered by the Episcopal Church, the same church that oversees Bruton Parish Church in Williamsburg.

———

Sir Francis Bacon and Dr. John Dee had collaborated to remove something from Glastonbury to America. There is evidence that whatever it was may have been buried in "Bacon's Vault" beneath the Bruton Church in Colonial Williamsburg, Virginia. Bacon's propensity for constructing such vaults has been independently established.

In 1911 a Dr. Orville Owen, convinced that Bacon had been the true author of the Shakespeare works, came from Detroit to England to search for Bacon's secret manuscripts. Clues he had found in one Bacon text led to an expedition to Wales. Beneath the silt in the Wye River in southeast Wales, he found a stone and cement vault with coded inscriptions (see the chapter on decoding inscriptions in this text). The vault itself was empty, and Dr. Owen and his associates believed the works had been there but had later been removed to an even more secure location.

In Sylva Sylvarum, Bacon described preserving documents through the use of mercury, placing parchments in quicksilver for long-term preservation. He also wrote of constructing artificial springs by using stone, sand, and ferns. These facts were brought to the attention of Oak Island treasure seeker Gilbert Hedden by Burrell Ruth, a student at Michigan State University, in 1939. Hedden acknowledged that

flasks of mercury had indeed been found in a dump on Oak Island.

Did Oak Island, Nova Scotia, became a refuge for Bacon's treasures? The time frame fits, considering that Nova Scotia was parceled during Bacon's time, and Bacon had links to Sir Francis Drake and John Dec, both of whom it can be shown to have had connections with Nova Scotia.

Bacon and two of his closest friends had received land in eastern Canada: William Rawley, who had protected Bacon's manuscript until his death in 1660, and Thomas Bushell, a mining engineer whose expertise was in extracting ore from flooded mines, both shared in Bacon's Canadian grant.

On 16 July 1582, John Dee recorded in his diary the acquisition of 10,000 acres of the "new conquest" from the patents of Sir George Peckham and Sir Thomas Gerard, which gave him possession of vast tracts in New England, including Westford, Massachusetts, where was buried Sir James Gunn of the Sinclair-Zeno Expedition. Three weeks later, on August 11th, Dee records (without details) a visit from Sir Francis Bacon.

Two years earlier, on 10 September 1580, Dee was granted by Sir Humfrey Gilbert "the royalties of discoveries to all the north above the parallel of the 50 degree of latitude." If the voyage had succeeded, Dee would have gained most of Canada, including Nova Scotia. After the death of Sir Humfrey Gilbert, Dee negotiated with Sir Humfrey's brother, Sir Adrian Gilbert, in the summer of 1583, in a grant "to discover and settle the northerly parts of Atlantis, called Novus Orbis. ...The said Adrian Gilbert, John Dee, and John Davis to be exempt from all customs, for ever." [Calendar of State Papers, vol.161, no.24] Therefore, both Dee and Bacon had ties to the Sinclairs and the Oak Island treasure mystery.

The writers (and Masons) Christopher Knight and Robert Lomas, in their masterful book The Hiram Key [Element

Books, Inc., Boston, 1998, pp.332-33], give an excellent assessment of Sir Francis Bacon in these words:

> ...No one in the king's group of Freemasons had more passion for the advancement of science and the opening up of thinking about nature. Bacon, however, let his Masonic knowledge mingle with his public aspirations when he published his book *The New Atlantis* which openly spoke of his plan for a rebuilding of King Solomon's Temple in spiritual terms. This pure Ezekiel-esque vision, he said, was to be "a palace of invention" and "a great temple of science"; it was visualized less as a building than as a new state where the pursuit of knowledge in all its branches was to be organized on principles of the highest efficiency. In this work the intellectual seed germ of the constitution of the United States of America was firmly planted.

National Cathedral in Washington, D.C.

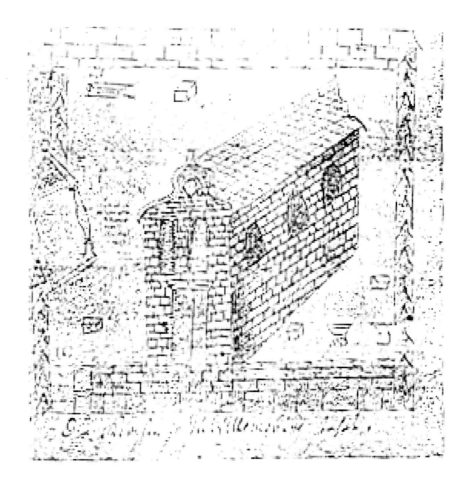

Bruton Church

Chapter Twenty-Two

The Sanpete Sanctuary

There was an arcane side to Isaac Morley of which most of his contemporaries were unaware. He is most often depicted as a strong and loyal general authority of the Mormon Church, beloved by the members over whom he administered, and renowned for his gentle and compassionate nature. But he was much more than this, as we were to learn from the Rosicrucian documents and his own carefully guarded journals.

Isaac Morley was a member of a secret society with strong connections to the Knights Templar. This society, known as the Philadelphes, claimed an authority by direct descent from the last Templar Grand Master, Jacques de Molay. When Jacques de Molay was imprisoned in France, shortly before his execution in 1314, he was visited by a Templar Knight named Larmenius upon whom de Molay conferred the Grand Mastership of the French Templars. Larmenius in turn conferred this title by charter upon a successor and the Order continued to exist in secret through succeeding generations. Many of the Grand Masters of the Philadelphes were members of the royal Bourbon family of France (of which Louis Philippe, the Citizen King, was a member), and the last known French Grand Master Bernard Fabré Palaprat.

The Philadelphes also had some illustrious members in addition, including the Marquis de Lafayette, Benjamin Franklin, Charles Nodier and Victor Hugo. Benjamin Franklin appears to have brought the Philadelphes to America where it was masked under his philanthropic and philosophical society called the Junto. Benjamin Franklin, in addition to having been Grand Master of the Rosicrucian Order (in succession from John Dee), was founder and Master of the Masonic Lodge of Pennsylvania. As such, he was in constant communication with the Sinclairs, Masters of the Scottish Lodge.

General Arthur St. Clair, who was descended from William Sinclair of Rosslyn, had served with the British military leader Sir Jeffrey Amherst in Nova Scotia. He fought on the British side against France during the American Revolution, but when asked to fight against the American colonies, he resigned his commission and became a major general of the American army. He was clearly associated with Benjamin Franklin. He later fought against the Indians, and married the daughter of a wealthy French family but died in poverty. His tombstone inscription reads: "This stone is erected over the bones of their departed brother by the members of the Masonic society."

General Horatio Gates, who also fought under Amherst and was a close friend of George Washington, married the daughter of the Masonic grand master of Nova Scotia. George Washington had been sworn in as a Mason in 1752 at the age of twenty, and eventually became Grand Master of the Grand Lodge of Virginia. Lafayette noted how committed Washington was to his fellow Masons. Washington was sworn in by the Grand Master of New York, Robert Livingston, with the Bible of Saint John's Lodge of New York. Patrick Henry and Richard Henry Lee were Masons. John Hancock, Dr. Joseph Warren and Paul Revere were members of the Scottish Lodge, which in America had a degree of rank called the "Knight Templar."

The dollar had and still has Masonic symbols, including the unfinished pyramid, the "all-seeing eye," and a scroll proclaiming a "new secular order." Masonry triumphed in the United States; the utopia of Bacon came to fruition.

Sir Jeffrey Amherst, mentioned above, led a regiment called the Royal Scots and drove the French out of Nova Scotia in 1758. It was Amherst, wishing to increase the population, who divided the territory and created the document known as the Shoreham Grant, in 1759. For the first time, Oak Island officially had an owner.

Many New England families, fearing the threat of revolution in America, went north to Nova Scotia. Many Highland families from Scotland also migrated to "new Scotland." Amherst chartered the first British lodge in America and trained such fellow Masons as Ethan Allen, Benedict Arnold, and George Putnam. Lieutenant Colonel John Young, who served under Amherst, had been appointed deputy grand master of the Scottish Lodge by none other than William Sinclair of Rosslyn. In 1761 Young turned over the lodge to Lt. Col. Augustine Provost, who became the grand master for all the Scottish lodges in America. Augustine Provost was of the family of Etienne Provost, the French-Canadian trapper and explorer who penetrated what became the state of Utah and established a fort and trading post at a site which today bears his name—Provo, Utah.

Lt. Col. John Young was a direct descendant of Richard Young, whom John Dee refers to in his diary as his "brother," which means that Young must either have married a member of the Fromonds family, or been a brother or brother-in-law of an earlier wife. Richard Young had been one of the most virulently anti-Catholic judges of his age; nearly every reference to him in the *Calendar of State Papers* concerns his judgements against papists and recusants. For example, an item dated January 1590 (vol. 230, no. 30) deals with information against one Mrs. Dewse, and "her desire to be revenged of her enemies, one of whom was that thief, Justice Young, who lived by robbing papists; the others were Sir Rowland Hayward and others, whose pictures of wax she would have made and then prick them to the heart." Richard Young's daughter Margaret married, in 1573, to Hugh Platt (1552-1608), writer and alchemist and "kinsman" of John Dee.

On 6 March 1583, John Dee entered this notation in his diary: "I, and Mr Adrian Gilbert and John Davis, did meet with Mr Alderman Barnes, Mr Towrson and Mr Yong and Mr Hudson, about the N W voyage."

"Mr Hudson" was the legendary Henry Hudson the younger, who explored extensively in search of the "Northwest Passage," and for whom Hudson Bay and Hudson River were named. His fateful last expedition was in 1610-11. Etienne Provost explored the region which became Utah under the auspices of the Hudson Bay Fur Company.

With these connections our story begins to coalesce. Henry Gunn, ancestor of Lucy Gunn (wife of Isaac Morley) and a direct descendant of Sir James Gunn (the Westford Knight), removed from the Highlands of Scotland to Great Burstead in England shortly after the year 1600. A family record states that Henry Gunn's wife, Sarah, was delivered of a son "in the Highlands of Scotland" only days before their arrival at Great Burstead. That son, Jasper Gunn, was christened at Great Burstead on 9 August 1606. [LDS Gen. Soc. AFN: 8TH3-F6.]

Jasper Gunn had little opportunity to know his father. Henry Gunn, who was a renowned sailor, with considerable knowledge of the coastline of America, either from the benefit of personal experience or from maps and charts of his ancestors, or both, had come to England to join the Hudson Expedition. As such, he would have necessarily worked closely with John Dee, who already had copies of the maps of the Sinclair-Zeno Expedition, and backed the Hudson exploration.

Gunn family tradition maintains that Henry Gunn perished with the Hudson company while searching for a Northwest Passage in 1610-11, when his son Jasper was only four or five years of age.

John Dee had backed the Adrian Gilbert—Henry Hudson explorations beginning in 1583, but Dee had died in 1609, a year before Hudson's final fateful expedition. There seemed to be a concerted effort to pursue Dee's earliest urgings to explore North America; he was the shadowy figure behind nearly every major voyage of exploration of the last half of the 16th century and the beginning of the 17th century.

Following the death of Henry Gunn in 1610-11, Jasper Gunn became a ward of none other than William Sinclair of Rosslyn, a very significant fact indeed, for it is a strong indication that the Gunns and Sinclairs of Scotland were closely allied with the planned explorations promoted by John Dee in the New World. Jasper Gunn was educated, at Sinclair expense and sponsorship, in the art of medicine at Edinburgh, and received a degree as Doctor of Medicine.

In 1615 his mentor, William Sinclair, was condemned to death for allowing a Jesuit priest to conduct the Catholic Mass at Rosslyn; the priest was hung and William was pardoned to an exile in Ireland. Mobs destroyed the Sinclair home and chapel searching for their rumored treasure [*The Sword and The Grail*, Andrew Sinclair, p.185], but it had been removed to America in 1545 by Oliver Sinclair. William Sinclair, Grand Master of Scottish Masons, was eventually restored to his property at Rosslyn, though considerably diminished of wealth and much in need of replenishing the family coffers.

It seemed to us more than coincidental that it was just at this time when Dr. Jasper Gunn emigrated to America. He arrived at Hartford, Connecticut, between the years 1632 and 1635, and established himself as America's first official physician. He wrote a medical guide—*Dr Gunn's Book of Medicine*—that became a standard for American doctors for the next century. Dr. Gunn's Book was steeped as much in mysticism as medicine, and some believe that he coded hidden messages within the text.

Even though he made his home in Hartford, Connecticut, Dr. Gunn spent most of his early years conducting a series of excavations in the vicinity of Springfield, Massachusetts, not far from the town of Westford, where his ancestor, Sir James Gunn, the Westford Knight, was buried in 1398. Some of his excavations took place near Fall River, Massachusetts, where the Taunton River empties into Assonet Bay. On the east side of the bay is "Dighton Rock," inscribed with strange symbols; and at Fall River in 1831 was found the skeleton of a man in armor believed to have been the remains of Sir James Gunn. When Dr. Jasper Gunn died at Hartford on 12 January 1671, his son Nathaniel (1636/40-1663) continued the excavations. Eventually the family moved to Massachusetts permanently, settling at Montague.

Dr. Jasper Gunn had a large family by his wife Mary Christian, many of whom intermarried with some of New England's most prominent families: the Websters, Judds, Wyatts, Gillettes, and more. Among those intermarriages was that of Nathaniel Gunn (1693-1779) to Esther Belding, whose aunt Elizabeth Belding (1663-1735) married on 31 January 1682, at Springfield, Massachusetts, Henry Gilbert, a descendant of Adrian Gilbert, John Dee's partner in exploration.

Asahel Gunn (1757-1834) married, on 12 September 1776, his cousin Lucy Gunn (1756-1790). Lucy's grandmother, Mary Russell, had also married her distant cousin, Joseph Root; both Mary Russell and Joseph Root were direct descendants of Sir Francis Russell, second Earl of Bedford, one of John Dee's closest associates. In fact, the Gunn family intermarried for several generations with cousins—the

Gunns, the Roots, the Marshes, the Russells, the Morleys—almost as though it was designed (see Appendix: Genealogy).

Asahel Gunn, aforementioned, was born 5 February 1757 at Montague, Massachusetts, a son of Asahel Gunn, Sr., and Thankful Marsh. At the outbreak of the American Revolution, he enlisted in the regiment of none other than Major General Arthur St. Clair, serving not only in the Revolutionary War, but afterwards in several Indian campaigns. The daughter of Asahel Gunn and Lucy Gunn, whose name was also Lucy, married her cousin Isaac Morley.

Lucy Gunn was born 24 January 1786 at Montague, Massachusetts. Her mother died when she was only four, and her father remarried two years later to Submit Bardwell. Her cousin, Isaac Morley, became her childhood sweetheart.

Isaac Morley was born at Montague on 11 March 1786, a son of Thomas Morley (1758-1844) and Editha Marsh (1762-1843); Editha's father, Ebenezer Marsh, Jr. (1716-1800), was brother of Thankful Marsh (1728-1817), who married Asahel Gunn, Sr. Those relationships, though complex, are very important.

Isaac Morley's immigrant ancestor was Thomas Morley (1665-1712), who was born in Bottesford, Lincolnshire, England, and came to America at about the age of twenty-five, settling first at Salem, Massachusetts, where he married (8 Dec. 1681) to Martha Wright. Shortly after his marriage, Thomas Morley removed to Westford, Massachusetts, site of the memorial to Sir James Gunn! Then, if this were not "coincidence" enough, he left Massachusetts to migrate to Hartford County, Connecticut, where he became one of the founders of the town of Glastonbury!

The next three generations of the Morley family were born in Glastonbury, including Isaac's father, Thomas, in 1758; but Thomas migrated to Montague, Massachusetts, where he married Editha Marsh

(14 Feb. 1783). And at Montague their son Isaac was born in 1786.

———

In previous chapters we have recounted the history of Isaac Morley. We mentioned that he married his cousin and childhood sweetheart, Lucy Gunn (20 June 1812), in the midst of the War of 1812. By 1810 he had constructed a cabin in the Western Reserve, at a place which became the town of Kirtland, Ohio, and following his service in the War of 1812, he settled permanently on his farm near Kirtland.

Initially a Presbyterian, in 1828 Isaac was baptized into the "Campbellite" church by Pastor Sidney Rigdon. This church, founded by a Scotsman, Alexander Campbell, was based in West Virginia, but was gaining converts rapidly along the expanding frontier. However, the following year brought about a major development of considerable significance. Isaac Morley and Sidney Rigdon traveled to Cincinnati to hear a debate between Alexander Campbell and the great Welsh reformer, Robert Owen. Because they did, we discovered a strong connection between Isaac Morley and the Madoc cult—and ultimately to John Dee and the Rosicrucians.

———

By the year 1791, near the time of Benjamin Franklin's death in America, correspondence in the *Gentleman's Magazine* and the *Public Advertiser* in England had led to the formation of an influential Madoc cult among quite a number of Welsh literary figures, some missionary arms of the Free Churches, and the large Welsh colony in London, which had formed a branch of the Cymmrodorion Society.

The prime mover in the establishment of this Madoc "school" was Edward Williams, better known as the bard Iolo Morganwg (1740-1826), an Eisteddfod oracle who developed an obsessive interest in the stories of Madoc. With his friend, Dr. W. Owen-Pughe, he wrote a series of notes in defense of the Madoc legend in the

Gentleman's Magazine, the *Cambrian Biography* and the *Cambro-Briton*. Together these two men revived interest in Madoc, chiefly by popularizing ancient bardic odes, in the case of Iolo Morganwg, while Owen-Pughe, who was the author of the *Dictionary of the Welsh Language*, collected ten different accounts of Madoc, all confirming his discovery of land in the west.

It seemed their purpose was to promote and publicize the Madoc legend, to what end is not clear, except that it perpetuated the same cult begun by John Dee two centuries earlier. Dr. Owen-Pughe was responsible for popularizing Madoc as a subject for literary discussion in London. They formed a literary circle which met regularly at a place with which by now we were quite familiar—the "Gentleman's Club of Spalding." This Club was a well-known meeting place for those involved in arcane and esoteric pursuits, and among its alumni were Benjamin Franklin, Sir Isaac Newton, Robert Boyle, and at least two of Joseph Smith's ancestors: Robert Smith and Thomas French.

No sooner had Iolo Morganwg and Owen-Pughe established their Madoc cult than they began to recruit new members from among their friends and associates. The next to join them was their common friend, the poet Robert Southey (1774-1803); and with Southey we had a firm connection. Robert Southey had been a partner with poets William Wordsworth and Samuel Coleridge in the establishment of a socialistic endeavor called "Pantisocracy," and was a strong advocate of the cause of the French Revolution.

Southey joined the Madoc movement with his friend, the redoubtable Dr. Samuel Johnson, and he set out immediately to pursue and further the Madoc story. Southey decided to immortalize Madoc in an epic poem, and leased a house in Wales where he lived for many months to absorb the atmosphere and scenery. Some of his material was obtained from Iolo

Morganwg, to whom he paid tribute in his poem:

> Iolo, old Iolo, he who knows
>
> The virtue of all herbs of mount or vale,
>
> Or green wood shade, or quiet brooklet's bed:
>
> Whatever lore of science, or of song
>
> Sages and bards of old have handed down.

And Southey wrote in his poem Madoc, which he composed in 1805, the year of Joseph Smith's birth:

> Not with a heart unmoved I left thy shores
>
> Dear native isle! Not without a pang,
>
> As the fair uplands lessen'd on the view,
>
> Cast back the long involuntary looks!
>
> The morning cheered our outset; gentle airs
>
> Curl'd the blue deep, and bright the summer sun
>
> Played o'er the summer ocean, when our barques
>
> Began their way.

Iolo Morganwg's passion for the Madoc legend was such that he announced his intention of visiting America to search for the "Madogwys" who, he claimed, were the descendants of Madoc and his colony. This trip never materialized, so he turned his obsession towards translating the Madoc story from what he claimed were genuine Welsh medieval texts. The finished product appeared in the third series of *Triads in the Myvyrian Archaiology* and was received as a real historical revelation.

The tenth of these Triads claims to be a

record of three great mysteries of the sea: the first that of *Gafran ab Aeddan* (Aeddan or Aidan was the father of King Arthur) and his followers who set out in search of the Isles of Llion and were never heard of again; the second, that of *Merlin*, the bard of Aurelius Ambrosius, and his nine Cylfeirdd, who sailed away in the Glass House into oblivion; the third, that of *Madoc ab Owain Gwynedd* who "went to sea with three hundred men in ten ships and nobody knows where they went to." We were reminded that it had first been John Dee who put forth this claim to Richard Hakluyt and others, though Geoffrey of Monmouth's *History of the Kings of Britain*, finished in around 1136, listed King Arthur's and King Malgo's conquests overseas.

In 1791, Iolo Morganwg headed an arcane society composed of literary giants of his day, including Robert Southey. But Iolo had also long maintained a correspondence with Benjamin Franklin on the subject of the Welsh Indians. Franklin informed Iolo that more than thirty years earlier, when he had conducted peace negotiations with the Six Nations near Carlisle, Pennsylvania, he had been told by members of the Indian delegation that remnants of a tribe which spoke words of Welsh lived in the vicinity of "the Big Bend of the Susquehanna, at a camp they call Towanda."

Now we encountered another phase of Iolo Morganwg's plan to prove the Madoc legend. Two other men entered the scheme, two very wealthy men, who financed Iolo's grand design of sending agents all over Wales in quest of ancient manuscripts and books, prior to his publication of the Triads. These same two men also supported Iolo's unusual plan of practicing Druidical rites on Primrose Hill. The two men who financed Iolo's dreams and schemes were Owen Jones, a prosperous furrier of Upper Thomas Street (who purchased furs through the Hudson's Bay Company), and the other was John Hoppner (1758-1810).

Hoppner was the illegitimate son of King George III, and half-brother of Augustus Frederick (1763-1827), Duke of Sussex, the latter of whom was fellow Mason with Giovanni Belzoni in the St. James Lodge, and Belzoni was a procurer of Egyptian mummies in Egypt, which came into possession of Joseph Smith. Moreover, John Hoppner, financier of Iolo Morganwg's search for Madoc, was the teacher of Henry Salt at the Royal Academy in 1800, and Salt was the English Consul in Egypt, and the uncle of Michael Chandler, who sold the Egyptian mummies and papyri to Joseph Smith in 1835, from which Smith "translated" the Book of Abraham and other Mormon doctrinal works.

During the French Revolution, Benjamin Franklin set aside Towanda, Pennsylvania, as a refuge for French aristocrats fleeing the Terror. Among those who sought refuge there were Louis Philippe, the Citizen King, and his brother the Duke of Beaujolais. Louis Philippe, curiously, donned the garb of a frontiersman and for several years wandered throughout Kentucky and the Carolinas, and as far north as New York, looking for adventure—or something more tangible. His sister Pamela had a daughter who lived at Palmyra, New York.

At about the same time came William Wordsworth, Samuel Coleridge, and Robert Southey, who envisaged an American Utopia, along the same lines as that proposed by Sir Francis Bacon, a socialistic order they called "Pantisocracy." The site they chose to establish this ideal society was none other than Towanda, Pennsylvania.

Pantisocracy never got off the ground, and the primary reason was that the movers put most of their finances behind another project—which had some connection to Towanda—a project to find something connected with Madoc which would provide authority to establish all of America as a giant "Pantisocracy."

It began when William Owen, one of the alumni of the Madoc cult from the "Gentleman's Club of Spalding," was very much taken with a strange character calling himself "Chief" William Bowles, who appeared in London wearing his chieftain's headdress and recounting stories of Welsh Indians in America. William Owen soon eagerly reported to the *Gentleman's Magazine* that he and Richard Williams had met Bowles and were satisfied with his evidence. That evidence concerned an early connection with Utah! Owen wrote:

When Chief Bowles was asked why he thought the white Indians were Welsh, he replied, "A Welshman was with me at home for some time. He had been a prisoner among the Spaniards and worked in the mines of Mexico. By some means he contrived to escape, got into the wilds and made his way across the Continent, and eventually found himself with a people with whom he could converse and stayed there some time."

Amongst other particulars, he told me that "they had several books, which were mostly religiously kept in skins, and were considered by them as mysteries. These they believed gave an account from whence they had come. These people told the Welshmen that they had not seen a white man like themselves, who was a stranger, for a long time."

It must be remembered that in the late 18th century, "Mexico" was considered to be the Rocky Mountains, and not merely the southern country to which we now refer. The "mines of Mexico" refer to the Spanish gold mines in the Uintah Basin region of what is now Utah, as we shall see. The fact that the natives possessed books which recorded their ancient history is reminiscent of both John Dee's *Secret Book of Madog* and Joseph Smith's *Book of Mormon*.

Bowles' enthusiasm soon spread to his new-found comrades in the Madoc cult, who revived an old interest in sending an expedition to America in search of the Welsh Indians. As early as 1 March 1733 a group of Welshmen wrote a letter to the British Missionary Society in London urging such an expedition. The letter stated:

"It is not unknown to you that Madoc Gwynedd, a Prince of Wales, did about five hundred years ago, sail westward. ...Some relics of the Welsh tongue being found in old and deserted settlements about the Mississippi make it probable that he sailed up that river. And we, being moved with brotherly love to our countrymen, are meditating to go in search of them, but are discouraged by the distance of the place and the uncertainty of the course we would steer. If you can give us any information and direction together with some help to bear expense we shall find men adventurous enough to undertake the expedition, having no other end in view than to carry the gospel of peace among our ancient brethren; and believing it will be to the enlightenment of the British empire in America and a proof of prior right to the whole continent should we happily succeed."

We remain, gentleman, your loving countrymen,

(signed)John Davis,

David Evans,

Nathaniel Jenkins,

Benjamin Griffith,

Joseph Eton.

Inspired by Bowles and the enthusiasm of the Welsh missionary societies, the members of the literary cult of the Gentleman's Club soon formulated a plan of raw expedition. In 1791 William Owen approached Iolo Morganwg and Thomas Pennant with the proposition, and they in turn incorporated the support of Robert

Southey and his Pantisocracy associates, Wordsworth and Coleridge. The Welsh reformer, Robert Owen, donated funds in support of the expedition, as did Owen Jones and John Hoppner, to mention only a few.

Iolo Morganwg had originally intended to be the one to make the pilgrimage, but at the last moment he was too involved in his zealous claim to have rediscovered the ancient ritual of the Druids, and another had to be found to take his place. The man who was finally chosen was an unknown twenty-one year-old named John Evans from the village of Waunfawr, near Caernarvon, Wales.

Evans sailed for America near the end of summer in 1792, and set out on his quest for the Welsh Indians in the spring of 1793. Evans studied his maps and decided that the Indians he sought lived somewhere high up the Missouri River. He considered the northern route to reach them and even sought letters of introduction to the Governors of Canada, but ultimately chose a route from the south. In March 1793, Evans crossed the Allegheny Mountains to the Ohio River, down which he sailed for seven hundred miles until he reached the Mississippi. He proceeded by boat up the Mississippi for another two hundred miles to that river's junction with the Missouri at St. Louis. After some adventures, which included two years in prison, Evans connected with a Scotsman named James Mackay.

Mackay was a member of the Scottish clan that had been an ancient enemy of the clan Gunn. He had arrived in Nova Scotia as a member of the Royal Scots, which had first arrived in Nova Scotia under the command of Sir Jeffrey Amherst. Mackay, in company with other fellow Scots, worked as a trapper in Canada for the Hudson's Bay Company (where he worked with Etienne Provost, who later explored Utah), during which time he had gained important experience in organizing exploring expeditions. The Spaniards, learning his reputation, first secured his services and then, impressed with his abilities, gave him Spanish nationality. Within a short time they gave him the title of Principal Explorer and Director of Indian Territory in the Missouri Company, which had been established by the Spaniards to build a series of new forts. The new territory had to first be explored and charted, and the Spaniards hoped that by following the Missouri River to its source they might eventually find a tributary connecting westward to the Pacific Ocean. It was hoped that Mackay's 1795 expedition would succeed where others had failed. Mackay employed John Evans in the hopes that if the story of the Welsh-speaking Indians was true, Evans, acting as interpreter, might interrogate them as to the Pacific route. Evans was appointed second in command to Mackay.

We had more than passing interest in James Mackay, for only as little as two or three years earlier, he had been in charge of escorting Lord Edward Fitzgerald down the Mississippi to New Orleans on his way to visit the "Mexican mines." And we were reminded that Lord Fitzgerald had married the mysterious Pamela, sister to Louis Philippe, and that the daughter of Pamela would, in a few years, come to reside in Joseph Smith's home town of Palmyra, New York, and subsequently helped finance the publication of the Book of Mormon.

Lord Fitzgerald's mysterious journey to the "Mexican mines" seemed to us a convenient excuse for something else. Official records are mostly silent, except to state that Fitzgerald came from Canada, where he had been formally admitted into the Bear tribe, along the Missouri River past St. Louis, where he engaged Mackay to escort him down the Mississippi to New Orleans to seek permission from the Spanish Governor Miro to proceed to the Mexican mines, but that permission was denied.

It seems apparent that Lord Edward Fitzgerald had met the Mandans on the Missouri, and they had told him something of the Indians who resided in Mexico (Utah region) where they labored in the gold mines of the Spaniards, perhaps that they were related and were also descendants of Madoc. Immediately thereafter, John Evans joined James Mackay to find the Mandans and through them learn a route through the Rocky Mountains. But after several years of wandering the upper headquarters of the Missouri, though finding the Mandans, Evans and Mackay had to admit defeat. Evans settled at New Orleans, where he became a member of the household of Don Manuel Gayoso de Lemos, the new Governor of New Orleans. By 1797 John Evans, the "pious and virtuous" Welshman from a Methodist family, was a declared traitor to his country, a drunkard who lay stupefied in brothels for days at a time, and in declining health. The Spaniards, to keep him quiet, offered Evans employment as a land surveyor, an annuity for life, and a two thousand dollar down payment in cash. Don Lemos asked Evans to map out the frontier between Spanish and British and United States possessions. The map was completed according to a letter which President Thomas Jefferson wrote to Captain Meriwether Lewis on 13 January 1804, in which he stated: "I now enclose a map of the Missouri as far as the Mandans. It is said to be very accurate. It was done by a Mr. John Evans by order of the Spanish Government."

Where did Jefferson (who succeeded Franklin as Rosicrucian Grand Master) obtain Evans' map? We found the answer in the National Archives, and the revelation made the circle of connections complete. According to the files of the Lewis and Clark expedition, Jefferson obtained the map from none other than Louis Philippe, the Citizen King!

Louis Philippe (1773-1850), son of the Duke of Orleans by Louise Marie Adelaide de Bourbon, was the godson of Marie Antoinette, and close friend of Charles Nodier and Victor Hugo (both Grand Masters of the Prieuré de Sion). In 1796 the Directory offered to release his mother and

two brothers from the Bastille on condition that he would go to America. He arrived to Towanda, Pennsylvania, in October 1796, and for the next three years he wandered through the wilderness, dressed in the garb of a frontiersman, leading "hunting" expeditions into the North Carolina-Kentucky frontier.

Louis Philippe was in New Orleans during the summer of 1798, and was a guest at the palace of Governor Manuel Gayoso de Lemos, and there apparently met John Evans, who was a member of Don Lemos' household, and from him obtained a copy of the map. Louis Philippe maintained friendly relations with the Spaniards; eventually, his son Antoine Philippe married the younger sister of Queen Isabella of Spain.

The question thus arises: Why was Louis Philippe interested in a map of the Upper Missouri, drawn by a Welshman, delineating the location of the Mandan villages? The only feasible answer is that Louis Philippe, soon to become King of France, whose niece would soon settle at Palmyra, New York, was searching for the Welsh Indians! To what end is uncertain, but we found it significant that when Louis Philippe returned to France, and so exiled himself almost immediately to England with his brothers, the mansion which was offered him in Twickenham was arranged for by none other than John Hoppner as agent for King George III (Hoppner's father). And, of course, we cannot ignore the fact that Louis Philippe was brother-in-law of Lord Edward Fitzgerald.

As for John Evans, on 20 May 1799, Don Manuel wrote to Mackay: "Poor Evans is very ill. I perceived that he deranged himself when out of my sight, but I perceived it too late. The strength of the liquor has deranged his head; he has been out of his sense for several days, but with care he is doing better, and I hope he will get well."

He didn't. John Evans died before the end of the month in New Orleans at the age of twenty-nine.

It seems fairly certain, based upon available evidence, that several opposing arcane societies were vying for the same "treasure" in the Palmyra-Towanda region. Benjamin Franklin, Grand Master of the Rosicrucians, established a colony for French refugees at Towanda, Pennsylvania, at the Big Bend of the Susquehanna River, where descendants of Prince Madoc once had a village.

A German dissenter named George Rapp established a socialistic-religious colony at Towanda which the "Rappites" called Harmony. William Wordsworth, Samuel Coleridge, and Robert Southey established their own socialistic-utopian society at Harmony which they called "Pantisocracy." One of their partners and investors in Pantisocracy was the reformer Robert Owen, a Scotsman who belonged to the Madoc cult which met at the Gentleman's Club of Spalding.

Robert Owen purchased Harmony, Pennsylvania, from the Rappites where he hoped to establish his own socialistic community with a Baconian-type government. Eventually Owen chose another site in the state of Indiana, which he called "New Harmony." New Harmony was a communistic society, where all residents shared equally all possessions and all responsibilities.

Having established his model society, Owen began a series of lectures to recruit new members to his philosophy. In 1829 he was challenged to a debate by Alexander Campbell, founder of the "Campbellite" religion, who took exception to his philosophy, and they met in public debate at Cincinnati. Isaac Morley and Sidney Rigdon, recent converts to the Campbellite religion, came down from Kirtland to attend the debate and support Campbell in his defense of their faith; however, after listening to the debate and meeting personally with Robert Owen, Morley and Rigdon instantly defected from the Campbellite

church, returned to Kirtland, and established their own communistic society on Morley's farm, which they called *The Family*. The members of The Family held all things in common, which was the condition they believed existed in the early church.

In 1830, Mormon missionaries visited Kirtland, and when they returned to New York, Sidney Rigdon went with them, to meet the Prophet Joseph Smith. Almost immediately, Smith moved the whole body of the Church to Kirtland. Morley converted and was baptized, Joseph Smith moved into his home, and eventually married one of Isaac's daughters as a plural wife.

The secret societies were searching for something—something that had been hidden up in America long before, something that would give them the power and authority to establish the Kingdom of God on Earth in the last days. The evidence leads to only one conclusion—that those relics were the Ark of the Covenant, the Stone of Scone, and the sacred contents of the Temple of Solomon, without which there could be no establishment of a New Jerusalem.

Chapter Twenty-Three

The Sign and The Seal

John Brewer found a cave and ruined his life; but what he discovered may have changed the history of the world. He may have found the key to an ancient mystery when he discovered two mummified corpses—a man and a woman—and a number of stone boxes containing metal plates bearing strange inscriptions. The plates, the mummies, the symbols on the stone boxes, and the ancient inscriptions on ledges throughout the Sanpete region offered the very first clues to solving the mystery of Sanpete Valley.

In the concluding chapter we will advance a hypothesis, based upon our investigations, about what once lay hidden—and may yet repose—in some secret vault in the Sanpete Valley region. We will leave it ultimately to the readers to draw their own conclusions.

———

America was inhabited and visited far more anciently than generally believed. Philosophers such as the Greek scholar Plato (427-347 B.C.) and mystic-scientists like Sir Francis Bacon and Dr. John Dee, believed that America was synonymous with the ancient "Lost Continent" of Atlantis. They believed that it was inhabited by an advanced race whose ancient king was Atlas; his subjects were called Atlanteans or Aztlans. We believe they were the ancestors of the Aztecs.

Later, America or Atlantis was equated with the Garden of Eden, the Promised Land, a land more choice than any other, where the government of a "Kingdom of God" would be established in the Last Days. The land had been prophesied from ancient times to become the "New Atlantis," the "New Jerusalem," the "New Zion" of the Last Dispensation.

Ancient America was something else, too; it was the source of the greatest deposit of gold in the world! It was known from very early times as the land of the legendary "Golden Fleece," the "Gold of the Gods," "El Dorado," the "Seven Cities of Cibola," "King Solomon's Mines," and "Carre-Shinob."

Circa 1194 B.C. Jason and the Argonauts sailed from Greece to the kingdom of Colchis in quest of the Golden Fleece. Colchis was the land of the ancestors of the Aztecs, within the region encompassing the present State of Utah. All doubt seems to be dispelled by a statement of John Dee in the preface of his work, *The Secret Book of Madog*, wherein he states that:

...the ancient inhabitants of that land [Atlantis, i.e. America], as it is written, lived far inland near a great body [of water] which they called Sal Mer [the Salt Sea]. ...The people there are called Aztlans, so writ Madog, Prince of Gwynedd, who have g [i.e. gold] in great abundance. The g is the purest kind, from which they fashion all the forms of their adornment. ...The Aztlans have great stone temples, and so writ Noahtl, a scribe of that nation, that every dram of g therein was of a weight and measure equal to the stones of their foundation...

John Dee's "Sal Mer" can only be the Great Salt Lake, one of only two inland salt seas in the world (the other being the Dead Sea). One is tempted to see the name of "Noah" in the name "Noahtl," but it is likely only coincidental. The native language of the Aztecs is "Nahuatl," and this appears to be a more logical source.

The ancient Colchians lived in a land plentiful with gold and they built stone temples and adorned them with the sacred gold. They were the guardians of the "Golden Fleece," which was certainly synonymous with the fabulous trove which the Native Americans called "Carre-Shinob." The Golden Fleece was quite possibly something else too: it may have been a solid gold statue of a ram that stood on an acropolis atop the temple mount of their city, according to established traditions connected to the Order of the Golden Fleece.

Our hypothesis, derived from a compilation of all the evidence, postulates that the Sanpete Valley and its environs comprised the ancient land of Colchis, existing from before 2000 B.C. The ancient King of the Colchians was the legendary Atlas, guardian of the greatest source of gold in the world, deep in the volcanic caverns of the nearby Uintah Mountains.

Aeas was the city of the Colchians when Jason and the Argonauts arrived there circa 1194 B.C., and Aeetes was their king. Aeas may have stood where the city of Manti now stands, and the Argonauts built a temple to Athena on Temple Hill, wherein the rites of the Orphic Mysteries were performed; and the Golden Fleece was its altar.

Space does not permit a full study of the significance of the Golden Fleece, beyond that which we have already explored; suffice it that it was inextricably connected to both the Orphic Mysteries and the Philosopher's Stone (as Sir Walter Raleigh pointed out in his *History of the World*). Part of its sacred nature was due to the fact that its gold was used by alchemists to transmute other base metals into gold, and into a mysterious red powder said to grant immortality (the Greek's "Nectar of the Gods"). In some of the Orphic rites, the Golden Fleece is even equated with the Golden Calf of the Exodus (and sometimes Moses is equated with Orpheus).

Many of the secret societies adopted an "Order of the Golden Fleece" as part of their rites. In addition, the Order of the Golden Fleece was one of the most illustrious chivalric orders in Europe. It had been inaugurated by Philip, Duke of Burgundy, in 1429, and later split into two branches, being awarded by the King of Spain and the Holy Roman Emperor, respectively. It is also noteworthy that William Sinclair, builder of Rosslyn Chapel and guardian of the Templar treasure, had many titles including "the Knight of the Cockle and Golden Fleece."

The fabulous caverns of gold in the Uintah Mountains (which now appear to have been lava tubes that filled with molten gold) became the source of ancient legends throughout ensuing centuries. The presence of Jason and the Argonauts (or at least Greek presence) in the Sanpete region seems to be confirmed by the Greek inscriptions found there, as well as carved sculptures of the Athenian school mentioned in a previous chapter.

Jason escaped with the Golden Fleece circa 1194 B.C., but Greeks continued to visit the land of Colchis during the centuries that followed. In about 950 B.C. the Greek navigator Milesius sailed for the New World and returned with shiploads of gold for the construction and adornment of Solomon's Temple; Solomon and Milesius were brothers-in-law. The Temple contained, among many other things, the Ark of the Covenant, the Coronation Stone, and other holy relics and treasure of immense value and significance. In addition, the caverns beneath the Temple on Mount Moriah were filled with gold, brought from the land of Colchis.

When Solomon's Temple was destroyed by the army of Nebuchadnezzar in 587 B.C., the Prophet Jeremiah managed to remove the Ark of the Covenant and probably the Coronation Stone, and escaped with them first to Egypt and then to Ireland, together with Tamar (Tea) Tephi, the daughter of Zedekiah, last King of Israel.

Tamar Tephi married Eochaidh, Heremon (King) of Ireland, while standing on the Stone, with Jeremiah officiating. Tamar and Eochaidh brought together the prophetic lineage of Pharez and Zarah, and became the ancestors of Jesus. Tamar died suddenly after giving birth to her only child and heir, a son who sired a long line of Irish and Scottish kings who were crowned on the Stone. Tamar's tomb was erected within the sacred hill of Tara, and called the "Mergech" ("Repository" in Hebrew). It was constructed to the exact dimensions of the Tabernacle and the Holy of Holies in Solomon's Temple (as was Rosslyn Chapel), and enshrined in this sacred cavern next to the mummified body of Tamar Tephi were the Holy Relics: the Ark of the Covenant, the Sword of Methuselah, David's Harp (which image adorns the modern flag of the Republic of Ireland), and other Temple treasures.

The Coronation Stone, which the Irish called Lia Fail (Stone of Destiny), was placed above the Mergech, and thereon were crowned all of the kings of Ireland for more than a thousand years, from Eochaidh in 586 B.C. to the 131st Ard-Righ (High King) named Murcheartach (Murdock). In 513 A.D., Murcheartach "loaned" the Stone to his brother Fergus on which to be crowned King of Alba (Scotland) and it was never returned. The kings of Scotland were crowned upon the "Stone of Scone" (as they called it) until the year 1296, when King Edward captured it and removed it to England, where it was placed beneath the Coronation Chair in Westminster Abbey.

But the Scots claim to have had the last laugh. When Edward demanded that they turn over to him the Stone of Scone, the abbot of Arbroath Abbey hid it up and produced instead a stone step from the abbey, which the English never questioned. Tradition maintains that the sacred Stone was placed under the guardianship of the Sinclairs of Rosslyn, and that Robert the Bruce was secretly crowned upon it. After-

wards it was removed, with the rest of the treasure of Rosslyn, to the New World. It may well have become one of the hidden treasures of the Sanpete Valley. This is verified by Laurence Gardner [*Bloodline of the Holy Grail*, Barnes & Noble Inc., (1997) pp.298-99] as follows:

"Princess Tamar (Teamhair) gave her name to Tara, the seat of the High Kings of Ireland, and she married Ard Ri (High King) Eochaidh, ancestor of Ugaine Már (Ugaine the Great). Subsequently, over a millennium, Eochaidh's successors were crowned in the presence of the sacred Stone. The Irish heritage then progressed into Scotland, where the relic of Judah became synonymous with the Kings of Dalriada. King Kenneth I MacAlpin (844-859) later moved the Stone to Scone Abbey when he united the Scots and the Picts. By the time of William the Lion (d. 1214), the Stone of Destiny bore witness to nearly a hundred coronations in sovereign descent from King Zedekiah.

"On declaring himself Overlord of Scotland in 1296, Edward I of England stole what he thought was the Stone of Destiny. What he actually got was a piece of sandstone from a monastery doorway, which has since rested beneath the Coronation Throne at Westminster Abbey. This piece of rubble is 26 inches long by 11 inches deep (c.66 x 28 cm) and weighs about 335 lbs (c. 152 kg). Royal seals of the early Scots kings depict a much larger installation rock, but this rock was not the sacred Stone of Destiny - no more than is the medieval masonry prize of King Edward. The real stone of Destiny is said to be smaller, more naturally rounded, and is of inscribed black basalt, not of hand-cut sandstone. It was hidden by the Cistercian Abbot of Scone in 1296, and it has remained hidden ever since. The Columban tradition tells that, on secreting the Stone, the Abbot prophesied that one day 'The Michael' would return to his inheritance. It is of importance to note that the x sign, which became so hated by the Roman Church, was identified with the archangel Michael (Melchizedok) onwards from Old Testament times. The heritage of St. Michael was the dynasty of high Zadok priests - a heritage that prevailed in the continuing Messianic line. The relationship of St. Andrew with the saltire was a later development....In relation to the real Stone, the Revd J. MacKay Nimmo of St. Columba's Church, Dundee, has since stated, 'When Scotland achieves self-government, the Stone will reappear...Until then, we will continue to guard this ancient symbol of our national identity.'"

During the Crusades the Templars were organized at Jerusalem and began excavating beneath the ruins of Solomon's Temple. What they discovered there made them wealthy and powerful, and they transported it to France where it was deposited in their Paris preceptory.

At this time there came to France one Madoc, Prince of Wales, who became Grand Master of the Cambrian Order of Templars, and he was given something significant that had been found beneath the Temple. In 1170 A.D., Madoc sailed away with the relic to the New World. Madoc, himself a descendant of the clan Gunn (Möre), established colonies in both North and Central America and, according to tradition, became King of the Aztecs. Native Americans of the inter-mountain region all claim descent from the "Welsh Indians."

It is our contention that Madoc brought one of the several copies of the Ark to the New World and placed it in a temple (perhaps remnants of the Athenian-Orphic temple of the Golden Fleece) on Temple Hill in Sanpete Valley.

It would be logical to conclude that when the Aztecs migrated south to Mexico they would have carried the Ark away with them, but this does not seem to be the case. The Aztecs held the Uintah Mountain region sacred, primarily due to the gold source and the caverns from which they believed their race derived, and over the centuries Aztec priests made pilgrimages to

the region, establishing what the Utes refer to as the "Trail of the Old Ones," to obtain ceremonial gold and to pay respects to their gods. Due to the Utes' continued reverence for the sacred valley of Sanpete, and Temple Hill, it seems logical to conclude that something significant reposed there. In the concluding chapter we hope to present even stronger evidence.

We have shown the relationship between the Sinclairs and the Gunns, and that through their auspices the Temple treasure was removed from Scotland to the New World between 1398 and 1545. The "Money Pit" of Nova Scotia has long been believed to be its hiding place, but every effort to expose it has met with failure. Sir James Gunn lost his life at Westford, Massachusetts, and Sir James was the direct ancestor of Lucy Gunn, wife of Isaac Morley. We have also shown that the Morley, Gunn, and Sinclair families had a common origin with the clan Möre of Norway (as also Madoc ap Owain Gwynedd). They appear to have been a chosen lineage, destined to alter the history of the world and of mankind.

The Gunns had been among the earliest discoverers of America, and Gunnar, an early navigator and explorer, had been the discoverer of Greenland in the early part of the tenth century A.D. Indeed, it may well have been the Gunns who gave America its name. Contrary to popular belief, America was called by that name long before the advent of Amerigo Vespucci.

Vespucci, a wealthy ship-chandler in Seville who did not sail to the New World until 1499, seven years after Columbus, was erroneously given credit for the name by an obscure clergyman named Waldseemüller, from the monastery of St. Deodatus in the Vosges Mountains in the Duchy of Lorraine on the French/German border. With a small group of associates, Waldseemüller printed a 103-page volume in April 1507 they called *Cosmographie Introductio*. Therein they gave Amerigo Vespucci credit for discovering the "fourth part" of the world, adding that "...I see no reason why any one should justly object to calling this part Amerige (from the Greek 'ge' meaning 'land of'), i.e. the land of Amerigo, or America, after Amerigo, its discoverer, a man of great ability."

Because Waldseemüller's book was the first printed reference, the credit stuck, and even when he made a public recantation, no one paid it any heed. It is still erroneously taught in public schools that America was named in honor of Amerigo Vespucci.

In fact the name "America" had been known since before the time of Jesus. It was associated with a mystical star called "Merica." The name was recorded by the Mandaeans, who were direct descendants of the Nasoreans (which was the sect to which Jesus belonged), who were the same group as the Qumranians, the people who buried their secret scrolls under Herod's Temple in 68 A.D. The forefathers of the Mandaeans were the authors of the scrolls which the Templars unearthed, which told of a mystical land beneath a star called "Merica." The Templars learned about the wonderful promised land beneath the bright lone star from the scrolls, and it is believed they sailed west to find it. Masonic writers Christopher Knight and Robert Lomas have written, "Maybe Templar descendants had been involved in naming the new continent; maybe the Templars themselves actually went in search of a land under the evening star they knew from their discoveries to be called 'Merica.'" [*The Hiram Key*, op.cit.p.77]

The proof is found in Rosslyn Chapel where carvings in the interior architecture show aloe cactus and Indian maize, both New World plants that were supposedly unknown outside that continent until well into the sixteenth century; and the carvings were made in Rosslyn Chapel prior to 1470, at least twenty-two years prior to Columbus' voyage.

Also in Rosslyn Chapel, carved into the wall of the underground crypt, is the coat-of-arms of the clan Gunn—a Viking ship with sails unfurled, sailing West towards the mystical star called "Merica." The same coat-of-arms appears on the same memorial to Sir James Gunn at Westford, Massachusetts, and on a ledge at Oak Island, Nova Scotia, indicating that they made it. Knight and Lomas also made the connection:

Whilst the Grand Master [Jacques de Molay] was being crucified, many Templars had slipped the net. A large part of the Templar fleet had been in harbour at the Atlantic sea port of La Rochelle and they must have been tipped off or picked up some rumours, for as the sun rose on the morning of Friday 13 October, the would-be arresting guards could see only water where the fleet had been tied up the night before. The ships of the Order were never seen again, but their battle flag, the skull and crossbones, was.

We now needed to establish what happened to those Templars that managed to escape the clutches of King Philip. From our investigations we found that their presence can be detected in two places soon after the escape: Scotland and America.

...They point their bows exactly due west and set sail on what is now the forty-second parallel in search of the land marked by the star they knew from the Nasorean scrolls was called Merica, which these French knights referred to as "la Merica," a name that later became simply America. They almost certainly landed in the Cape Cod or Rhode Island area of New England in the early weeks of 1308, setting foot on the New World nearly a century and a half before Christopher Columbus was even born.

This is a strong claim, but irrefutable evidence is already in existence to show that the Templars did reach America, settled there and that they carried out journeys to and from Scotland. In the small town of Westford, Massachusetts, there is an image of a knight carved as a series of punched holes into a slab of rock. The now-famous knight can be seen to be wearing a helmet and the habit of a military order and the sword shown in the weathered carving that has been identified as having a pommeled hilt of the style of a European knight of the fourteenth century. But for us the most fascinating feature is the shield which has a clear and simple design upon it; it depicts a single masted medieval vessel sailing west....towards a star. [*The Hiram Key*, op.cit., pp.288-89.]

The mystical coat of arms of the clan Gunn—which were quartered in the arms of the Sinclairs—has a very ancient pedigree and pedantic history. While it may have originated in Norway, it is first found on the arms of the kings of the Isle of Man from the reign of King Olaf the Black, who invaded the Sutherlands late in the fifth century. Olaf's son, Gunnar, a great navigator, maintained the arms, and is often credited with establishing the clan name of Gunn, though the name itself was already well established in the islands from as early as 279 A.D., and as we have noted may have been of Pictish origin.

One "King Gunn," who may well have been the father of Guinevere, allied with King Arthur to fight against the Saxons. We have also noted that John Dee claimed that Arthur sent navigators to Greenland and beyond to "Friseland" and even to "Estotiland"—America. And Dee's "secret" pedigrees showed Templar descent from King Arthur, which meant also of the Gunns, and he claimed the same descent for Queen Elizabeth I. It is clear that the Gunn family played a significant role in history. They appear to have been the secret power behind the throne of every Sea King from at least the fifth century to the sixteenth, a period of more than a thousand years.

As hereditary kings of Orkney, and through intermarriage, the Gunns empowered the Sinclairs to become Earls of Orkney. When the Sinclairs, by virtue of their descent from King Malcolm of Scot-land, became the rulers of Caithness, they did so again by the consent of the Gunns, the "Crowners" of Caithness.

The Gunn arms next appeared on the wall of a crypt in Rosslyn Chapel, where a number of Gunn knights were entombed with the Sinclairs. Sir James Gunn, of the "Crowners of Caithness," accompanied the Sinclair-Zeno Expedition of 1398 to Nova Scotia and Massachusetts, probably as chief navigator; the Gunns had been familiar with the New World for centuries. He left the Gunn arms engraved on ledges of rock at Oak Island in 1398 and at Westford, Massachusetts, the site of his death, in 1399, nearly a century before Columbus.

Two centuries later, Sir James Gunn's descendant, Dr. Jasper Gunn, emigrated from Scotland and settled in the vicinity of Sir James' death and burial site, and spent many years excavating the region around Westford, Massachusetts, apparently searching for something of great importance which could only have been connected in some fashion to his mysterious ancestor.

No less significant was the arrival of the Morley family in Massachusetts not long after the Gunns. The Morleys and Gunns were cousins and continued to intermarry, much as the Gunns had intermarried with their cousins the Sinclairs in Scotland. The Morley ancestors had been closely associated with the mystical Invisible College of the Rosicrucians, and some of them were close associates of Dr. John Dee. No sooner did they arrive in America than they helped to found the town of Glastonbury, Massachusetts. And we have shown that John Dee and Sir Francis Bacon discovered something very significant hidden up in Glastonbury Tor, England—all evidence indicates that it was the Ark of the Covenant—and removed it to America.

The Morleys were closely associated with Dee in England. Their presence in the vicinity of Sir James Gunn's burial place and the founding of a nearby town named

Glastonbury is more than coincidental. Like Dee, the Morleys and the Gunns were passionately absorbed in searching for treasure. And the Morleys and Gunns of New England were all members of Masonic orders and philosophical societies, with roots in the Templar movement.

Isaac Morley, educated in Salem, Massachusetts, continued the Morley family's association with the Rosicrucians. He established "The Family," based upon Robert Owen's order of "Harmony," similar to the "United Order" of Joseph Smith's "Mormon" Church, and Robert Owen was a member of the Madoc cult, first established by John Dee. Isaac Morley was instrumental in the foundation of the Mormon Church, and was party to Joseph Smith's purchase of the Egyptian mummies in 1835. He founded the majority of cities established by the Mormons, was instrumental in building their temples, and led the second migration of Saints to Utah in 1848. Almost immediately he was singled out by Chief Walker of the Utes to colonize the Sanpete Valley. Within a short time thereafter he was made privy to the secret of Carre-Shinob, and chose the site for the construction of a temple on Manti Hill.

More than thirty years ago I had the opportunity of meeting a descendant of Isaac Morley who resided at San Jose, California. This individual was also a member of the American order of Rosicrucians (A.M.O.R.C.) and was connected to that order's Egyptian museum, one of the finest collections in the world.

But the most interesting surprise was a private collection in the basement of this man's home. This collection had once belonged to Isaac Morley, and had been brought across the plains by him following the death of Joseph Smith. According to the curators of this private collection, and independently confirmed by LDS Church Archives, Morley brought a wagonload of "private" Church records West (including the "Nauvoo Bell" from the Nauvoo Temple) while Heber C. Kimball brought a wagonload of general Church records. A story was circulated that Morley's wagon was lost through the ice of the Mississippi River. It wasn't.

Morley's collection was astounding in diversity and content. There were numerous original documents in bales, tied with string and in some cases ribbon; there were ledgers and journals; there were rows of books, many of them very old and including the works of John Dee, Nicholas Flamel, Newton, and other esoteric writers. But the most amazing part of the collection were the artifacts. The centerpiece of these was an Egyptian mummy, ostensibly the mummy of Pharaoh Necho II, kept in a glass case. This mummy had been part of a number of mummies purchased by Joseph Smith in 1835, through the auspices of the societies. The artifacts also included a "seer stone," an ancient sword, and a Masonic dagger, among other things.

Of immense value historically were the journals of Isaac Morley. They were astutely kept and delineated the greater part of his life in detail. They confirm that he belonged to an ancient order which, though he never mentions by name, is clearly connected to the Rosicrucians. His association and close friendship with Chief Walker comprise a touching and informative part of his journals, and his detailed directions to Carre-Shinob enabled me to fulfill a lifelong dream to see the sacred caverns high in the Uintah Mountains. [see *The Gold of Carre-Shinob*, op.cit.]

———

The evidence is strong: a number of Arks were placed in various locations around the world, throughout various periods of history, under the auspices of the Templars, their predecessors and successors. At least one of these Arks found its way to the intermountain region of America under the care of Madoc ap Owain Gwynedd and may have reposed in a temple on Temple Hill in Manti.

Sir Francis Bacon and Dr. John Dee

acquired an Ark from the maze beneath Glastonbury Tor and removed it to America as part of their plan to establish a "New Jerusalem" in the New World. That Ark was secluded in a subterranean vault beneath the old Bruton Church in Williamsburg, Virginia, and subsequently disappeared. Sir Francis Bacon's coat-of-arms, a boar, seems to contain a cryptic code which shows the location of an Ark in the intermountain region.

If the Templar societies intended to establish a utopian government in America, the intermountain region would be the logical place for a capital, inasmuch as it was the source of sacred gold from which the Arks were made, and which adorned ancient temples. As we have seen in preceding chapters, this region had long been regarded as a sacred place, the land of Colchis and Atlantis, the Promised Land. Carre-Shinob, the "Mexican Mines," the repository of Montezuma's treasure, was the catalyst for myriads of searches through the centuries, from Jason's quest for the Golden Fleece, to Lord Edward Fitzgerald's search for the "Mexican Mines" in the American West.

Another possibility for what might have been hidden up in the Sanpete region of Utah is the Stone of Scone. We have shown previously that this ancient Stone, upon which were crowned the Kings of Israel, Ireland and Scotland for more than two thousand years, had been given over to the care of the Sinclairs of Rosslyn, and eventually removed to the New World with the bulk of the Temple treasure. If the Rosicrucian-Freemasonic orders intended to establish a New World government, with one of their own as King (and Laurence Gardner makes a strong argument for this in his masterful book *Bloodline of the Holy Grail*), then they would need the sacred Stone upon which to crown their monarch.

Finally, what may also be hidden up in Sanpete Valley or environs is the whole or part of the Templar treasure removed from Rosslyn, Scotland, to the New World. By all indications, the site chosen for the repository was Oak Island, Nova Scotia, but all efforts to solve the mystery of the so-called "Money Pit" have been met with failure. Henry Sinclair and Sir James Gunn spent as much time in the Massachusetts region as they did at Nova Scotia, and in light of the continued interest shown in that region by the Gunns and Morleys during the succeeding three centuries, it is logical to conclude that something was deposited there, near the burial place of Sir James Gunn.

Of all the possibilities of what may repose in the Sanpete Valley region, the strongest evidence points with certainty to the Ark of Covenant. In the concluding chapter we will present that evidence.

Chapter Twenty-Four

The Knight and The Ark

John Brewer found a cave in the hill behind the Manti Temple, and in the cave he discovered the mummified remains of a man and a woman. He made pen-and-ink sketches of the mummies, reposing in large stone sarcophaguses, and removed stone boxes containing metal plates from a second cave and took photographs of them.

Brewer himself made no professional assessment of his discoveries, though he appears to have accepted others' suggestions that the mummies were the remains of Book of Mormon characters, notably a "Jaredite King and Queen." Others were quick to note "Asian" features of the corpses and further pointed out what appeared to be a "Chinese dragon" motif in the carvings on the stone coffins. If the mummies were indeed "Jaredite," they would necessarily be more than 2500 years old, or more. While this is not impossible, the garments worn by the two ancient bodies preclude them from being Jaredite and in fact identify them quite readily.

Focusing specifically on the male mummy: *the attire is clearly the uniform of a Knight Templar*! The splayed cross across the mantle of the knight's chest is the most telling feature, but so is the helmet, and the sword. He is buried in true knightly fashion, indicating (as with the Gunns and Sinclairs at Rosslyn) that he was of nobility.

The splayed red cross—Maltese or Trungated Cross—was worn exclusively by the Knights Templar; no other order was ever authorized to display it. The helmet is the same "basinet" style helmet that identified the Westford Knight (Sir James Gunn) as a fourteenth century knight. The sword is clearly the squared-hilt type preferred by the Templars, and the buckler (a small shield) is of a pointed type found only in the northern islands of Britain during the fourteenth and fifteenth centuries (though used by Vikings much earlier). The Sanpete Knight, in the same fashion as the Westford Knight, is buried with his sword rested (hilt upward, blade towards the feet) on top of his body, a purely Templar burial. There can be no doubt whatsoever that the Sanpete mummy was once a Templar knight.

Not only can we identify the mummy as a Templar, we can even narrow down his personal identity because one of the stone boxes found in the second cave contains the clan Gunn coat-of-arms!

The coat-of-arms, a Viking ship with unfurled sail and three distinct oars, is painted black on white-lime on the side of the stone box. Interestingly, this is the "early" version of the Gunn arms, the version utilized by the Gunn Kings of the Isle of Man. On this version, the ship is clearly Viking, with Norse-type sail and oars, sometimes beneath a crescent; the second or later version, adopted when the Gunns became Crowners of Caithness, shows a double-decked ship with triangular sail beneath the star "Merica." Both are legitimate versions and are quartered in the arms of Sinclair.

There are three distinct possibilities for the identity of the Sanpete Knight: 1) He was a Gunn; 2) He was a Sinclair; 3) He was Madoc ap Owain Gwynedd! It seems logical to conclude that the knight was a member of the Gunn family because of the Gunn coat-of-arms; on the other hand the Sinclairs quartered the same coat-of-arms on their own shield and so were entitled. Was this knight the mysterious Oliver Sinclair who disappeared from Scotland in 1545 with the last of the Rosslyn treasures, never to be heard of again? Did he establish his own kingdom in Sanpete? We are reminded, for example, that the Scotsman Thomas Blake joined the Coronado-Cardenas Expedition near the same time, searching for something in the Uintah Mountains...and Blake had served with Sinclair in the army of Scotland. None of this suffers the indulgence of coincidence.

It cannot be ruled out that the mummy is that of the great Madoc ap Owain Gwynedd himself. Madoc was a Templar and therefore the uniform is easily explained. The helmet and buckler are more typical of those worn by knights of the isles during the latter part of the fourteenth to the early part of the fifteenth century; but both are originally Viking in origin and were used from at least the year 1000 A.D., and it must be remembered that Madoc was a descendant of the Scandinavian kings of Dublin and therefore of the Gunns, and would have been entitled to the Gunn arms quartered in his Welsh shield. Because the Gunn coat-of-arms on the stone box represents the early version, the date more nearly represents the time of Madoc.

Then there are the two "dragons" which appear on the sarcophagus of the knight. A close examination reveals that these symbols are not "dragons," but "griffins," and the griffin is the symbol of Wales, home of Madoc. The griffin was also adopted as a symbol by the Aztecs, and Madoc became King of the Aztecs, as we have noted elsewhere.

A good argument might be made that the mummy is Madoc, Prince of Wales, simply because the second cave contains stone boxes with engraved plates, for as we have already noted, John Dee maintained that Madoc recorded the history of his voyages and of the Native American people on metal plates, specifically gold. And we were soon to discover that the same charac-

ters recorded by John Dee as being transcribed from Madoc's gold plates are found on the plates found by Brewer; and are the same as some of the "Anthon Transcript" characters copied by Joseph Smith from the gold plates of the Book of Mormon; and are the same as some of the inscriptions found on the ledges in and around the Sanpete Valley.

We have examined the history of the Templars, the Rosicrucians, the Mormons, the Aztecs, the Gunns, Sinclairs and Morleys, all at great length, and it would be too much to suppose that all of the conjoining events are mere coincidence. The historical evidence is quite clear, but circumstantial. Ultimately, it was the inscriptions that provided answers.

We made a comparison from varied sources: the rock inscriptions at Sanpete, the Oak Island inscriptions, various Masonic scripts and Templar symbols, John Dee's "angelic" alphabet and "Adamic" language from his diaries, Dee's translation of *The Secret Book of Madog*, Joseph Smith's *Anthon Transcript* characters, the *Hermetic Emerald Tablet* of the Rosicrucians, and copies of characters taken from the plates found at Carre-Shinob, as well as other known ancient sources. What follows are copies of each of those symbols, after which we will attempt an explanation.

Random symbols from the Emerald Tablet of Hermes (ancient Chaldee):

Symbols on inscribed stone found at ninety feet on Oak Island, Nova Scotia, in 1802:

From a copied version of the Oak Island inscription (believed to be ancient Iberian):

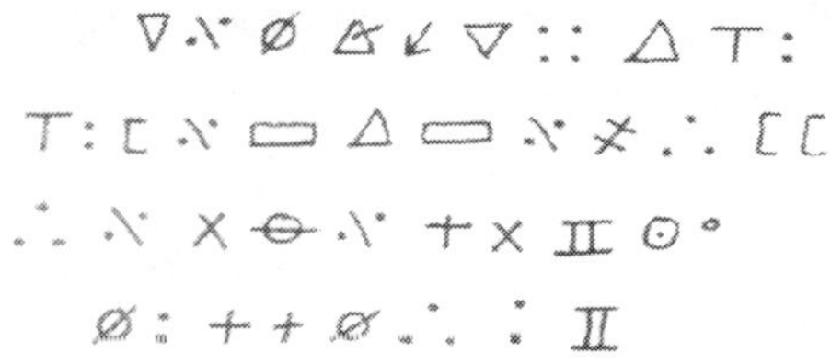

∇ᛈ Ø ⍝ᐪ ∇ :: △ T:
T:[ᛃ □ △ □ ᛁ ✕ ∴ [[
∴ ᛁ ✕ ⊙ᛈ +✕ Ⅱ ⊙°
Ø: + + Ø ∴ : Ⅱ

Masonic Signatures (from Sacred Geometry by Nigel Pennick):

MEDIEVAL SCOTTISH

SARACEN

EGYPTIAN

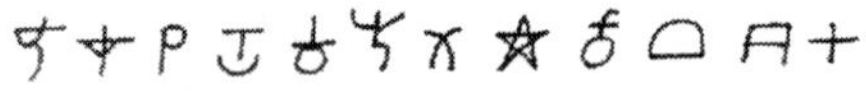

PERSIAN

MURISTANI

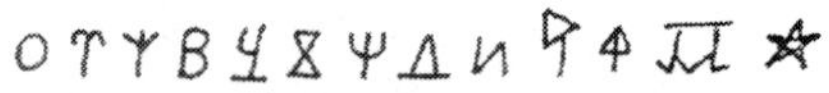

SYRIAN

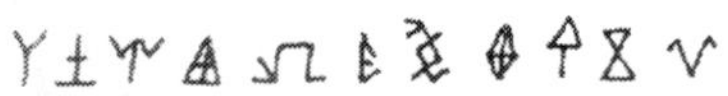

JERUSALEM

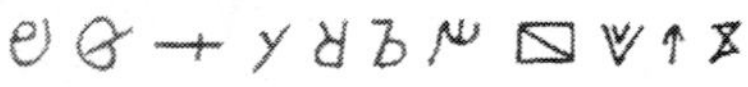

MEDIEVAL ENGLAND

MEDIEVAL FRANCE

NINETEENTH CENTURY
ENGLISH & SCOTTISH

John Dee's Diary:

"He [an angel] took from under the table a thing like a great globe, and set that in the chair, and upon that globe laid the book. He pointeth to the characters, and counteth them with his finger, being 21: and beginning from the right hand, toward the left."

— John Dee's Diary, Tues. 26 March 1583

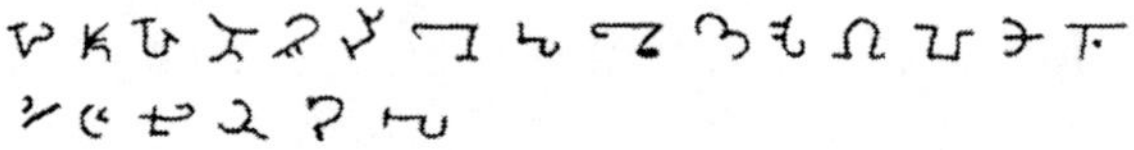

"28 Apr. [1583] Sunday: after dinner, about 4 of the clock. As I and E.K. had divers talks and discourses of transposition of letters: behold, suddenly appeared the spiritual creature, IL, and said: 'Here is a goodly disputation of transposition of letters. Choose whether you will dispute with me of transposition, or I shall learn you.'

" 'I had rather learn than dispute. And first I think, that those letters of our Adamical alphabet have due peculiar unchangeable proportion of their forms, and likewise that their order is also mystical.'

"IL: 'These letters represent the Creation of man: and therefore they must be in proportion. They represent the workmanship wherewithal the soul of man was made like unto his Creator...'"

ꭤ ꭚ ꭣ ꭤ ꭣ ꭣ ꭧ ꭦ ꭢ ꭧ ꭨ
ꭞ ꭧ ꭤ ꭢ ꭣ ꭦ ꭩ ꭤ ꭪ ꭫ ꭬

Key to symbols used by John Dee in his Diaries:

(Days of the week)

☽ Monday ☿ Tuesday ♀ Friday
♄ Saturday

(Planets & Astrology)

♄   Saturn   △   Trine (30°)
♃   Jupiter   ✳   Sextile (60°)
♂, ♂ Mars   ⋈   Quartile (90°)
☉   Sun   ♉   Taurus
♀   Venus   ☺   Cancer
☿   Mercury   ♌   Leo
☽   Moon   ♎   Libra
☍   opposition   ♐   Sagittarius
☌   conjunction   ♓   Pisces

(Personal Life)

△   John Dee   ⊕   Pars fortunae;
                         money
♅ Queen Elizabeth ☿   Messengers
⚦ Sexual Intercourse
(from the symbols for
Venus & Mars)

◎ Daytime   〰 Menstruation

(Alchemy & Science)

☿   Transaction, mercury   ☽ Silver
♀   Copper   ♀ Gold
♄   Lead   〰 Liquid,
                                water
✶   Sal ammoniac   □ Earth

It is important to note that Dee used certain symbols interchangeably, as did the Templars before him. In fact many of the symbols used by Dee are known Templar symbols, e.g. ☉ gold, ☽ silver, ♂ Mars, □ Earth, ⊕ money or treasure, etc. Often these symbols could be altered in meaning by combinations and/or additions. For example, the symbol for gold ☉ (which is the same as for the Sun) can be altered to ☺ which is sometimes represented as ⊗ which means "gold treasure" or "sacred gold." By the addition of points, such as ✧ we have the more specific meaning "Templar treasure" or "Templar gold." The points are believed to represent the buckler which is also evident on the Sanpete Knight. Before making further comparisons, it is important to present the symbols found at Manti, and elsewhere throughout the intermountain region.

Directly east of Temple Hill, Manti, Utah:

♀ ꝫ ⚕ ☉ Ʊ

Near Cedar City, Utah:

Near Nephi, Utah:

[These are engraved vertically]

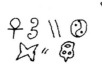

South Manti area: (above stone quarry)

Ogden, Utah:

(this character obliterated)

Pocatello, Idaho:

(large portion obliterated)

Provo, Utah:

Fillmore, Utah: (Chalk Creek Canyon)

Silver City, New Mexico:

Del Norte, Colorado:

[These are partially obliterated and difficult to read]

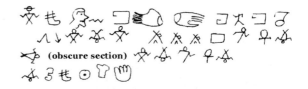

Grand Junction, Colorado:

(obscure section)

Near Cedar City Site (shown previously):

(not clear — may be a skull)

Fillmore Site (removed—in possession of Del Allgood of Fillmore):

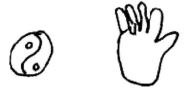

"Map Rock" near Fillmore:
(compare with Emerald Tablet characters—Chaldee)

From gold plates at Carre-Shinob

W𝔁ᵧ⧓⨳⨎𝐘⋔✦⊖ℱ℘𝐘Ω𝒵⫧𝐓𝓜 𝓡X✝𝐀

Carre-Shinob (type B):

Ω℥⊐✵⨎⫻⫻⫦⊙𝑢Ψ▢𝔁✦⟩⟨𝔁̂

Carre-Shinob (type C):

〰⟶Ψ"𝑦𝟸∟∟𝑢 ⊔ ⃝𝓏⫧ ss ⧓ℱℂ⧓ 𝟞𝔁 ℰ ∞
𝒟⟩∧𝟮𝒢ⅅ𝜖𝒵̂⫻⫻ 𝗂𝗂𝗂𝗂𝗂 ⫴⫧✝𝟫𝒵 ⚏𝛴𝟫𝟫W⊻G
⌣𝟤𝟙𝓜⟩𝒵𝈨⊐𝠀𝒵𝔁⤿ 𝔁⚶Ҥ⊔✦𝔁

Anthon Transcript:

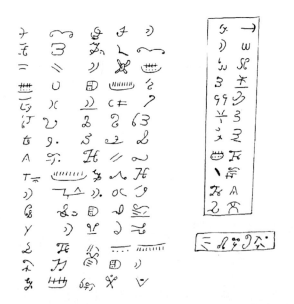

Recently discovered characters supposed to have come from the gold plates of the Book of Mormon

This profusion of characters becomes somewhat overwhelming, but within the numerous symbols are keys to solving the Sanpete mystery. The answer lies in a comparison of the symbols from various sources and locations. If a majority of the symbols match, a reasonable conclusion can be made that the characters have a common origin. And that is exactly what we find.

Emerald Tablet	Oak Island	Masonic	John Dee	Intermountain Inscriptions	Carre-Shinob	Book of Mormon
9					9	9
x	x				x	
4		4			4	
+	+	+		+	+	
	△	△	△			
○	○			○	○	○
⊙	⊙		⊙	⊙	⊙	
		✡		✡		
			Ω	Ω	Ω	Ω
		⟊				⟊
↓		↑		↓		
		Y			Y	Y
[					[	[
		L			LL	LL
		♂		♀	♀	
□	⊠		□	□	□	
		卐		卐	卐	
			3	3	3	3
	⊠					

Emerald Tablet	Oak Island	Masonic	John Dee	Intermountain Inscriptions	Carre-Shinob	Book of Mormon

Many other comparisons could be made, for there are literally thousands of such characters extant, but we have presented enough to indicate that most of the symbols have a common origin, and that that origin is Templar/Masonic. It also arguably proves that the Sanpete Valley inscriptions are of Templar origin rather than Jaredite or any other ancient species. The fact that some of the characters resemble ancient Egyptian, Chaldean, and Iberian, merely confirms the source, because the Templars (and later the Masons) based their symbolic language upon a reformed version of those ancient scripts. We are also reminded that Joseph Smith claimed that the characters of the gold plates of the Book of Mormon were "reformed Egyptian."

It should also be noted that the inter-mountain inscriptions show a number of symbols representing hands in various positions. A careful study of these make it clear that they are a representation of the Templar/Masonic hand signals used much like Indian sign language...(Did the Native Americans learn it from the Templars, or did the Templars learn it from the Native Americans?).

We will not be so presumptuous as to attempt an interpretation of the symbols, even though enough is known about them to make their meaning known, in most cases. With a little of their own research, readers should be able to draw their own conclusions.

However, there is one set of characters that we will offer an interpretation of, because we have an official source as verification of its meaning. Where they were found and who inscribed them is also significant. It also offers firm evidence of what lies hidden in or near the Sanpete Valley.

We have mentioned previously the efforts of Dr. Owen of Detroit to discover the hidden vault of Sir Francis Bacon, which he did discover, beneath the river bed of the River Wye, in Wales. The vault proved to be empty, its contents having been removed (probably to America) by Sir Francis Bacon early in the 16th century. The authenticity of the Vault was proved by the discovery of the coat-of-arms of Sir Francis Bacon (the boar) inscribed on one wall of the vault. On an opposite wall, facing West, was found another inscription and another coat-of-arms, offering irrefutable evidence that the former contents of Bacon's vault were connected with whatever was hidden in Sanpete Valley, half a world away. The inscription and arms were these:

With only very minor differences the symbols are clearly a replica of those found east of Temple Hill near Manti, Utah, and the coat-of-arms are without question those of the clan Gunn!

The genesis of the inscriptions on the vault and their subsequent interpretation is most enlightening. Dr. Owen claimed to have found copies of the inscriptions among the writings of Sir Thomas Herbert (1597-1682), a contemporary of Dr. John Dee and a personal friend of Sir Francis Bacon. Moreover, Sir Thomas Herbert wrote extensively about Madoc ap Owain Gwynedd [Sir Thomas Herbert, op.cit.]. Herbert, like John Dee, had access to the valuable collection of ancient manuscripts in Raglan Castle, seat of the Earl of Pembroke, before they were all destroyed during the English Civil War. Herbert's notes on the inscriptions appear to have derived from some of the Brechfa odes pertaining to Madoc's voyages, indicating that the inscriptions had some significance to Madoc. When we examine Herbert's interpretation of the inscriptions, which he specifically identifies as being "of the style of mysticall writing common among the Templar order of Scotland."

Herbert's inscriptions, based upon his discoveries at Raglan Castle and from his association with Sir Francis Bacon, are as follows:

- ☥ The Ankh, Egyptian symbol of both mortality and eternal life

- ⸎ an Adamic character relating to God or holiness

- ☥ unification Ankh representing "above as it is below"

- ♂ the symbol of gold utilized for sacred purposes

- ⎈ Templar symbol for "Arca Testamenta"—the Ark of the Covenant

Herbert's interpretation: "Here reposes the sacred golden Ark of the Covenant, source of eternal life and link between Heaven and Earth."

At least two of the Manti symbols—⸎ and Ω—appear in John Dee's "Adamic" alphabet which he, like Joseph Smith, claimed to have obtained from angelic beings. It is impossible to attribute the appearance of even one of these symbols simultaneously in Dee's diaries, on Bacon's vault, and on the ledges at Manti, to mere coincidence. Then consider the odds of finding all five of the above symbols two continents distant, stemming from the same source, some three centuries apart.

Only one conclusion can be drawn from all of the preceding evidence: the Ark of the Covenant, considered by archaeologists to be the greatest treasure relic in the world, once reposed, or may yet repose, in the Sanpete region. This particular Ark—and we have demonstrated that there were several in existence—was most likely deposited here by Madoc. Or maybe it was brought here by the Sinclairs or Gunns. Or

maybe by Sir Francis Bacon himself, or his associates. Or were they instead hunting for Madoc's Ark, for purposes unknown to us?

We have presented evidence that the mummy found in Brewer's cave was a Knight Templar, and bore the Gunn coat-of-arms. On the other hand, because the arms were painted on one of the ancient stone boxes, are we to conclude that it derives from the time of Madoc, two hundred years before the Sinclair-Gunn expedition? We have shown that Madoc was a Gunn descendant, but it is doubtful that he bore their arms. Was there a Gunn present in one or both of Madoc's expeditions? Perhaps as a navigator, because the Gunns had discovered America centuries prior to Madoc's voyages. We can only speculate, but we cannot deny the evidence. Perhaps, armed with this new information, someone will discover something more to broaden our knowledge on the subject.

By presenting our evidence and discoveries, the authors have not precluded other possibilities, nor do we intend to discount other hypotheses and beliefs. No inference should be made that we do not believe in the existence of the Jaredites and other races and peoples mentioned in the Book of Mormon. In fact, our researches tend to confirm much of the story of former inhabitants of the Americas as propounded by that source.

Moreover, the obvious connections between Joseph Smith, John Dee, and the Book of Mormon do not infer that any other version of the Book of Mormon origins are invalid. Indeed, our discoveries merely expand upon the former accounts and are not intended as a theological dissertation. Our interest here has been entirely historical and should in no way reflect upon individual beliefs and theologies. This narrative does not preclude the possibility that nations such as the Jaredites and Nephites could not have existed in this region; what we have shown, however, is solid evidence that the discoveries in the Sanpete Valley, at least, were of Templar origin, and of a somewhat later genesis. And we have further shown what the treasure of Sanpete Valley is most likely to be: the sacred Ark of the Covenant and possibly treasure from Solomon's Temple; and if the evidence is valid, there may also be stacks of engraved plates proving once and for all the true history of the ancient inhabitants of America.

The following photo's are courtesy of: Terry L. Carter

Indian Reservation, Ute

Gusher, Utah

Lone Pine, California

200

Lone Pine, California

Rockville, California

Austin, Nevada

Castle Craigs, California

Austin, Nevada

Austin, Nevada

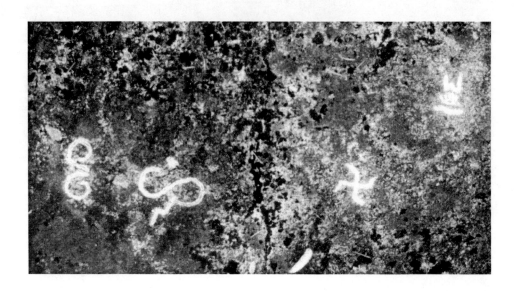

Castle Craigs, California

Castle Craigs, California

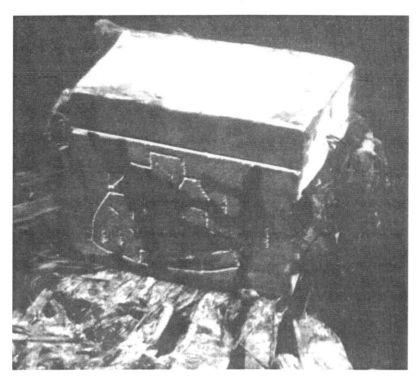

Brewer's Cave Discovery

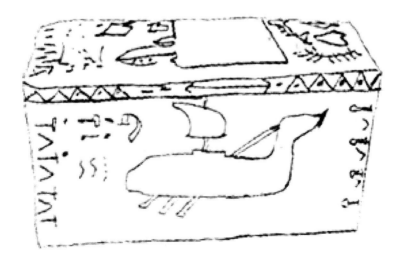

This is one of the stone boxes discovered in Brewer's Cave. Note the Viking ship, symbol of the Gunn Clan.

Brewer's Cave Discovery
Stone Box with Lid and Plate

Brewer's Cave Discovery

Brewer's Cave Discovery

Brewer's Cave Discovery

Plate

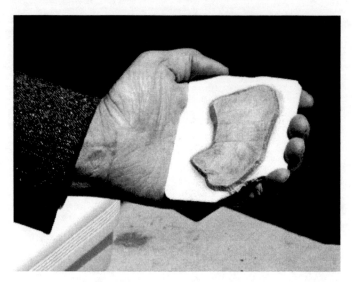

Brewer's Cave Discovery

Gold Plate, clay mold impression

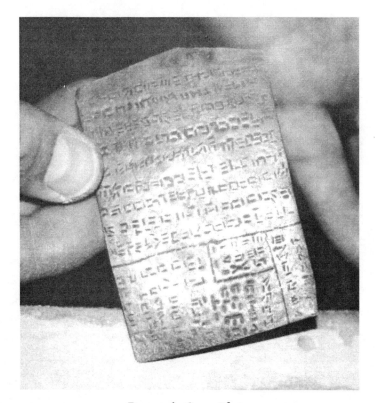

Brewer's Cave Plate

Brewer's Cave Plate

Tomapha, Nevada

Genoa, Nevada

Genoa, Nevada

Southern Utah

Southern Utah

The following pictures are courtesy of: Jeff Hanks, Manti, Utah

Brewer's Cave Discovery

Ogden, Utah

Fillmore, Utah

Provo, Utah

Manti, Utah

Manti, Utah
(North Panel) Near Manti Temple

Above Nephi, Utah

Ceder City, Utah

Fillmore, Utah—Chalk Creek

Appendix-Genealogy

TAMAR (TEA) TEPHI

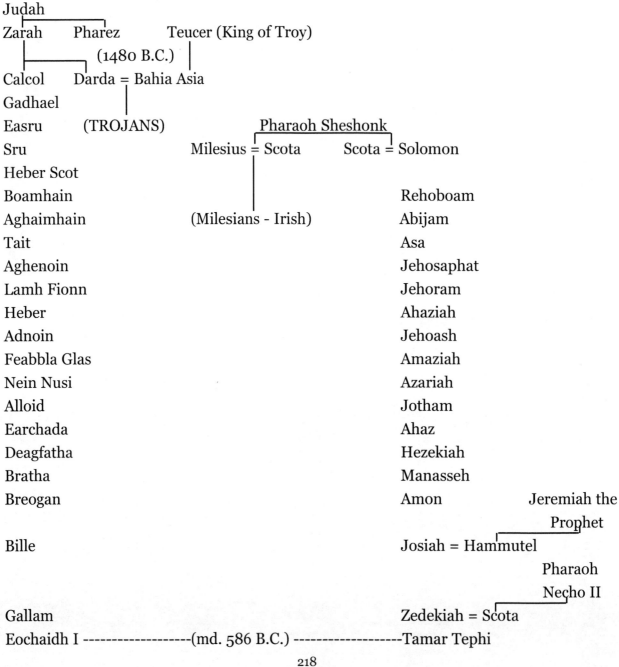

Judah
Zarah   Pharez   Teucer (King of Troy)
           (1480 B.C.)
Calcol   Darda = Bahia Asia
Gadhael
Easru   (TROJANS)   Pharaoh Sheshonk
Sru   Milesius = Scota   Scota = Solomon
Heber Scot
Boamhain   Rehoboam
Aghaimhain   (Milesians - Irish)   Abijam
Tait   Asa
Aghenoin   Jehosaphat
Lamh Fionn   Jehoram
Heber   Ahaziah
Adnoin   Jehoash
Feabbla Glas   Amaziah
Nein Nusi   Azariah
Alloid   Jotham
Earchada   Ahaz
Deagfatha   Hezekiah
Bratha   Manasseh
Breogan   Amon   Jeremiah the
                                                      Prophet
Bille   Josiah = Hammutel
                                          Pharaoh
                                          Necho II
Gallam   Zedekiah = Scota
Eochaidh I ------------------(md. 586 B.C.) -------------------Tamar Tephi

THE WESTFORD KNIGHT

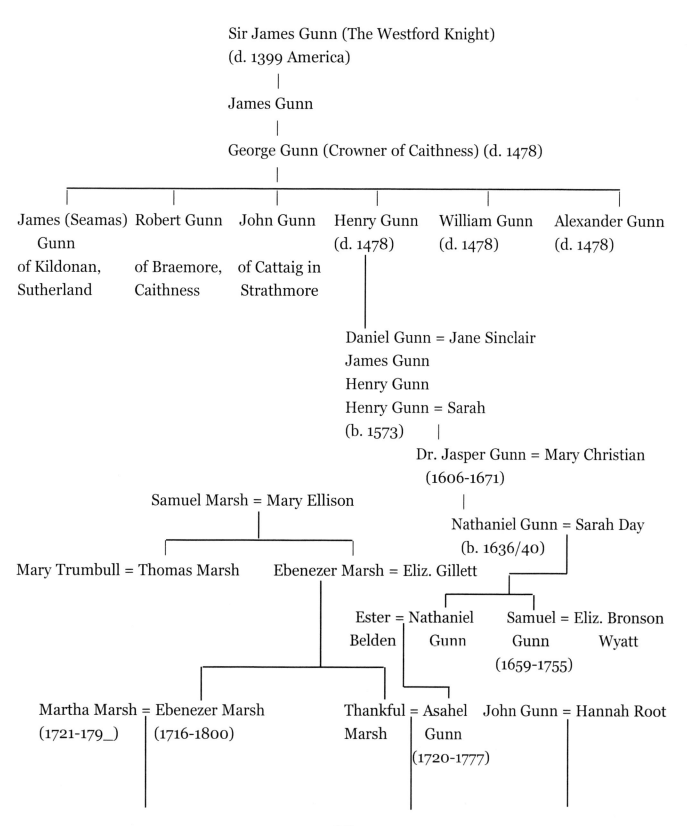

Sir James Gunn (The Westford Knight)
(d. 1399 America)

James Gunn

George Gunn (Crowner of Caithness) (d. 1478)

James (Seamas) Gunn of Kildonan, Sutherland

Robert Gunn of Braemore, Caithness

John Gunn of Cattaig in Strathmore

Henry Gunn (d. 1478)

William Gunn (d. 1478)

Alexander Gunn (d. 1478)

Daniel Gunn = Jane Sinclair
James Gunn
Henry Gunn
Henry Gunn = Sarah
(b. 1573)

Dr. Jasper Gunn = Mary Christian
(1606-1671)

Nathaniel Gunn = Sarah Day
(b. 1636/40)

Samuel Marsh = Mary Ellison

Mary Trumbull = Thomas Marsh

Ebenezer Marsh = Eliz. Gillett

Ester = Nathaniel
Belden   Gunn

Samuel = Eliz. Bronson
Gunn   Wyatt
(1659-1755)

Martha Marsh = Ebenezer Marsh
(1721-179_)   (1716-1800)

Thankful = Asahel
Marsh   Gunn
(1720-1777)

John Gunn = Hannah Root

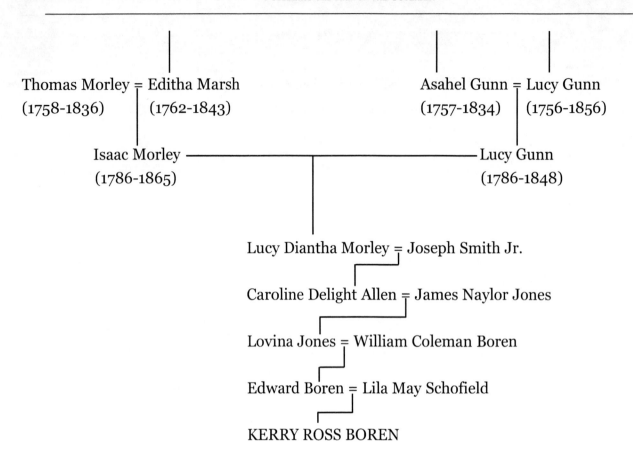

Thomas Morley = Editha Marsh
(1758-1836)   (1762-1843)

Asahel Gunn = Lucy Gunn
(1757-1834)   (1756-1856)

Isaac Morley ——————————————————— Lucy Gunn
(1786-1865)   (1786-1848)

Lucy Diantha Morley = Joseph Smith Jr.

Caroline Delight Allen = James Naylor Jones

Lovina Jones = William Coleman Boren

Edward Boren = Lila May Schofield

KERRY ROSS BOREN

JOSEPH SMITH - ISAAC MORLEY

Edward I (King of England 1239-1307)
Joan "of Acre" = Gilbert de Clare
Eleanor de Clare = Hugh le Despencer
Edward le Despencer
Margaret le Despencer = Robert Ferrer   (Lords of Möre)
Lord Edmund Ferrer
Lord William Ferrer   (Lords Morley)
Ann Ferrer = Sir Roger Vychan, Jr.
Thomas Vaughn = Sybil Devereaux   John Morley = Lacon ———————
Watkin Vaughn = Elizabeth Baskerville   William Morley = Eleanor Skipworth
Sybil Vaughn = John Scudamore   Edmund Morley = Margaret Hopkinson
*John Scudamore = Joan Payne   Edmund Morley = Philippa Bowyer
William Scudamore = Frances Lechmere   Thomas Morley = Mary Dolman
Mary Scudamore = Thomas French   Marmaduke Morley = Mary Brewer
Mary French = Robert Smith   Thomas Morley = Martha Wright
Samuel Smith, Sr. = Rebecca Curtis   Thomas Morley - Elizabeth Wickham
Samuel Smith, Jr. = Priscilla Gould   Timothy Morley = Mary Wood
Asael Smith = Mary Duty   Thomas Morley = Editha Marsh
Joseph Smith, Sr. = Lucy Mack   Isaac Morley = Lucy Gunn
Joseph Smith, Jr. (1805-1844) ——— (plural wife) ——— Lucy Diantha Morley

* Sir John Scudamore (ca. 1542-1623) | Caroline Delight (Allen) = James Naylor Jones
Gentleman usher to Queen Elizabeth, | Lovina Jones = William Coleman Boren
patron of the mathematician Thomas | Edward Boren = Lila May Schofield
Allen, and benefactor of the Bodleian
Library. His second wife Mary was
one of John Dee's most loyal friends
at court, and with Blanche Pary had
tried to obtain for him the mastership
of the Hosptal of St. Cross at Winchester   Kerry Ross Boren

Sinclair

Walderne de St. Clair (d. 1047)

William de St. Clair (Baron Rosslyn 1057) = Dorothy of Raby

Henri de St. Clair (B. Rosslyn, Crusader, Templar) = Rosabelle Forteith

Henri de St. Clair (B. Rosslyn, Scots Privy Councillor) = Margaret Gratney

William de St. Clair (B. Rosslyn 1180) = Agnes Dunbar (d/o Patrick/ 1st Earl of March)

Henri de St. Clair (B. Rosslyn) = Katherine (d/o Earl of Strathearn)

Henri de St. Clair (d. 1270) = Margaret (d/o Earl of Mar)

William de St. Clair (Ambass. To France) = Matilda (d/o Magnus, 35th Jarl of Orkney)

Henry de St. Clair (B. Rosslyn, commander of Knights Templar of Bannockburn 1314) = Alice de Fenton

William de St. Clair (d. 1330 Spain)

William de St. Clair (B. Rosslyn, d. 1358) = Isabel (d/o Malise II, 40th Jarl of Orkney)

Henry Sinclair (B. Rosslyn, Earl of Orkney, sailed to America 1398, d. 1400)

Earls of Orkney to Sinclair

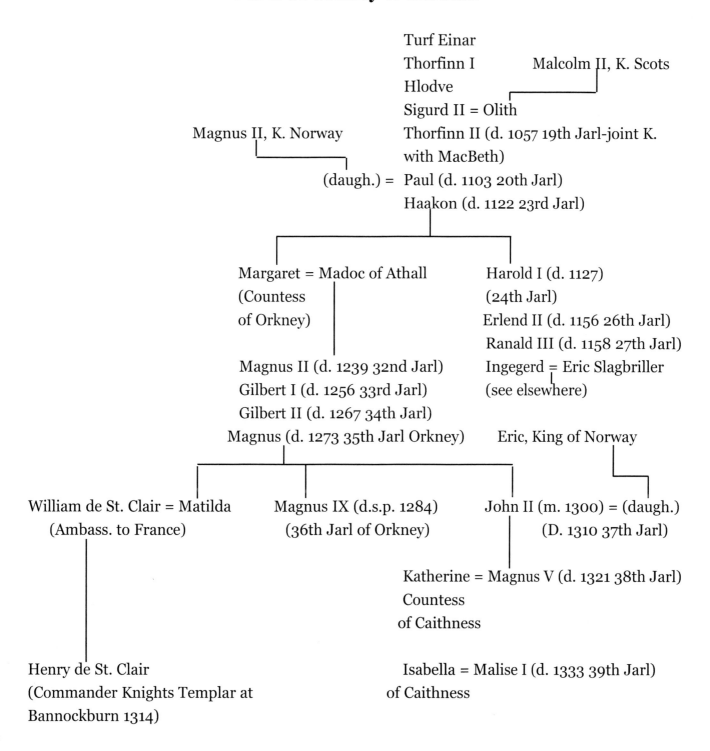

Turf Einar
Thorfinn I   Malcolm II, K. Scots
Hlodve
Sigurd II = Olith
Thorfinn II (d. 1057 19th Jarl-joint K.
with MacBeth)

Magnus II, K. Norway

(daugh.) = Paul (d. 1103 20th Jarl)
Haakon (d. 1122 23rd Jarl)

Margaret = Madoc of Athall   Harold I (d. 1127)
(Countess   (24th Jarl)
of Orkney)   Erlend II (d. 1156 26th Jarl)
                                     Ranald III (d. 1158 27th Jarl)
Magnus II (d. 1239 32nd Jarl)   Ingegerd = Eric Slagbriller
Gilbert I (d. 1256 33rd Jarl)   (see elsewhere)
Gilbert II (d. 1267 34th Jarl)
Magnus (d. 1273 35th Jarl Orkney)   Eric, King of Norway

William de St. Clair = Matilda   Magnus IX (d.s.p. 1284)   John II (m. 1300) = (daugh.)
(Ambass. to France)   (36th Jarl of Orkney)   (D. 1310 37th Jarl)

                                        Katherine = Magnus V (d. 1321 38th Jarl)
                                        Countess
                                        of Caithness

Henry de St. Clair   Isabella = Malise I (d. 1333 39th Jarl)
(Commander Knights Templar at   of Caithness
Bannockburn 1314)

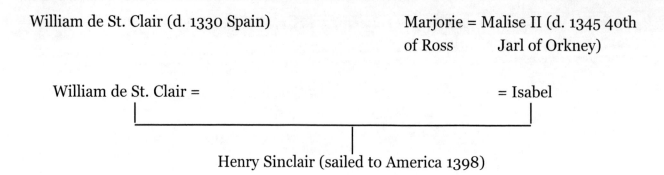

Gunns - Earls of Orkney

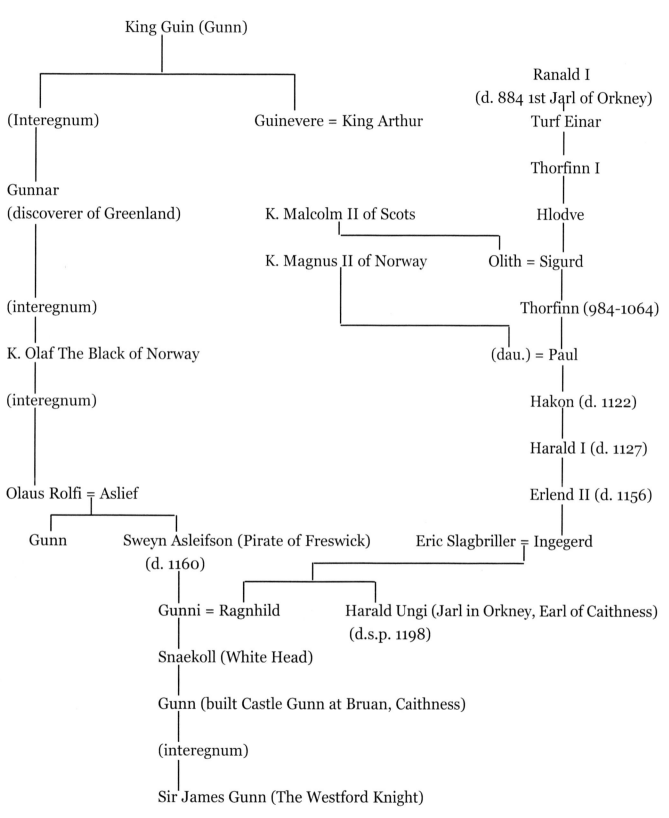

King Guin (Gunn)

(Interegnum)

Guinevere = King Arthur

Ranald I
(d. 884 1st Jarl of Orkney)

Turf Einar

Gunnar
(discoverer of Greenland)

K. Malcolm II of Scots

Thorfinn I

Hlodve

K. Magnus II of Norway

Olith = Sigurd

(interegnum)

Thorfinn (984-1064)

K. Olaf The Black of Norway

(dau.) = Paul

(interegnum)

Hakon (d. 1122)

Harald I (d. 1127)

Olaus Rolfi = Aslief

Erlend II (d. 1156)

Gunn

Sweyn Asleifson (Pirate of Freswick)
(d. 1160)

Eric Slagbriller = Ingegerd

Gunni = Ragnhild

Harald Ungi (Jarl in Orkney, Earl of Caithness)
(d.s.p. 1198)

Snaekoll (White Head)

Gunn (built Castle Gunn at Bruan, Caithness)

(interegnum)

Sir James Gunn (The Westford Knight)

Ancestry of St. Clair

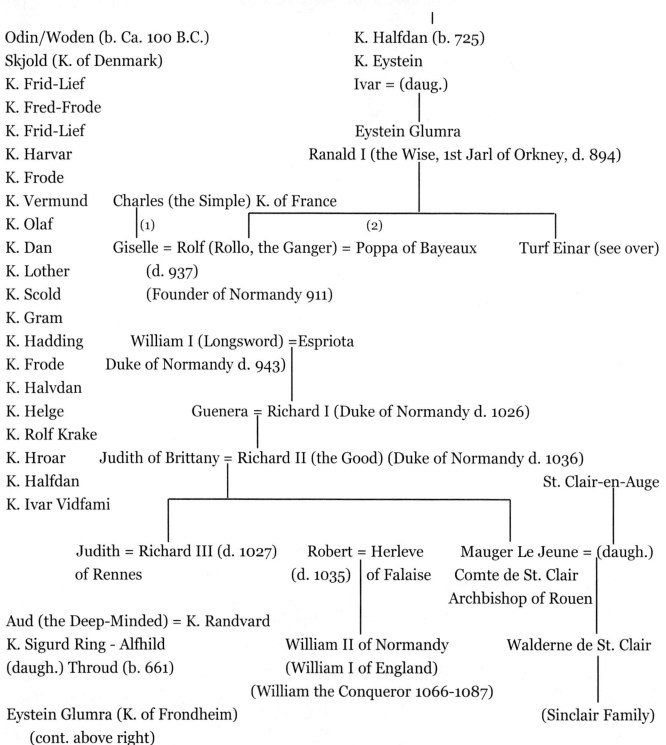

Odin/Woden (b. Ca. 100 B.C.)

Skjold (K. of Denmark)

K. Frid-Lief

K. Fred-Frode

K. Frid-Lief

K. Harvar

K. Frode

K. Vermund

K. Olaf

K. Dan

K. Lother

K. Scold

K. Gram

K. Hadding

K. Frode

K. Halvdan

K. Helge

K. Rolf Krake

K. Hroar

K. Halfdan

K. Ivar Vidfami

K. Halfdan (b. 725)

K. Eystein

Ivar = (daug.)

Eystein Glumra

Ranald I (the Wise, 1st Jarl of Orkney, d. 894)

Charles (the Simple) K. of France

(1)

(2)

Giselle = Rolf (Rollo, the Ganger) = Poppa of Bayeaux

(d. 937)

(Founder of Normandy 911)

Turf Einar (see over)

William I (Longsword) =Espriota
Duke of Normandy d. 943)

Guenera = Richard I (Duke of Normandy d. 1026)

Judith of Brittany = Richard II (the Good) (Duke of Normandy d. 1036)

St. Clair-en-Auge

Judith = Richard III (d. 1027)
of Rennes

Robert = Herleve
(d. 1035) | of Falaise

Mauger Le Jeune = (daugh.)
Comte de St. Clair
Archbishop of Rouen

Aud (the Deep-Minded) = K. Randvard

K. Sigurd Ring - Alfhild

(daugh.) Throud (b. 661)

William II of Normandy
(William I of England)
(William the Conqueror 1066-1087)

Walderne de St. Clair

Eystein Glumra (K. of Frondheim)
(cont. above right)

(Sinclair Family)

King Arthur's Descent From Joseph of Arimathea

Joseph of Arimathea (1-82 A.D.)

Anna = Bran the Blessed

Penardun = King Marius of Siluria (74-125 A.D.)

Coel I of Camulod (125-170 A.D.)

Lleiffer Mawr (K. Lucius, 170-181 A.D.)

Gladys = Cadwan, Prince of Cumbria

K. Coel II (d. 262)

Cunedd

Confer of Strathelyde

Fer

Cursalen

Clemens (Cluim)

Quintillius (Cinhil)

Cynloye

Ceretic Guletic (ca. 450)

Cinuit

K. Dyfnwal Hen of Strathclyde

Ingenach = Brychan II

Princess Lluan of Brechin = K. Gabran of Scots

Aidan mac Gabran of Dalriada (Uther Pendragon)

KING ARTHUR (Ard-Ri and Warlord 559-603) = Guinevere

KING ARTHUR (Ard-Ri and Warlord 559-603) = GUINEVERE
JOSEPH OF ARIMATHEA TO MADOC AP OWAIN GWYNEDD

Joseph of Arimathea

Anna = Bran the Blessed

Beli (Heli)

Avallach

Duvun

Onwed

Anguerit

Angouloub

Gur Dumn

Guiocein

Cein

Tegid Pies Rudawg

Patern Pesiut

Octern

Cunedda Wledig = Gwawl

Einian Yrth (ca. 46)

Cadwallon Llaw Hir

Maelqwyn Gwynedd (ca. 535-548)

Rhun

Beli

Iago (Jacob) (d. 616)

K. Cadfan of Gwynedd (616-625) = Acha

Cadwallon II, K. of Gwynedd (d. 634) = Helen
(continued above - next column this page)

Cadwaladr, K. of Gwynedd (654-664)

Edwal, K. of Gwyneed (664 -)

Rhodri Molwynog, K. of Gwynedd (d. 754)

Cinan Tindaethwy (754-816)

Merfyn Vrych (825-844)

Rhodri Mawr, K. of Gwynedd (844-878)

(interegnum)

(Cont. on chart - *Madoc's Scandinavian Descent*)

Olaf - King of Man & Isles

Somerled(d. 1164) = Ragnhild   (daugh.) = Conan, King of Gwynedd

Gruffyth ap Conan (d. 1137/38)

Chrisiant = Owain Gwynedd (d. 1169)

Madoc ap Owain Gwynedd

MADOC'S SCANDINAVIAN DESCENT

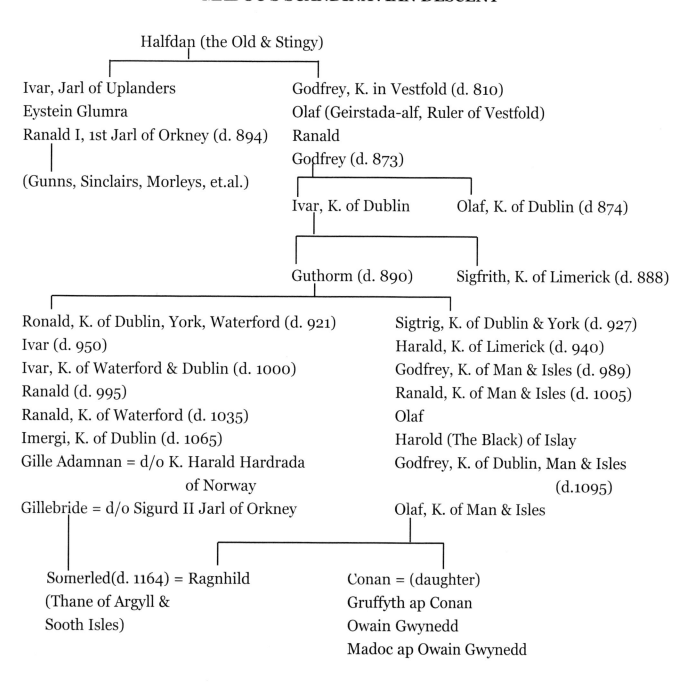

Halfdan (the Old & Stingy)

Ivar, Jarl of Uplanders
Eystein Glumra
Ranald I, 1st Jarl of Orkney (d. 894)

(Gunns, Sinclairs, Morleys, et.al.)

Godfrey, K. in Vestfold (d. 810)
Olaf (Geirstada-alf, Ruler of Vestfold)
Ranald
Godfrey (d. 873)

Ivar, K. of Dublin   Olaf, K. of Dublin (d 874)

Guthorm (d. 890)   Sigfrith, K. of Limerick (d. 888)

Ronald, K. of Dublin, York, Waterford (d. 921)
Ivar (d. 950)
Ivar, K. of Waterford & Dublin (d. 1000)
Ranald (d. 995)
Ranald, K. of Waterford (d. 1035)
Imergi, K. of Dublin (d. 1065)
Gille Adamnan = d/o K. Harald Hardrada
          of Norway
Gillebride = d/o Sigurd II Jarl of Orkney

Sigtrig, K. of Dublin & York (d. 927)
Harald, K. of Limerick (d. 940)
Godfrey, K. of Man & Isles (d. 989)
Ranald, K. of Man & Isles (d. 1005)
Olaf
Harold (The Black) of Islay
Godfrey, K. of Dublin, Man & Isles
          (d.1095)
Olaf, K. of Man & Isles

Somerled(d. 1164) = Ragnhild
(Thane of Argyll &
Sooth Isles)

Conan = (daughter)
Gruffyth ap Conan
Owain Gwynedd
Madoc ap Owain Gwynedd

GUNN DESCENT FROM EARLS OF BEDFORDSHIRE

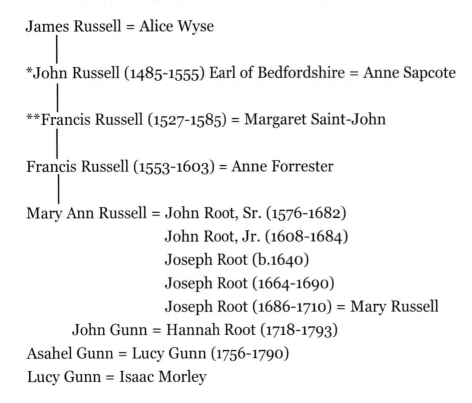

James Russell = Alice Wyse

*John Russell (1485-1555) Earl of Bedfordshire = Anne Sapcote

**Francis Russell (1527-1585) = Margaret Saint-John

Francis Russell (1553-1603) = Anne Forrester

Mary Ann Russell = John Root, Sr. (1576-1682)

John Root, Jr. (1608-1684)

Joseph Root (b.1640)

Joseph Root (1664-1690)

Joseph Root (1686-1710) = Mary Russell

John Gunn = Hannah Root (1718-1793)

Asahel Gunn = Lucy Gunn (1756-1790)

Lucy Gunn = Isaac Morley

* Sir John Russell was created 1st Earl of Bedfordshire by Henry VIII. Sir John was a courtier at the court of Henry the VIII with his close friend and associate Sir Francis Bryan (1490-1550), Grand Master of the Rosicrucians who was succeeded in that office by Dr. John Dee.

** Sir Francis Russell and his wife Margaret were intimate friends of Dr. John Dee, and his strong advocate at the court of Queen Elizabeth I.

Suggested Reading

The Diaries of John Dee, Edward Fenton, ed., Day Books, Oxfordshire, 1998.

John Dee: The World of an Elizabethan Magus, P. French, London, 1972.

The Principal Navigations, Voyages, Traffiques and Discoveries of the English Nation, Richard Hakluyt, 8 vols; London, 1907.

"Shows in the Showstone: a theater of alchemy and apocalypse in the angel conversations of John Dee (1527-1608/9)," D. Harkness, *Renaissance Quarterly*, 49, 707-37, 1996.

The Alchemical Writings of Edward Kelly, E. Kelly, A.E. Waite, ed., London, 1893.

John Dee's Action with Spirits, C.L. Whitby, 2 vols. (1581-83); London and New York, 1988.

The Hiram Key, Christopher Knight & Robert Lomas, Element Books, Inc., USA, UK, Australia, 1997.

Ark of the Covenant, Holy Grail, Henrietta Bernstein, De Vorss & Co., Marina del Rey, CA, 1998.

The Real History of the Rosicrucians, A.E. Waite, London, 1887.

The Rosicrucian Enlightenment, Frances Amelia Yates, London and Boston, 1972.

The Mystery of Francis Bacon, William T. Smedley, Health Research, U.S.A., 1967.

The Golden Legend, Jacobus de Voragine, F.S. Ellis, ed., London, 1900; trans. And adapted from Latin by Granger Ryan and Helmest Ripperger, Arno Press, New York, 1969.

The Glastonbury Legends: King Arthur and St. Joseph of Arimathea, Joseph Armitage Robinson, Cambridge, 1926.

Glastonbury, ancient Avalon, New Jerusalem, Anthony Roberts, ed., London, Rider 1978, 1992.

The History of the World, Sir Walter Raleigh, London, 1614.

Francis Bacon and His Secret Society, Mrs. Henry Pott, London, 1911.

Our Story of Atlantis, Written Down for the Hermetic Brotherhood and Future Rulers of America, W.P. Phelon, M.D., The Philosophical Pub. Co., Quakertown, PA, 1937.

American Indian Freemasonry, Arthur C. Parker, New York, 1919.

Sacred Mysteries Among the Mayas and the Quiches, Dr. Augustus Le Plongeon, New York, 1909.

Foundations Unearthed, Quest for Bruton Vault, Marie Bauer Hall, Veritas Press, Los Angeles, CA 1940, 1974.

America's Assignment with Destiny, Manly P. Hall, Philosophical Research Soc., Los Angeles, 1931.

The Secret Destiny of America, Manly P. Hall, Philosophical Research Soc., Los Angeles, 1944, 1972.

"Legends of Glastonbury Abbey," Manly P. Hall, *P.R.S. Journal*, vol. 18, no. 2.

The Secret Teachings of All Ages, An Encyclopedic Outline of Masonic, Hermetic, Qabbalistic, and Rosicrucian Symbolical Philosophy, Manly P. Hall, Philosophical Research Soc., Los Angeles, 1928.

The Secret History of Francis Bacon, Alfred Dodd, Rider, London, 1941.

John Dee: Scientist, Geographer, Astrologer and Secret Agent to Elizabeth I, Richard Deacon, London, 1968.

Les Mystères Templiers, Louis Charpentier, Paris, 1967.

Holy Blood, Holy Grail, Michael Baigent, Richard Leigh, Henry Lincoln, London, 1982, 1983; New York, 1983.

New Atlantis, Sir Francis Bacon (Begun by Lord Verulam Viscount St. Albans and continued by R.H. Esquire), London, 1627.

The Glastonbury Tor Maze: At the Foot of the Tree, Geoffrey Ashe, Glastonbury, 1979.

The Lost Treasure of the Knights Templar, Steven Sora, Destiny Books, Rochester, VT, 1999.

Sir Francis Drake, James A. Williamson, Crief, Lives-Collins, London, 1951.

"Westford's Mysterious Knight," Lawrence F. Willard, *Yankee Magazine*, vol. 22 (1958).

"Rock Sketch Hints Scottish Invasion," Emille Tavell, *Christian Science Monitor*, Oct. 2, 1957.

"Eskimo and Viking Finds in the Arctic," Peter Schledermann, *National Geographic*, vol. 159, no.5, 1981.

Viking Scotland, Anna Ritchie, B.T. Batsford, London, 1993.

Prince Henry Sinclair, Frederick J. Pohl, Clarkson N. Potter, New York, 1974.

The Big Dig, D'Arcy O'Connor, Ballantine Books, New York, 1988.

A History of the Sinclair Family, Leonard A. Morrison, Damprell and Upman, Boston, 1896.

"Comprehensive Evidence for Viking and Gaelic Sites in the Americas and Elsewhere," unpub. ms., Fletcher Library, Medford, Mass.

The Vinland Sagas, Magnus Magnusson, Penguin Books, New York, 1965.

The Iberian Stones Speak, Paul MacKendrick, Funk and Wagnalls, New York, 1969.

The Gunn Salute, Herbert B. Livesay, vol. 17, no.3, 1987.

"The Fourteenth Century Discovery of America by Antonio Zeno," William H. Hobbs, *Scientific American*, vol. 72, January 1951.

Maps of the Ancient Sea Kings, Charles H. Hapgood, E.P. Dutton, New York, 1966.

The Sign and The Seal, Graham Hancock, Crown Pub. Inc., New York, 1992.

The Greek Myths, Robert Graves, Penguin Books, New York, 1955.

Guinevere, Norma Lorre Goodrich, Harper Perennial, New York, 1955.

The Golden Bough, Sir James Fraser, Macmillan, New York, 1922.

America B.C., Barry Fell, Quadrangle Books, New York, 1976.

Secrets of Rennes-Le-Château, Lionel and Patricia Fanthorpe, Samuel Weiser, Inc., York Beach, Maine, 1992.

Bacon Is Shakespeare, Sir Edwin Durning-Lawrence, John McBridge, New York, 1910.

Nordic Expedition Communicator, Pete Cummings, ed., Worcester, Mass., 1990 (self-publication).

The Oak Island Quest, William S. Crooker, Lancelot Press, Hantsport, Nova Scotia, 1978.

Lost Cities of North and Central America, David Hatcher Childress, Adventures Unlimited Press, Stelle, Ille, 1992.

Francis Bacon: The Temper of a Man, Catherine Drinker Bowen, Little, Brown, & Co., Boston, 1963.

They All Discovered America, Charles Michael Boland, Doubleday, Garden City, N.Y., 1961.

America's Secret Aristocracy, Stephen Birmingham, Berkley Books, New York, 1987.

The God-Kings and the Titans, James Bailey, Harper and Row, New York, 1987.

The Secret Doctrine of the Rosicrucians, Anonymous, Barnes and Noble, New York, 1993.

The Norse Discovery of America, Rasmus B. Anderson, Norroena Society, London, 1906.

Bloodline of the Holy Grail: The Hidden Lineage of Jesus Revealed, Laurence Gardner, Element, 1996.

The Widow's Son: The Esoteric History of the Prophet Joseph Smith and The Origin of Mormonism, Kerry Ross O'Boran (Boren) and Lisa Lee O'Boran, priv. pub., Salt Lake City, 1997.

The Gold of Carre-Shinob, Kerry Ross Boren and Lisa Lee Boren, Bonneville Books, Springville, Utah 1998.